# Interpreting Dreams and Visions

*"A dynamic and fresh approach to a spiritual resource long neglected."*

**Revd Dr Russ Parker,** author of *Healing Dreams*

*"Quoting the prophet Joel on the day of Pentecost, the apostle Peter underlined that dreams and visions were to be one of the primary ways in which God would communicate the revelation of His heart to His people under the New Covenant. Nevertheless, the interpretation of dreams and visions has often been marginalized and overlooked or even rejected in the Church; either because it was misunderstood, or simply because the necessary tools were missing. In this incredibly practical and down to earth book, Liz Evans combines her years of personal experience, with proven biblical wisdom and fascinating practical examples and exercises, to provide the reader with a comprehensive handbook that will serve many seeking to grow in their understanding of how, when and to whom God speaks through dreams and visions. I commend it wholeheartedly!"*

**Wes Hall,** Principal, Revival Training Center
of Stuttgart, Germany

*"Having worked with Liz and welcomed her to teach dream interpretation at our church, I am delighted that she has now made her work available through this book. Liz's ministry is solidly bible based, highly inspirational and easily accessible to everyone. Above all her passion for Jesus, love for people and integrity for truth, combined with amazing spiritual sensitivity, makes her prophetic ministry unique and trustworthy. This book is an essential tool for anyone serious about interpreting dreams and taking this ministry into the market place. The potential is both transformational and limitless."*

**Revd Clive W. Corfield,** Senior Pastor, City Church,
St Albans and Founding director, REAP

# INTERPRETING
# DREAMS
## *and*
# VISIONS

*A practical guide for using them
powerfully to impact the world*

## LIZ EVANS

MONARCH
BOOKS

Published by Monarch Books
an imprint of
**Lion Hudson IP Ltd**
Wilkinson House, Jordan Hill Road,
Oxford OX2 8DR, England
Email: monarch@lionhudson.com
www.lionhudson.com/monarch

ISBN 978 0 85721 779 0
e-ISBN 978 0 85721 780 6

First edition 2017

**Acknowledgments**
Every effort has been made to trace and contact copyright holders of material used in this book. We apologize for any inadvertent omissions or errors.
p. 28: Extract from *Understanding Dreams and Visions* by John Paul Jackson copyright © 2005, John Paul Jackson. Used by permission of Stream Ministries.
p. 74: Extract from *Celtic Daily Prayer Book Two: Farther Up and Farther In* copyright © 2015, HarperCollins Publishers Ltd. Used by permission of HarperCollins Publishers Ltd.
Scripture quotations taken from the Holy Bible, New International Version Anglicised. Copyright © 1979, 1984, 2011 Biblica, formerly International Bible Society. Used by permission of Hodder & Stoughton Ltd, an Hachette UK company. All rights reserved. "NIV" is a registered trademark of Biblica. UK trademark number 1448790.
Scripture marked NET quoted by permission. Quotations designated (NET) are from the NET Bible® copyright ©1996-2006 by Biblical Studies Press, L.L.C. http://bible.org All rights reserved.
Extracts marked KJV from The Authorized (King James) Version. Rights in the Authorized Version are vested in the Crown. Reproduced by permission of the Crown's patentee, Cambridge University Press.
Scripture quotations marked ESV are from The Holy Bible, English Standard Version® (ESV®) copyright © 2001 by Crossway, a publishing ministry of Good News Publishers. All rights reserved.
Scripture quotations marked NRSV are from The New Revised Standard Version of the Bible copyright © 1989 by the Division of Christian Education of the National Council of Churches in the USA. Used by permission. All Rights Reserved.
Scripture quotations marked ISV are from the International Standard Bible. Used by permission. All rights reserved.
Scripture quotations marked BBE are from Bible in Basic English. Used by permission of CrossReach Publications. All rights reserved.
Scripture quotations marked NLT are taken from the Holy Bible, New Living Translation, copyright © 1996, 2004, 2007 by Tyndale House Foundation. Used by permission of Tyndale House Publishers, Inc., Carol Stream, Illinois 60188. All rights reserved.
Scripture quotations marked WEB are taken from the World English Bible. Used by permission. All rights reserved.

A catalogue record for this book is available from the British Library

Printed and bound in the UK, November 2017, LH29

This book is of course dedicated to God's great gift to me, my family.

To Dave: some twenty years ago you made me a promise on our wedding day, and I've lived in the circle of it ever since. Thank you is such a tiny word for all your love.

To AnnaElouise and Jonny: It never occurred to me when you joined our family that you would bring so much fun and hilarity with you.

AnnaElouise, you are a joyous mix of gifting, wit, and beauty. How can anything so tiny be so wise?

Jonathan, you have filled the house with fun, guitar music, and athletics medals. I love the way you defend people and care for them. With you every day is a party.

The sheer quality of who you both are and the strength that is in you, is awesome. We believe in you and who you are made to be.

In memory of my father, Arthur Kenneth White, 1930–1997, a consummate teacher and pastor, a countryman who taught me to honour God, serve His people, and love words.

# CONTENTS

# ACKNOWLEDGMENTS

Thank you to my PA Leigh Giles. Our latest adventure was to write a book. My children say that in ministry we make up one person and you are three-quarters of it. Thank you for researching obscure references, typing endlessly, and bringing order to my world. If it's true that those who serve will be called to sit at the head of the table, then the rest of us will wave to you from its foot. I'm in awe of your grace and commitment.

Thank you, Feel Good Community, because this book has been written as we've lived the material in it together. You've made generosity and kindness watchwords, and you carry His power with understated grace. Pioneering, ministry, family, and fun in creative, vibrant community: bliss.

A particular thank you to my father-in-law, John Evans, whose encouragement to keep going while I wrote this manuscript meant more than he will know.

And to Carolyn Cooper, with whom the Love has a Voice ministry was birthed as we travelled and trained together. Your wisdom is a powerful force in the ministry. You and Judith Hoffman have carried so much of the DNA and weight of the teaching and outreach ministry, respectively, over the years – thank you for your support. I've seen spiritual daughters grow into weighty ministers of God.

Thank you to the seers, whose dreams and visions are in this book for us to learn from, for sharing your revelation stories with us.

And finally, thank you to Jenny Hewett and Chris Giles for weighing the exercise interpretations in team.

# FOREWORD

The moment we turn our light out at night and settle our head into the pillow we embark on an adventure, and it is an adventure in the dark. Sooner or later we lose our awareness of the world we have inhabited during the day, and our mind slips into a world of apparently random and disordered thoughts and feelings that, several times during the night, congeal into experiences that we call "dreams". These are highly visual, and yet we can only observe them with our eyes closed, because they can only be witnessed by our inner eyes. Come the morning, when we awake from our night's rest, we can sometimes remember scenes and feelings from these dreams. They tell us that we have visited an extraordinary world where the normal rules of life do not apply: we meet people who have died long ago; we play instruments we have never learned; we become weightless and float over the trees. Even if we only remember fragments of them, some dreams manage to capture our longings, and others capture our dreads or our shame. Some horrify or terrify us – those that we call "nightmares". Most we quickly dismiss the moment we open our curtains and walk into the daylight hours. Such dismissals can mean we miss the pearl of great price, for something was ringing out in our souls as a message to be heard. But because we have not understood the language, we have shrugged our shoulders and assumed it was simply a figment of our imagination that is best left in the dark.

While dreams take place in the hours of sleep, visions and visual impressions in the mind are more likely to come to us in our waking hours. Humans have a wonderful capacity to see things that are beyond the scope of our mortal eyes, and the Bible is full of stories of people who see in this way: Abraham and his smoking fire-pot and flaming torch (Genesis 15:17), Ezekiel and his remarkable creatures (Ezekiel 1), and Amos and his plumb-line (Amos 7:7) to name but a few. But it is not just the great prophets of old who are given such visions – we all have the capacity to be open to such things if only we will trust the inner eyes of the soul.

When Jesus walked the pathways of this world, He taught the people in a variety of ways. One of the most intriguing was His use of storytelling. The Gospel writers called these stories "parables". They were stories with a message. But the message was not always obvious. Matthew, in chapter 13 of his Gospel, writes of how on one occasion Jesus was sitting in a boat at the edge of lake and told lots of stories to His fascinated listeners sitting on the shore. One of these stories Matthew records in detail – the story of a sower spreading the vital seed on the land, with some falling among the weeds, some falling on the pathway, and some settling into the good earth. Later in the day His rather puzzled disciples ask him why He speaks in parables, and you get the impression that they are a bit annoyed that He won't give them this teaching straight. "Just tell us what to believe, and we'll get on and believe it," you can hear them saying. In response, Jesus refers them to some words of Isaiah, the great prophet who once upon a time had a vision that changed his life when he saw the Lord high and lifted up in the Temple (Isaiah 6). Jesus repeats the words issued during that prophetic experience of Isaiah: "Though seeing, they do not see; though hearing they do not hear or understand." But he goes on to tell his disciples, "but blessed are your eyes, because they see, and your ears because they hear." (Matthew 13:13–16). In other words, Jesus wants to bless all who choose to follow Him with the gift of seeing and hearing in a new way. He trains them to see with different eyes.

Dreams and visions are similar to parables. They are stories that need to be "perceived". To take them literally is no good. They come with a language that needs to be learned. It is a language of the soul, and it is a language in which the Holy Spirit has a particular interest (see Joel 2:28). If we wish to grow in our understanding of God, of ourselves, and of this world in which He has placed us, we will need to learn the language of these parables perceived by the inner eye. Liz Evans, in this beautiful book, is our tutor for this language. I have known Liz for several years and greatly appreciate her ministry. She is a wonderfully clear teacher. So many people in the "dream business" set themselves up as gurus who dazzle us with their impressive skills. Because Liz is a deeply humble and pastoral teacher, her aim is not to set herself up as this kind of guru, even though her knowledge and research into the subject is truly impressive. It will soon become apparent as you read this book that her deep desire is to equip each of us to learn the language of dreams and visions, and to help others to discover the same. Liz is deeply missional and uses her understanding of this language very sensitively in her missional work with those who have not yet discovered Christ. The learning of this gift is vitally important for our mission to a world that is longing to understand the language of the inner world of dreams and inspiring visions.

In the pages of this book Liz has provided for us a very helpful and thoroughly practical handbook. As she says, the learning will take time and we can't expect to crack the subject in just a few sittings. Though there is much practical teaching in this book, it is not a "ten easy steps to dream and vision interpretation" book. There are no short cuts in this world. Liz invites us into a listening lifestyle for which, over time, we will learn the language. But if we put our minds and hearts into learning the basics, we will open the doorway of revelation. We will become those who see and perceive with the eyes of the heart. We will learn to hear the voice of the Lord coming to us through our dreams and visions. But as we make our way through this book we find we are not just learning some useful tools of the trade, but we are actually on a voyage of discovery.

It is hard to read this book and not be changed as we encounter the God who loves to reveal His wonders to His children. By the end of it you will not only have acquired skills, you will also have gained wisdom, a wisdom that our world so desperately needs.

**Michael Mitton**
Writer, speaker, spiritual director

# THE DREAMS AND VISIONS IN THIS BOOK

Please note, all the dreams and visions in this book are genuine revelations. They reflect the hopes, fears, and experiences of real people, and contain a little piece of their lives. As such we hold them as precious. As living pieces of revelation, some of them may speak into your life, as well as teach you to understand dreams and visions.

You may notice further levels of revelation, in addition to the answers; at this stage you and I are becoming an interpretation team, as each one of us has a part of the interpretation. Occasionally a more sensitive part of the interpretation has been left unsaid. But the interpretations in the book have been checked and calibrated against the real-life story into which the dream or vision spoke, so you can be confident of their validity.

We have kept the seer's own words, each telling their dream or vision, so that you can hear them speaking through it.

Some of the names and details in the dreams and visions have been changed to protect people's privacy.

All the Bible references in this book are taken from the New International Version UK unless otherwise stated.

## Disclaimer

This book is written out of our experience in teaching people to interpret dreams and visions and to use them in a wise and responsible way. It speaks into both the "dis-use" and the "mis-use" of the biblical gifts of dream interpretation and receiving visions from God.

Some people answer the problem of the "mis-use" of these gifts with the suggestion that "dis-use" is the best safeguard. But that answer doesn't solve the problem, because sooner or later people will pick up the gifts again, without proper scriptural guidelines or experienced common-sense suggestions for their use.

This book is written to promote "right use". It includes an essential component of scriptural guidelines and practical wisdom for safe practice. The headlines of these are that messages from God and how they are handled should line up with the loving values of Scripture: "'Love the Lord your God… and love your neighbour as yourself.' There is no commandment [or dream or vision] greater than these" (Mark 12:30–31). There are also wise protocols included for each type of dream or vision we interpret.

Please note that, in the New Testament, revelation and interpretation are used within the loving accountable community of God's people, where what we see is tested before being given or acted upon (1 Corinthians 14:29).

There are many forms of misuse, and before you volunteer observations, please be careful in what you say, what interpretations you offer, and to whom you offer them. It's best to be general and humble in your interpretation. There is a limit to your knowledge. I recommend you use phrases like, "It seems to me," "I suggest." And if you are not sure about something, seek the advice of those you consider wise. Be appropriately cautious, be sensitive, and think twice before you speak.

Please note that I can accept no responsibility for any misuse of the material in this book.

# HOW TO USE THIS BOOK

*Immediately you open the pages of the Bible
and look for the subject of dreams,
there is a startling contrast with today's
popular scepticism of their usefulness.*

Revd Dr Russ Parker[1]

I recently received a phone call from a pastor who was dealing with a heartbreaking and perplexing pastoral situation. One of the people involved had had a compelling dream. Over the phone, we interpreted that dream together. The dream story brought to light the root of some inexplicable and outrageous behaviour, giving those looking on a considerable measure of understanding.

The pastor's response summed up all that I have found out about dreams and visions: "It just goes to show the majesty and genius of dreams; to receive these messages at this time, in an incomprehensible situation."

This book contains a very practical collection of dreams and visions, stories which illustrate their potential, and graded exercises to take you on a journey to interpret revelation. It will help you to understand dreams and visions and learn to use them effectively.

I've written the later chapters with the intention that they will become a handbook for those who want to use dreams and visions on outreach and in the life of the church, as well as in their own lives.

It's important to follow the chapters through from the beginning (I state that because I rarely read a book that way). They lay out both the foundation and a pathway to develop a rounded skill base and to practise the mechanics of interpretation.

Dreams and visions were released, just as God had promised in the book of Joel, when the Holy Spirit was poured out on all flesh. Revelation was loosed, and God began to communicate with His people in a new

---

1     Russ Parker, *Healing Dreams*, SPCK, 1998, p. 7.

and living way. As John states, "He will take what is mine and declare it to you."[2] This is not just about information; it has substance. It brings life.

The goal of this book is not only to teach you a skill; it is also to explore the meeting place between a person's life and the messages that God speaks in dreams and visions. It is to show you how God works with dreams and visions to release healing and revelation which will change people's worlds. And how to partner with Him to do that.

When I heard about the outreach opportunities that come with dream interpretation, I read widely and booked balanced, respected ministers to come in and teach our church about it. I learned a lot, both academically and biblically. But I still couldn't actually interpret dreams or visions.

Before the expert instructors left, I asked them for a number of dreams and their meanings. I gathered some of the church leaders together and we began to interpret the dreams, to assess and calibrate our answers, to find out where and why we were wrong. Checking the answers and gleaning teaching points for each dream gave me a process to start learning the practice of interpretation. This book reproduces that proven method of learning for you. The theory you need is woven in among the stories and exercises, so you can learn to use it practically, and access a hidden world of revelation. But "knowledge is only part of understanding. Genuine understanding comes from hands-on experience".[3] With understanding, people begin to realize, *I can do it*. Understanding brings confidence, allowing the gift of interpretation to mature. As you learn, you will be able to practise, and the more you practise the more you will learn, and so your confidence and understanding will grow.

The explanations throughout are firmly rooted in clearly laid-out biblical principles, so you can confidently learn from them. Understanding dreams and visions is both scriptural and attainable.

As you go through the book, you will begin to notice recurring themes and patterns in the dreams and visions described, which shed light on how they work. These recurring themes are not surprising when

---

2        John 16:14 (ISV).
3        Seymour Papert, *Mindstorms: Children, Computers, and Powerful Ideals*, New York: Basic Books, 1980.

you consider how much of our culture arises from shared experience. The symbolism on which we draw is to some extent a common pool. But some symbolic meanings are totally unique to the seer's own life, giving them their own particular dream or vision story. You will begin to be comfortable with that ambiguity.

The teaching points are repeated in summary at the end of each chapter, and the exercises systematically help you apply and absorb each teaching point. Every dream and vision exercise you study will teach you something – especially those you get wrong!

Our own interpretations are given at the end of each chapter, to help you check on how you are doing and encourage you to express things sensitively and well.

Throughout the book you will be given sensible safeguards to help a rookie interpreter learn and practise wisely – just in case, having bought this book, you are suddenly presumed to be the local expert!

Interpretation is not a science. It is a way of listening – to what both God and the seer are saying in the dream or vision, even though part of the process is thought through and based on experience. As you look at the exercises, there are some things you can learn, and some that you can only see or hear in that "aha!" moment of unlocking, when the meaning of the dream or vision suddenly becomes apparent to you. It comes as God brings understanding.

It's a devotional process that is fun. There's a humility and rest that comes as we learn to rely on God for both the meanings and the skills we need: "Your fruitfulness comes from me" (Hosea 14:8, NET). Sometimes we will pause on the journey and listen to the message of a dream or vision, taking time to apply what God is saying through its story, allowing its message to touch our lives with its life, hope, and peace.

It takes an average of three to five years to become fully fluent in understanding and to grow an instinctive gift of interpretation. It is a journey with the Holy Spirit, which will enrich your life and your scriptural understanding, as well put you in a position to interpret dreams and experience visions.

When training in the gifts of the Spirit, of which interpretation is one, John Wimber used to tell people, "Of course you can!"[4] We've

---

4    A founding leader of the Vineyard Movement (a US evangelical charismatic denomination), John Wimber did pioneering work in the 1980s, teaching systematically from

trained many hundreds of people in interpretation, on our courses, and it's always fun to see them realize they too can hear God, see visions, and begin to understand their dreams.

I asked God to show me a vision for the people who will read this book. He showed me a nail about 15 cm long. It represented those small pointed pieces of revelation which God puts in a dream or vision to speak to people. As I watched, a scene began to unfold before my eyes: the nail was embedded in an ancient shop door, on an ancient stone street. A sign hung from it saying, "Open".

God has shown me this shop before. It represents a shop window where His people display to the world His grace and giftings so that others can experience the realities of His goodness as He touches their lives. When you interpret the messages that God has put in the world's dreams and visions, the people of God are open for business.

> *They will be called oaks of righteousness,*
> *a planting of the Lord*
> *for the display of His splendour.*
> *They will… restore the places long devastated.*

> Isaiah 61:3–4

God is pouring spiritual capital into places that have been long devastated, and opening spaces where people can hear Him speak again.

The vision moved on to focus on the door, which was now partly open, and the "Open" sign became a very personal invitation to you:

Come… buy and eat!

> *…without money and without cost.*
> *Why spend money on what is not bread,*
> *and your labour on what does not satisfy?*
> *Listen, listen to me, and eat what is good,*
> *and you will delight in the richest of fare.*
> *Give ear and come to me;*
> *listen, that you may live.*
> *I will make an everlasting covenant with you…*

the New Testament on the practical application of signs and wonders.

*nations you do not know will come running to you,*
*because of the Lord your God,*
*the Holy One of Israel,*
*for he has endowed you with splendour.*

Isaiah 55:1–5

It's typical of God to invite us to a rich feast of His goodness, to give us His splendour and then to display His plentiful supply to a world in need.

"So," as they say, "if you are sitting comfortably, I will begin…"[5]

---

5      The words with which the daily story on the long-running BBC children's radio programme *Listen with Mother* always began.

18

*Chapter 1*

# AN INTRODUCTION TO DREAMS
# AND VISIONS

*In the last days, God says,*
*I will pour out my Spirit on all people.*
*Your sons and daughters will prophesy,*
*your young men will see visions,*
*your old men will dream dreams.*
*Even on my servants, both men and women,*
*I will pour out my Spirit in those days,*
*and they will prophesy.*

Acts 2:17–18

Dreams are a normal part of our lives. Medical research has discovered that we spend, on average, six years of our lives dreaming.[6] We have all overheard or had conversations which began, "I had a dream last night…"

Twelve years ago I began my journey to understand dreams and visions, but I was not expecting my own world to be changed so much. It was as if someone had turned the lights on. I could see where I was, where I was going, and how to get there. It was, quite literally, a revelation.

I had discovered a rich, sparkling stream of revelation, which had been hidden beneath the surface of my everyday world and welled up

---

6     *The Times*, 28 February 2009. Dr Rubin Naiman, Clinical Assistant Professor of Medicine, Dr Andrew Weil's University of Arizona Centre for Integrative Medicine.

through my dream life and into my visions. It became something of an oasis where life and freedom streamed into my full and active life.

As we trained other churches, and did life together, my whole prophetic team started to talk about our dreams, and we began to understand much more about how God cares about us. It was like finding a personal manual explaining our lives and thoughts. We began to notice God's healing and help. And our nights became laced with dream stories He sent to encourage and direct us. By the time we had formed the Love has a Voice ministry,[7] to train and mentor people from all walks of life, dreams and visions had become a natural part of our lives.

There also seemed to be a soul commentary, a processing, going on at night, often far deeper than our daytime thinking. During a lifetime of dreaming, our souls have some very interesting things to say, particularly in recurring or memorable dreams.

Now and then we received warnings about things we had planned. I must admit that, at first, we often discovered the wisdom of listening to this information the hard way. We ignored the warnings as fanciful initially because listening to our dreams was new to us.

> At first glance our dream might be fairly unimpressive,
> and our conscious mind, the one that likes things
> clear, rational and acceptable, rolls its eyes and tells
> us there are more important things to be getting on
> with. But I've got impatient with those rolling eyes,
> and increasingly I like to take hold of the dream and
> give it a fair hearing, because, as likely as not, it has
> something important to say to me.[8]

Soon we began to be told of other people's dream stories and to hear accounts of God touching people's lives. I love to tell the following story on my interpretation courses because I saw God take a little piece of heaven's wisdom and put it in a dream. He gave the dream to a child and, when that dream was interpreted, hope and a measure of healing came. Love reached down and spoke to her. And then I saw Him move decisively to fulfil the promise in the dream.

---

7      lovehasavoice.org (accessed 23 August 2017).

8      Michael Mitton, *Dreaming of Home*, Bible Reading Fellowship, 2012.

The story began when I received a phone call from a family asking me to go and visit them. A seven-year-old girl called Rose had been through a tumultuous time and had asked to see me.

I travelled to her grandmother's house, and when I arrived I found both Rose and her mother excited about a dream Rose had had the night before. My heart sank as I realized what God had done. I had prayed that God would give me something from Him to say, but at this time I was far more comfortable with Scripture or prophecy than I was interpreting dreams.

We encouraged the child to go and play, and I took the dream, which they had written down for me, and asked God for His help. God was very gentle with me: the dream was mostly straightforward:

> In my dream a war was going on. I was watching
> it from the window in Granny's house. There was a
> good wolf and a bad wolf and dogs who turned into
> leopards and attacked people. At the end of the dream,
> the good wolf lifted up his paw and the war stopped.
> In the middle of the dream I was taken to a bedroom.
> It looked totally different and it had a bathroom in
> it; everything was all pink. My hair was washed and
> washed and then wrapped in a big fluffy pink towel.

Rose's family lived in suburbia, not on a safari park, so this was obviously not a literal dream! It's framed in metaphor, the picture language of a little girl looking from the sidelines at an unfolding story which she doesn't fully understand. The events play out using animal characters and symbolic language.

These particular symbols are not uncommon in dreams and visions. In fact, as we have explored interpretation, we have uncovered two surprising trends: not only are there occasional patterns of commonly occurring symbols, but also certain dreams appear again and again, right across cultures and nations, drawing on our common human and environmental heritage. Because, however, they are our own dreams, they also contain language that is meaningful and individual to us. That's a paradox.

> *Our Western dualistic minds do not process paradox*
> *very well. Without a contemplative mind, we do not*
> *know how to hold creative tensions. We are better at…*
> *demanding a complete resolution to things before we*
> *have learnt what they have to teach us. This is not the*
> *way of wisdom.*[9]

Maturity has the ability to hold two truths in tension: to recognize both uniquely individual and corporate, common symbols. I'm expecting the experience you will glean on this process will lead you to be able to do just that. You can, of course, start afresh and not use any of the symbols and patterns that other people have noticed. But if you do, you are certainly taking the long way round! The debate on these matters rages hotly and is explored in chapter 3.

The symbols and meanings appearing in Rose's particular dream were as follows:

- Good wolf – God, the positive spiritual influence in the story

- Bad wolf – an evil spiritual influence

- Window – place of revelation

- Window in Granny's house – watching from a safe place

- Dogs – friends/protectors/loyal companions

- Leopard (appearing in this dream story as negative, threatening) – danger, fighter, vengeance (the positive would have been a powerful leader, strong and permanent)

- Bedroom – place of safety and rest

- Bathroom – place of cleansing from something we have done, or something that has happened to us

- Pink – colour of love

Rose's dream story is a window on her world. Her heart was expressing her distress at the situation around her. But there is more to the story than that soul commentary – the dream carried a message of comfort and healing from God. As I read the dream, I was able to separate

---

9       Richard Rohr, *Falling Upward*. SPCK, 2012.

out the different messages in the story. Some of them were helpful for Rose to hear, but others simply gave me information about what was happening around Rose, and what God was going to do about that.

The dream story (using the wolves) spoke of a spiritual element to the events in which the family were caught up. But that was balanced by a foretelling statement, suggesting that God (the good wolf) was about to intervene in the situation.

It was important for me to put the interpretation very gently for a child, and to bring that same sense of peace and love that comes at the end of her dream story. As interpreter, I needed the wisdom to recognize what to tell and what not to tell Rose. I was coming into a situation where emotions were running high. "The tongue of the wise brings healing",[10] and I have learnt that wisdom weighs its words carefully. What could I say to help a child who had shown us a glimpse into her brave little heart?

I said to her, "This dream says to me it's as if you've been watching something that's felt a bit like a war. And perhaps even people you've felt safe with have seemed unpredictable recently. They may even have been cross with each other sometimes.

"But there are three special things in this dream. Even though it's been hard to watch and you may have felt upset and not known what has been going on, you are ok. You have a safe place at Granny's house. Who do you think the good wolf is?"

Rose's face looked up at me with her big eyes and cute freckles. She simply said, "God."

I carried on, "God is nearby to help you. And He is going to do something very special just for you. He is going to come and wash away some of the feelings you've been having and help you to feel more peaceful."

At this point we made sure Rose was cosy, sitting comfortably with her grandmother, and we prayed that God would come and take her back in her imagination into that lovely pink bedroom and into the safe bathroom and wash away those bad thoughts, memories, and experiences. At that point, Rose's face relaxed. I asked her how she felt. She breathed out a word on a long sigh: "Happeee."

---

10    Proverbs 12:18.

The message for Rose in the dream was that God wanted to come and bring her comfort and healing. The wisdom for me, from that same dream, was that I dealing with not only a family in distress, but also with a spiritual element that was influencing the events. It was important not to tell Rose that information, which would have been unnecessarily perplexing for many adults, let alone a small child. And the foretelling message of the dream, promising that the situation was going to change, had no timeframe and no specifics, and it's also possible that I could have been wrong. There could be no promises made to Rose. But these two pieces of information brought a prayer agenda, which was confirmed when Rose and her mother went home. I heard a little bit more about the situation from Rose's grandparents, and I recognized some familiar spiritual elements around fear and control, and my heart broke for the people caught up in the story. I began to feel angry on their behalf.

As soon as I was alone, I stood up to pray about the spiritual side of the drama, asking God to come and intervene on behalf of the family, and binding the specific spirits that were fuelling the fire. What I didn't know was that, right at that moment, a few miles away, a difficult discussion to try to bring order to the situation was ending in volatile failure. One partner got up to leave when, quite suddenly, the atmosphere and the feeling of the interaction totally changed. And unexpectedly, within the hour, a practical plan for the future was proposed and accepted, bringing a more peaceful way forward for all concerned.

The Good Wolf had lifted up His paw, and the forces that had been driving the situation were quieted for long enough to bring a breakthrough.

The next time I saw Rose, she danced up to me saying, "Liz! Liz! The Holy Spirit came to me in a dream last night." This seven-year-old child had the capacity to recognize and receive the wisdom of God speaking through her dreams – and you can too.

Like Rose, in our dreams and visions we can find ourselves and others in apparently bizarre series of events. It's important to note that though the picture language tells us a lot, the dream story is what delivers the message. While the symbols in Rose's dream story frequently reappear in dreams, it's really important not to take their meaning for granted. There is a flexibility in symbolism. In Rose's dream, the dog, a common dream symbol, appeared as a trusted friend, a protector. In another dream a dog growling may mean an unstable or angry friend. Or the dog may simply be a real pet which the dreamer used to own, which gives timing or context to the dream story.

It's the story that delivers the message. Think of Aesop's fable, *The Tortoise and the Hare*. It's easy to see that the tortoise and hare respectively represent the slow and the speedy, but it's the story that delivers the message. Without the story, the tortoise and the hare are just animals doing their thing in a field. Symbols play a part, but they are not the most important thing. I stress this point because many beginners focus on the symbols instead of the story. In this book all the symbols and their meanings – within the context of that particular dream or vision – are given to you. They are next to the exercise, to help you understand it.

Visions carry just as much impact as dreams. God's compassion comes through again and again. My team and I were interpreting dreams at a local café when a young woman from a Pacific island wandered in and sat with us. She was well groomed and beautiful. She had been in England for four years and had a good job. Penelope was early to meet her friends and, as we chatted, God showed me a picture for her. She was alone on the pavement with a big suitcase, but as a small child of about four. In my vision, a shiny, big, black car drew up, and out from the back seat got Jesus. He picked up her suitcase and brought her safely into the car.

The vision spoke about Penelope's feelings and family issues from that time in her life, at the age of four, when her father left the family, leaving her feeling isolated and alone. This vision showed that God had a place of safety and covering for her. Penelope, who had been heavily using cannabis to cope with the pain from her past, asked God to come and care for her life, and she joined our community. God reached out to her in her hidden sadness, proving again that He is the God who sees each person and cares deeply about the secrets of their hearts: "I, the Lord, reveal myself to them in visions, I speak to them in dreams" (Numbers 12:6).

My own vision of God is broadening too. From time to time, encounters in dreams and visions install an update on the tablet of my heart. The sketchy outline of a two-dimensional, high, and distant God is continuing to come alive, full of colour and personality, bringing a new level of love and relationship. During the songs in a weekly prayer-room worship set, I looked up and had a remarkable vision: for the first time ever, I saw Jesus' eyes. He was looking at me. His face was obscured but I gazed directly into His immense, bright eyes. And in Jesus' eyes was a flame. I knew that flame was salvation; it blazed furiously. Burningly strong, it was power to save, it was fury against evil. It was stronger than death. I'd never before understood the phrase, "Love is as strong as death."[11] But I saw it in His eye: nothing is equal to His salvation. I became acutely aware that Jesus is unchanging and unchangeable, the Lord of the universe. I saw the salvation in His eyes, and I knew in that moment that God never gives up on us or our situations. This is another creative tension. Difficulties may persist, or we have faced and lost battles, but even so God reveals Himself to us and we see that nothing surpasses His power. Our story isn't over yet, by a long chalk, and hope springs to life again.

In my vision, I looked again and I saw both eyes smiling at me; this time salvation was superseded by His kindness. It was like liquid kindness – all I could do was look and look. All I could think was, "You love me! You really love me!" He was smiling at me, with His heart in His eyes, and all I could think was, "How you love me!" It communicated to every part of my life. My heart relaxed and sang with the freedom that comes from His love.

Without revelation, we live with an underdeveloped idea of God, and the image of His reality remains indistinct. But when we see Him, we understand. We let go of the ground, cast down the idols of the fears which have held us back, and begin to fly. We begin to live from the revelation of who He is. And we live differently, generously, and victoriously, fuelled by the knowledge of God. Revelation infuses our world with the qualities of the Kingdom: of peace, joy, cleansing, and power: "But they that wait upon the Lord shall renew their strength; they shall mount up with wings as eagles; they shall run, and not be weary; and they shall walk, and not faint."[12]

Many times we simply have to laugh as we interpret dreams in

---

11      Song of Solomon 8:6.
12      Isaiah 40:31 (KJV).

community action events when, typically, young men sit poleaxed for long minutes, saying, "I'm shocked, I'm shocked, I'm shocked! How could you know that? I'm shocked!"

The experience has challenged their worldview. They don't realize that there, in their dreams, their heart and lives and friendship dynamics are on display. We see their strengths, what is happening spiritually, their attitudes, hopes, and fears.

It is my hope that, excited by this powerful and transformative ministry, you will still get well and truly stuck on some dream and vision exercises. When you do, you have a choice to make: Do I turn to the answer in the back? Or do I ask God to begin to show me the answer? To understand is deeper than to see. Dreams and visions speak in stories, and once you know how to look at them you are helped to understand and explain the meaning. God who created the earth and all creation has illimitable imagination. He can use anything to get His point across.

Jesus loved to tell stories when teaching people about His kingdom, their own personal challenges, and their lives. Some of these parables were hard to understand. Once, after listening to the latest story in His repertoire, the disciples, sounding a little grumpy and perplexed, came and asked Jesus, "Why do you speak to the people in parables?"[13] It's a question you may well find yourself asking as you approach a difficult vision or a dream. In the context of the disciples' relationship with Jesus, a conversation began. And Jesus was able to explain what He was saying through the story.

This is a scenario you will get used to. First He tells you or someone else a dream story or shows them a vision. It feels perplexing. Then – and it happens quite suddenly – you see. God reveals it to you. Revelation is making something known. This conversation happens in the context of a relationship, and there are some things about interpretation that you will learn, but there are also some things that you will begin to see and hear with God's help, as you open that conversation with Him. Simply ask Him questions and enjoy waiting to see how He will answer you. Jesus told His intimate friends that the hard of heart can't see the truths hidden in parables. No doubt, to

---

13      Matthew 13:10.

refer to Michael Mitton, they rolled their eyes and got on with more important things to do.[14]

This shows the importance of a curious, teachable spirit. Jesus said, "Truly I tell you, anyone who will not receive the kingdom of God like a little child will never enter it."[15]

John Paul Jackson explained it like this:

> *Unfettered, creative faith exists in our childhood.*
> *But [as we grow up] western culture has an implicit*
> *demand that we come to rely only on the logical, the*
> *reasonable and the objective.*[16]

One night when I was putting my small children to bed, AnnaElouise, then aged five, asked if we could ask God for a picture. I stopped our bedtime story and prayed very simply that God would give one of us a picture. With my adult arrogance, I assumed I would be the "one of us" who got the picture, but when I closed my eyes, I saw nothing. This was not good news; I wanted my children to be confident that God speaks to us. So I opened my eyes and asked the children if they had seen anything. "Yes" said AnnaElouise, "I saw a little girl carrying a basket of eggs. She dropped all the eggs and they broke." Again, not good news. I wanted a nice, cosy, settling picture for bedtime. So I asked her if she knew what it meant. "Yes," she said with a beaming smile, "there was one egg which didn't break. And that's me. I'm the egg which didn't break. Because God is my eggshell."

At the time of writing, AnnaElouise is eighteen, and in all the challenges of life, she remains unbroken. Her interpretation has stood the test of time.

## Ander's dream story: receiving the kingdom

This childlike quality of faith, which inherits the kingdom of God, was clearly illustrated in one dream I interpreted at the beginning of my interpretation journey. Ander's dream went like this:

---

14      See Mitton, *Dreaming of Home, 2012*.
15      Mark 10:15.
16      John Paul Jackson, *Understanding Dreams and Visions*, Institute for Spiritual Development, 2005.

> *In my dream, I was standing in a circle of people*
> *around my father. None of the people were really my*
> *siblings, but it was as if they were his children. My*
> *father asked what we wanted from him. One said she*
> *wanted a million dollars, one said she wanted his whole*
> *pay cheque every two weeks. I just said, "I just want*
> *you to help me when I need it." He told someone that I*
> *was the only one who would inherit his wealth.*

## Interpretation

This dream is speaking about the assurance of provision, proximity, and loving attention of God the Father. It carries an inherent commendation for the simplicity, trust, and purity of Ander's attitude. And it shows that this restful way of waiting on and trusting God for all we need is totally effective. Ander's dream is a very scriptural dream.

One day in my prayer time the Lord gave me a very firm instruction: "Remember who I am." Immediately I saw a vision of Jesus in Matthew 19:13, and He was laughing. He was holding out His hand to bless the children who were pressing in and surrounding Him.

This is what happens to us as we step out on the journey of interpretation in simple trust. We find Jesus, relaxed, and engaging, extending His hand, and blessing us with revelation. It's supposed to be fun:

> *Cultivate the habit of rejoicing in the assurance that*
> *the Divine wisdom is guiding you, even where you do*
> *not yet see the way… Abiding in Him, His wisdom will*
> *come to you as the spontaneous outflowing of a life*
> *rooted in Him.*[17]

Rose, AnnaElouise, and Ander were all encouraged and reassured by the interpretation of their dreams. In modern society we often turn to scientific research to inform ourselves, but understanding our dreams and visions can add a depth of insight that hard data cannot encompass.

The Bible takes it for granted that God spoke in dream stories and visions. They are accepted as providing the impetus for a complete

---

17      Andrew Murray, *Abide in Christ*, Whitaker House, 1979.

change of direction in the dreamer's life. In the Old Testament, tactless seventeen-year-old Joseph got himself into trouble for telling his large family of older brothers about his dreams, revelations of the future.[18] He saw his brothers' sheaves of corn bowing to his, their stars bowing to his. His brothers clearly understood the implications of these dreams – and they were enraged. There was a pecking order for brothers in that culture. They pecked him right into a hole in the ground, sold him as a slave, and the rest is history.

Years later, another biblical Joseph was perplexed and concerned on finding Mary, his wife-to-be, pregnant with a child he knew was not his. God chose a dream in which an angel of the Lord appeared, to reassure Joseph and explain this miraculous but alarming situation.[19] Further dreams warned him how to keep the child safe. Matthew the evangelist feels no need to defend the belief that God chose this way to speak to Joseph; it is, to him, an accepted and reliable method of receiving revelation.

The Gospel writer Luke, the doctor with the love of writing "an orderly account",[20] continues to give considerable weight to dreams and visions in the book of Acts. New Testament scholar Luke Timothy Johnson notes that "Luke has visions play an important role for his prophetic characters in the narrative".[21]

More than 30 per cent of the biblical text is composed of visions and dreams. It contains a pattern which demonstrates how God communicates, both with His people and with those who don't yet know Him. It was only after the Middle Ages that a culture of scepticism rose in tandem with increasing scientific sophistication, so that the understanding of dreams and visions as vehicles of divine communication fell out of favour.

In recent times, though, a cultural shift has manifested and there is renewed interest especially in dreams, from a world increasingly eager to explore beyond the material realm, searching for spiritual experience and purpose.

Popular, reputable, mainstream publications – BBC website articles, *The Times* newspaper, among others – now sometimes feature

---

18      Genesis 37:5–9.
19      Matthew 1:20.
20      Luke 1:3.
21      Luke Timothy Johnson, *The Acts of the Apostles*, Michael Glazier, 2006.

substantial articles on dreams, reporting increased attendance at dream interpretation groups and the emergence of practitioners offering to interpret dreams for substantial sums.

Now might be a good time to remind ourselves that prophecy and interpretation are gifts, not products. They belong to God. The phrase, "Cross my palm with silver," came from fortune-tellers selling their services. In the book of Acts, Luke tells us that when he and Paul were "going to the place of prayer, we were met by a slave girl who had a spirit of divination and brought her owners much gain by fortune-telling."[22]

When we interpret dreams and visions, it's important to model something different from the merchandizing of the world. "Serve, don't sell," is a helpful marker for the purity of motive and source of prophecy. We use that guideline with the public when we do dreams and visions outreach. It's one of a number of markers which we recommend to people as they work with those who are searching for spiritual input.

The postmodern world is rediscovering its need for the spiritual side of life. Part of that ontological shift is a curiosity about dreams and visions which prompts people to seek out their meaning.

As I travel in Europe, I encounter churches more at ease than ever with biblically sound, calmly practical, and competent prophetic revelation. But whereas in Bible times and early church history the interpretation of dream stories and visions was familiar and undertaken in a weighty and experienced tradition, modern-day interpretation, even when it is enthusiastic, is sometimes shallow and immature. The church has lost something precious, which is well worth uncovering again.

> *Though significant portions of the Christian Church*
> *eventually came to ignore or even disdain dreams,*
> *God in His patient, gracious love, has continued to*
> *communicate by this instrument. Church history bears*
> *this out. St Augustine, one of the most influential*
> *figures in Church history AD 354–430 referenced his*
> *dreams as an important way God speaks to humanity.*
> *St Thomas Aquinas AD 1225–1274 was an extremely*
> *influential theologian who was of the opinion*

---

22    Acts 16:16 (ESV UK).

*that dreams could have a spiritual origin. He also experienced visions.* [23]

Modern life has many challenges, which affect the church community as well as wider society. We know from our study of the Scriptures that God's methods of guidance include dreams and visions. It makes sense for us to take advantage of this torch to shine on paths presently too dark to make headway. Later on in the book (chapter 5) we will consider the importance of dreams and visions for church life and leadership. For now, we note that we are living in times when people have lost touch with wise traditions to guide them, yet are becoming ever more open to, and hungry for, this link with the spiritual dimension – with the wisdom of God. There is a tremendous need for balanced, well-trained interpreters to stand in the gap: people with wisdom, discernment, and biblical integrity, observing good practice and working within accountable relationships.[24]

We are especially hearing reports of many Muslim people who, particularly in areas where the church is repressed and even persecuted, have in increasing numbers found their way to Christian faith through their experience of the visitations of Jesus in dreams and visions. Faisal Malick tells of a Muslim man who, after experiencing the same dream several nights in a row, knocked at a church door and told his dream to the pastor. He said:

> *I have this dream where I see a huge high fence, and I begin to climb the fence. As I climb the fence I get up a little bit, and then I fall to the ground. Then I get up. I climb the fence again, and I fall to the ground. I keep doing this, and I'm getting frustrated. I know I must get to the other side of the fence, but I can't because I keep falling to the ground. I need to get to the other side, and I don't know how. I know this dream is from God, and I know God is trying to speak to me. Could you help me interpret what this means?*

23      John Paul Jackson, *Understanding Dreams and Visions.*, 2005
24      See the instructions given in 1 Corinthians 14:29 (NRSVA): "Let two or three prophets speak, and let the others weigh what is said."

He was offered the following interpretation:

> *You are trying to get to the other side which is Heaven, and you're trying to do it by your own works. That's why you keep falling to the ground, because you're not good enough to get there by your own works. But you can get to Heaven through the grace of the Lord Jesus Christ.*[25]

The Muslim man asked the pastor to wait a moment. He left, and then returned with five of his Muslim friends. As they talked together, all of them were born again, baptized, and now attend the church.

Faisal, an ex-Muslim turned Christian evangelist, records, "Statistically, around the world now, the number one way a Muslim comes to Jesus is by a dream or a vision."[26]

In this story Faisal tells of the Muslim man and his friends, it's interesting that the man sought out the pastor, not the other way round. Any barriers were lowered because it was he who made the enquiry and asked for advice. It is reminiscent of the story in the book of Daniel, where King Belshazzar requests the prophet's insights into his vision, saying, "I have heard that you are able to give interpretations and to solve difficult problems."[27]

I believe it's no coincidence that in many places, established and respected ministries have simultaneously begun to mentor whole groups of prophetic people in more depth. It seems to me that God is using these core ministries to raise and develop a wave of people who have wisdom in discerning spiritual things, who are able to interpret dreams and visions, and who have the maturity to stand securely in the love of Christ amid the curiosity and questioning of our age with its emerging spiritual awareness. It's beautiful to watch people encounter that wisdom as their dreams are interpreted, and to lead them through their encounters with the living God in their visions. We see them realize that God has stopped in a moment in time, reached down, and spoken to them. A frequent reaction makes

---

25    Faisal Malick, *Destiny of Islam in the End Times*, Destiny Image Publishers Inc. 2007.
26    Ibid.
27    Daniel 5:16.

me smile – people say, "I didn't know Christians knew about spiritual things." Love has a voice and people are ready and eager to hear what He is saying.

As we train and equip the *laos*, the household of faith, to respond to this hunger and searching, we help them to understand the four basic skills of prophetic ministry. Interpretation is one of the prophetic skills through which we hear God. Together, these four skills are:

- revelation, in which we hear or see what God is saying;

- interpretation, in which we interpret what that means;

- application, in which we apply it in the right situation;

- timing, in which we discern the time frame that God had in mind.

The four skills encapsulate an understanding of the prophetic process. We find their roots back in the Old Testament, where we see this comprehensive process of revelation and listening to God in the words, "Hear, O Israel…"[28] The Hebrew for "hear" is *Sh'ma*. It means to listen, to discern, to understand (interpret), to fully obey (apply), and to proclaim.

In this book we are looking at that prophetic process of listening to revelation in the form of dreams and visions, and understanding what they mean, in order to apply their meaning to our lives:

> *All men dream: but not equally. Those who dream by night in the dusty recesses of their minds wake up in the day to find it was vanity, but the dreamers of the day are dangerous men, for they may act their dreams with open eyes, to make it possible.*[29]

This book aims to help you become a dangerous dreamer of the day: possessing that rare blend of vision and action, to implement the tested messages within revelation. It aims to help you to add strategy to vision, to become one who breaks through, whose lamps keep burning in

---

28      Deuteronomy 6:4.
29      T. E. Lawrence (Lawrence of Arabia), *Seven Pillars of Wisdom*, Anchor, 1 June 1922..

testing times, who can scale a wall, advance in the face of enemies, and see darkness turn to light.[30]

But in stark contrast to these joyous and victorious words, a picture in the book of Proverbs keeps our minds focused on the importance of the task.[31] The Aramaic Bible translates the verse as, "Where there is no revelation a people is breached."[32] And the evidence of the serious consequences of this lack of revelation is everywhere to be seen.

History tragically and dramatically offers the lesson in the case of Abraham Lincoln, who believed in taking dreams seriously. For instance, in 1863 he wrote to his wife asking her to "put Tad's pistols away" because he "had an ugly dream about him".

According to the President's friend Ward Hill, Lincoln told his wife and a group of friends, just days before his death at the hands of gunman John Wilks, that he had dreamt of his own assassination, saying, "I slept no more that night and although it was only a dream, I have been strangely annoyed by it ever since."

Hill records that the President discounted the dream because he didn't recognize the corpse lying in state as his own, despite the fact that, in the dream story, he had asked the mourners who had died and was told, "The President." I don't, of course, know what increased security measures might have been available to Lincoln, had he rightly understood the dream, and whether they could have made a difference to the outcome. But if they could have done so, Lincoln paid a high price for a lack of sound interpretation.

The verse in Proverbs 29:18 goes on to say, "but blessed is the one who heeds wisdom's instructions."

When we *sh'ma* – when we heed and apply the word of the Lord as it comes to us – we become dangerous to the darkness. We begin to rebuild the walls around our lives, our families, and our communities: "Your people will rebuild the ancient ruins... you will be called Repairer of Broken Walls, Restorer of Streets with Dwellings."[33]

The church is learning to listen again, to understand and interpret the world's dreams and visions. In this age of mass communication,

---

30    See 2 Samuel 22:29–30.
31    Proverbs 29:18.
32    Martin McNamara, 1991.
33    Isaiah 58:12.

we are rediscovering one of the oldest scriptural methods of communication between God and His people.

But while you are learning, it's important to restrict yourself to general comments about other people's dreams and visions. This book will introduce, reinforce, and help you to apply the skills and knowledge you need to understand the language of dreams and visions, but it takes time to develop this skill, to avoid misreading the signs.

Swansea Council had a high-profile problem with interpretation of a bilingual sign, photographs of which were splashed all over the internet. Embarrassingly, the non-Welsh-speaking administrators failed to understand the automated email response which they received after emailing the translation department to translate their sign. Instead of instructions regarding heavy goods lorries reversing, in Welsh on the sign it read, "I am not in the office at the moment. Send any work to be translated." It's good to learn a language before using it in public.

This book is more than an introduction to a skill base. It is an invitation to apprentice yourself to a craft, to work with the One who speaks to bring life and transformation. It's an invitation to come back to the centre and listen to your own heart. It may have been quite some time since you paid any attention to your own inner voice. But you are not forgotten. In your dreams and visions God lifts your burdens and comes to find you when you are lost. He has so many things to show you. He wants to teach you not only how to understand those things but also to dream again, to lift your gaze, to become all that He made you to be: from the centre of His love right to the outskirts, the hem of His garments – where people come and find healing when we interpret their dreams and visions.[34]

Brother Lawrence, a seventeenth-century Carmelite lay brother who wrote a small treatise on prayer which has become a beloved classic, spoke of the soul as a small boat with the Holy Spirit as the wind in her sails: "Those who have the gale of the Holy Spirit go forward even in sleep."[35] As Richard Foster words it in his book, *Sanctuary of the Soul* – "Those who have been breathed on by the Holy Spirit move forward, even while sleeping."[36]

---

34    See Luke 8:44 – the woman who found healing when she touched the hem of Christ's garment.
35    Brother Lawrence, *The Practice of the Presence of God*, available in many editions.
36    Hodder & Stoughton, 2011,

In sleep, when we are entirely passive, our heart finds a voice. God communicates without running the gauntlet of our distractions and opinions. A God-initiated healing process begins to address the areas of strain in our life, bringing hope, rest, and new beginnings. He speaks to us about our life and our relationships, so that we can make good choices and adjustments to succeed. He reboots our emotional life.

As His revelation flows, *shalom* – that healing peace, happiness, safety, and completeness – begins to be established more and more in our life. And the rhythm of order and wholeness – where we breathe and sleep, wake, and live in well-being, is gradually restored. Our thoughts, experiences, and feelings are processed while we rest. God has set up a healing and processing dynamic while you sleep.

It's literally creative, and how very like God. After all, which parent hasn't gone to check on their sleeping child and whispered their love, removed things which weren't safe, reached out, and blessed them?

One of the big needs of our age is to hear Him, to truly hear the voice of God speaking to us. We are not orphans cut adrift upon the currents of our lives. In dreams and visions, God's hand comes down to touch and heal. His revelation creates a stream of life-giving consciousness within our own hearts and minds. His loving guidance guards and keeps our ways. He is the Father we have missed. And in the night, in pictures and visions, His kingdom comes – His revelation falls like fresh rain.

For some of you reading this book, there will undoubtedly be areas in your life that looked at first like pools of promise – maybe the beginnings of a relationship, a marriage, a child born to you; or something you started – perhaps a job, vocation, or ministry. But when you look at it now, instead of a clear pool of promise, you see a muddy puddle. What you need is fresh rain.

> "For my thoughts are not your thoughts,
> neither are your ways my ways," declares the Lord.
> "As the heavens are higher than the earth,
> so are my ways higher than your ways,
> and my thoughts than your thoughts.
> As the rain and snow come down from heaven,
> and do not return to it without watering the earth,

*and making it bud and flourish,*
*so that it yields seed for the sower and bread for the eater,*
*so is my word that goes out from my mouth:*
*It will not return me to empty,*
*but will accomplish what I desire,*
*and achieve the purpose for which I sent it.*
*You will go out in joy and be led forth in peace."*[37]

That's a picture of *shalom*. The wellness of the kingdom. The Septuagint, the Greek version of the Old Testament created in AD 70, translates the Hebrew "word" – used here in verse 11 ("so will my message be that goes out of my mouth") into the Greek word *rhema*, which resounds with life-giving creative energy and potential. It is not something written but a dynamic, living word spoken by God into a soul to bring faith to birth.

Dreams and visions act as the *rhema* of God, the in-breathing of His Spirit to bring life. Like rain in the desert causes it to bloom, dreams and visions fall on the dry riverbed areas of your life like a beautiful covering of fresh snow, to restore purity and put things back the way they were supposed to be. He restores your soul.

John Sentamu says, "God invites us to join Him in transforming both [the world] and ourselves. God trusts and believes in us implicitly. His love affair with us is such that He loves to transform us into those people we were meant to be."[38]

As we progress through the book we will look at how dreams and visions are sent to us with that purpose. As we interpret and apply the wisdom they contain, the arrow goes straight to its aim, the revelation achieves its intent.

If you can use this book with a friend, go through the exercises together. If you get stuck, separate and give yourself two or three days to ask God to show you the meaning of the dream or vision. He can, even while you are on the bus, having lunch, or sleeping. Then come back together and share your experiences. The best interpretations are done in a team. Give God time to lead you.

---

37     Isaiah 55:8–12a (NIV).
38     The Most Revd Dr John Sentamu, Archbishop of York, in *The Daily Telegraph*, 22 December 2002.

Don't always rush to the answers at the back. Your gift of interpretation will grow as you exercise it and you will learn something with every exercise you do. Practice makes perfect. Your ability, confidence, and understanding will all develop together.

And if you need help – come and see us on a dreams and visions course. We will spend time with you to see where and why there is a blockage. Our courses are always fun, and trained mentors will be alongside you.[39]

In the first book of Samuel (chapter 3), the story is told of Samuel's very first experience of God speaking to him, when he was only a little boy. A child oblate, he lived at the temple with Eli the old priest, and when he heard the Lord calling his name as he lay in bed he assumed it was Eli, and rushed to see how he could be of service. After this had happened three times, it dawned on Eli that little Samuel had heard the voice of God, and he told him how to respond next time it happened. He was to say, "Speak, Lord, because your servant is listening." Sometimes we can be like the young Samuel needing a prompt from Eli, and we are here to help you. This book is part of a collection of resources to help you on your journey, so you can understand what God is saying to you and to others.

"Speak, Lord, because your servants are listening."

## My prayer for you

Lord God, I ask that You will speak to those reading this book, as they come to ask You for wisdom. Please walk with them, and open to them the understanding they need. I know You can lead and guide them, and You want to do so. I bring them to You, asking You to put out Your hand and bless them. Let them hear your laughter, speak to them in dreams, reveal yourself to them in visions. Give them discernment, so they understand what You are saying.

Please mature the gift of interpretation throughout the body of Christ. I pray that You will raise a wave of interpreters who will take light into the world, so that many will recognize Your voice and hear what You are saying to them in the days ahead.

In Jesus' name, Amen.

---

39    Contact details for enquiries about dreams and visions courses can be found at www.lovehasavoice.org (accessed 10 August 2017).

## Teaching points from chapter 1

- Interpreting dreams and visions is more than analyzing the information in them. It allows people to listen to their own hearts and understand what God is saying through the dreams and visions. Its aim is to work with the meaning of the dream or vision until it fulfils its purpose of positive change or encouragement.

- It is important to balance the dream's story with its symbols. The symbols in the dream help, but they can mean different things person to person, culture to culture. It's the dream's story that holds the message. Some parts of a dream will be literal and some will be symbolic. You will learn to allow the context and the flow of the story to guide you. What is the story saying?

- Dream and vision interpretation is a skill, not a science. There are some things you can learn to apply; there are some things you can only discern or "hear".

- It will take an average of three to five years to become fluent in the language of dreams and visions. The four basic prophetic skills of revelation, interpretation, application, and timing make up a developed, mature understanding, but simple interpretation can easily be picked up.

- Relax and enjoy the exercises; prayerfully leave time if you get stuck – allow God to bring that moment of unlocking. "Do not interpretations belong to God?"[40]

## Some safe guidelines while you learn

In the learning stage, it is best to apply some straightforward guidelines for interpreting dreams and visions. Often it's a matter of using the right phrases and language. It's wise to learn to put something well. I recommend these guidelines as a constant when you use interpretation.

Be general and humble in your interpretation. There is a limit to your knowledge. Using phrases like, "I think…", "It seems to me…", or "I

---

40    Genesis 40:8.

believe this is speaking about…" gives the person who has received the dream or vision room to consider what you are saying and to peacefully accept or reject it.

"The one who prophesies speaks to people for their strengthening, encouraging and comfort" (1 Corinthians 14:3). Encouraging and comforting are like "over-the-counter medicines in a pharmacy – everyone can use them, with reference to the instructions by the manufacturer. In this case, be loving, use common sense, and respect people's normal everyday boundaries.

But certain categories of revelation are like behind-the-counter medicines. It takes a qualified, experienced pastoral practitioner to use them. We advise you to:

- avoid foretelling – saying what is going to happen;

- avoid direction – saying that a dream implies someone should follow a particular course of action;

- avoid correction – telling people not to do a particular thing;

- avoid giving warnings.

We'll guide you through the best way to give interpretations during the exercises, so that you develop a strong inner awareness of safe practice.

## A working definition of terms used in this book

It's helpful to understand the difference between a dream and a vision, which both encompass revelation which comes in picture form.

**Visions**, as we use the term in this book, are images or moving pictures you see while you are awake; this can be in your mind's eye, or you may see them openly.

Take a moment to picture a large birthday cake. See its colours, the plate it is sitting on. In your imagination, you "saw" a picture. A spiritual vision, however, comes unbidden; it is not deliberately summoned up in your imagination or the result of something your mind has been dwelling on. You usually notice visions first in worship or in prayer. You will learn to identify their source, which is a vital skill, to discern whether a vision or dream is from God, from the person's own mind, or from a dark source.

**Dreams**, on the other hand, are moving pictures you see in your mind's eye while you are asleep. They are easily forgotten, although this has more to do with the function of short-term memory than the nature of dreams. The duration of short-term memory, unless you reinforce the memory of the dream by recording or recounting it, is between fifteen and thirty seconds on average.[41] If we record our dreams, we capture those fleeting impressions that can hold meaning.

Some dreams recur or are very memorable and stay with us for a lifetime, but it's important not to be too serious about recording every single dream. That can become time consuming and bring a lack of peace.

The same symbolic language, along with our own very personal symbolism, is often found in dreams and visions. It is interchangeable.

**Seers** are those who see dreams and visions from God. When our dreams are interpreted, we find out that we all "see" to a greater or lesser extent, but seers see what is, what is to come, and what God wants to do. They notice spiritual activity and perceive the unseen issues of people's hearts. Discernment, a biblical filter, balance, common sense, and teamwork, with a healthy, loving base, are all key in the seer gifting, because the job description is necessarily subjective.

I have a special love for seers. It's an interesting way of life, a 3D technicolour way of living that is so far from the mundane everyday. We make a safe place for seers on our mentoring schools to help them learn to flourish in their lives and gifting.

In the book of Revelation, John is shown a vision, and he is told, "Write down what you have seen."[42] In Habakkuk it is put like this to the prophet, who has been watching to see what God would say to him: "Write the vision, make it plain... so that a runner may read it."[43] He is told to see it, record it, and make it clear, so that those who read it can run freely, with joy and passion, in the path that God has chosen for them. This is our life's work.

**Prophetic person:** In the context of this book we use this term to describe those who partner with God by using revelation, rather than those holding an office of prophet.

Take time to settle in and enjoy the journey!

---

41      Research by Alkinson & Shiffman (1971) cited in *Simply Psychology AS*, Oxford University Press, 2012.
42      Revelation 1:19 (NLT).
43      Habakkuk 2:2 (NRSVA).

*Chapter 2*

# BEGINNING YOUR PRACTICAL JOURNEY INTO UNDERSTANDING DREAMS AND VISIONS

*There was a man who never became a mathematician, because he believed the answers in the back of his textbook. Ironically, the answers were correct.*

Anon

Some time ago I was teaching at a conference when I received a text from a friend who worked with me in the prayer house. Alistair's name flashed up on my screen along with his message: "Dude, tell me my dream."

I replied, "Ali, I'm too busy to play with you now. Let's talk later!" And I carried on with my training session. Looking back, I wonder what would have happened if we had paused and played Alistair's game. Would God have shown me the dream if I had asked Him?

An Old Testament King asked the prophet Daniel the same question. Having had a disturbing dream, Nebuchadnezzar pulled in his wise men and, on pain of death, asked them to tell him *both* the content of his dream *and* the interpretation.

Daniel was thrown back on God and needed a 100 per cent revelation. God came through, as He always does when our backs are against the wall, and He showed Daniel both the dream and the interpretation.

We will make this journey much easier for you than it was for Daniel, and give you three things to reduce the amount of revelation you will need for interpreting each dream or vision in this book:

- We will give you the dream or vision!

- We will give you the context of the dream or vision story – helpful information about the people involved and their lives. Context gives meaning. The relevant part of the real-life story of the person helps you understand the meaning of the dream or vision.

- We will also give you questions to lead you along a path, like stepping stones, to unlock the interpretation during the early learning stages.

I'd like you to move lightly through the dream and vision exercises, to play with them. As you do, you will learn, because this mix of practical wisdom, growing experience, and revelation from God unfolds the journey into understanding dreams and visions. One of the questions I am asked most frequently is: can the interpretation of dreams and visions be taught? If it's a gift, how can training help?

The concept of a journey into understanding – while engaging with revelation – is very scriptural.

> The advance of the kingdom, the spiritual life, does not occur instantly, but over time... [We] do not instantly understand it all. But the Spirit of God illumines [our] understanding daily. Eventually, stumbling disciples will become bold ministers.[44]

Your journey begins by asking God to give you the prophetic gift of being able to understand dreams and visions.

"Keep on pursuing love, and keep on desiring spiritual gifts, especially the ability to prophesy."[45] The journey begins in a place of

---

44      Dr Allen Ross, "The Parable Of The Sower And The Seed (Matthew 13:1–23)", 2006, available at https://bible.org/seriespage/20-parable-sower-and-seed-matthew-131-23 (last accessed 10 August 2017).
45      1 Corinthians 14:1 (ISV). The Greek words used here are *dioko*, meaning "earnestly pursue"; and *zeloo* (for "desiring"), meaning "be ambitious for" – a strong word,

prayer, humility, and rest; it's a quiet place.

When I was a student, I became filled with a desire to hear God speak to me. From a conservative evangelical background, studying both the Old and New Testaments as part of my degree, this was new to me. I went down on my knees every Wednesday afternoon, praying that I would hear God's voice beyond Scripture. And I heard nothing. As the months went by, in the face of increasing frustration, I continued to present my request to God. I asked, I stopped, I listened. And I heard nothing.

But something happened as I lived my life: I began to see visions when I worshipped, to hear God speak to me when I walked in the countryside. At first it was peace-loving and secure, and then strong and powerful, affecting situations and lives. Several years on from those early days, I began to seek to interpret dreams and visions. It's so simple: we manifest what we carry, we carry what we are given, we are given what we seek. Gifting begins with a seeking, with an "earnest desiring". Then it develops and matures during a journey, through which God teaches you how to see and hear and how to understand. It's this journey into understanding that you and I are going on together through this book.

The second step of the journey is training. As Bill Johnson often says, while teaching on the subject of spiritual gifts: "Gifts are free. Maturity is expensive."[46] The gift is given, but the person needs to be trained. In the stories of the Old Testament prophets and in Paul's New Testament teaching, we see a training and learning process going on. I love the fact that Samuel continually got it wrong at the beginning of his ministry, but God persevered and brought someone to help him.

A similar gentleness marks the young Jeremiah's first visions:

> And the word of the Lord came to me, saying,
> "Jeremiah, what do you see?" And I said, "I see an
> almond branch."[47]

And God went on to tell him what it meant.

Learning to see and hear is the beginning of the journey. It's a sweet time. I often spend time with those who are at this stage in their journey

---

the root of the English "zeal".
46      Bill Johnson, senior pastor of Bethel Church, Redding, California, USA.
47      Jeremiah 1:11 (ESV).

into revelation; their wonder and sheer enthusiasm make me smile. They are far more excited when they see or hear something directly from God than if we prophesy to them. In our outreach ministry, I watch people who have never previously encountered God beginning to see visions and hear His inner voice, responding to Him – often for the first time – as their journey toward Him begins. They have experienced the reality of God as a real person who communicates with them and they marvel at what has just happened. But it takes time for them to begin to understand and interpret what they see.

In the New Testament, Paul teaches how to deal with revelation, how to establish order and protocol in its use. His instructions use the word "weigh" in the Greek, which can also be translated "discriminate, interpret, to recognize."[48] He trains us to use the gift.[49] As we are trained, our spiritual senses are matured, "trained by use to see…"[50] In effect, in this chapter, I'm asking you, just as God asked Jeremiah, "Reader, what do you see?" And I'm giving you some information and questions which will help you understand what you see.

## Getting started – key steps to observe in unlocking an interpretation

Three foundational questions will help you to interpret dreams and visions. In this chapter we take time to look at and practise these three foundational steps, so you begin to notice them instinctively:

• Who or what is the dream or vision about?

• What type of revelation is it?

• What protocol should I apply?

We are gradually building the layers of your understanding through teaching, examples, and exercises. The exercises will help you to use what we teach you so that it becomes second nature to you. It's important to be patient with yourself on the journey. I treat it as a game

---

48    For example, 1 Corinthians 14:29: "Two or three prophets should speak, and the others should weigh carefully what is said." "Weigh" is translated from the Greek *diakrino*, meaning "separate, distinguish, discern". From *dia*– meaning "thoroughly back-and-forth", which serves to intensify, and *–krino*, meaning "to judge".

49    Goodrick and Kohlenburger III, *The NIV Exhaustive Concordance*, Zondervan Publishing House, 1990, p. 1702.

50    Hebrews 5:14 (BBE).

of hide and seek, being amused and relaxed as I ask God to show me the hidden meanings in the revelation.

## Step one: who or what is the dream or vision about?

Asking who or what the dream or vision is about is the first step to understanding the revelation. Unless we learn to ask this, we may come up with many and varied interpretations, but they will not be what it is really about.

The majority of our dreams are about our own lives, but revelation about other things goes up if you have responsibility or pray, for other people and events. In the Bible we see God giving revelation through dreams and visions to leaders and intercessors so they can act and pray effectively in wider situations.

To identify what or who the revelation is about, ask yourself: is the person who had the dream or vision:

- a key part of the story? Then it's about them.

- a small part of the story? Then it's about something they play a part in.

- observing the story? Then it's about what they are observing.

Alan took a dream to his church leader because he felt it was about their church. At that time, Alan was learning to interpret dreams and visions at a local training school. Alan started off by explaining his dream: "I was driving my car, to pick up my son from his school…"

When we ask ourselves, "Who or what is this dream about?" we see at once that it's about Alan's own life, not the church, as he supposed, because none of the statements in the dream point to church:

- I was driving (he's in charge)

- my car (in this case his vocation)

- to pick up my son (Alan's growing interpretation gift)

- from his school (the training school where he was learning to interpret dreams and visions).

Alan's life and his new area of training, not his own church, are the main focus of the story. Everything belongs primarily to him. Approximately 90 to 95 per cent of all revelation is about the life of the person having the dream or vision.

"Who or what is the dream or vision about?" is a vital question to ask each and every time or we can mistakenly jump to conclusions. But also when we come to do an interpretation for someone else we can often be reminded of something going on in our own life, and overlay our life or opinions on to another person's dream or vision, especially if we identify with the story. Asking this question is a great safeguard because it puts boundaries around the dream or vision, isolating it from our own lives as interpreters.

Knowing that in his real-life context Alan had recently begun a new area of training helped us understand his dream.

The real-life context of the person who saw the dream or vision will always help you understand it more fully. Details make more sense when the context is explained.

I remember the parents of a girl called Emma contacted us to ask advice about their daughter's dream. We were able to understand it when Emma's mother told us the context of what was happening in Emma's life at the time. Emma's best friend Josie was suffering from anorexia. The girls were part of a supportive friendship group of which Josie had been the leader, and the stress of the situation was impacting all the girls. The situation was becoming serious as various children, including Emma, were beginning to stop eating and lose weight.

Emma told her parents, "I dreamt I was in a car with all of my friends. Josie was driving all over the road – it was erratic and dangerous. I knew we were going to crash. I asked her to stop and be careful. I knew that at thirteen she was too young to drive. But she said that this was how her mother had taught her to drive."

Now that we know the context, the dream itself carries more meaning: Josie's issues are not only impacting her health, but all the girls are at risk because of her behaviour. This dream is highlighting the negative influence that Josie has on Emma and the other girls at the moment.

Emma is a small part of this dream story. She is in the car with all her friends, but it is Josie in the driving seat. The dream is about the effect of what was happening in Josie's life on Emma and the rest of the friendship group.

We felt this flagged up an urgent priority to get Emma out from under Josie's leadership. Fast. Because we had responsibility for caring for this family, we had the freedom to suggest that they consider this option. A mutual friend was an expert psychologist in the field of eating disorders, and our initial thoughts were confirmed by her advice.

Emma's parents gently encouraged her to be healthier and more relaxed about her diet. We stepped in to help Emma's mother increase her own influence and friendship with Emma, and gradually Emma's eating habits returned to normal. The friendship group became increasingly dysfunctional and disintegrated, but Emma was able to transition to a healthy new group of friends. Meanwhile, Josie's own situation became more acute and she was given the expert care that she needed in a specialist unit and had time away from school to recover her sense of health and well-being.

Alan and Emma had dreams which were about their own lives, but one evening, an elderly lady asked me about a dream which had perplexed her. She told me, "In my dream I was watching two men. One of the men had a huge black spider on his neck."

Our dreamer was observing a dream story about the men, particularly about the man who was being attacked by the spider. This dream was not about the dreamer.

God shows us revelation about other people and other situations for various reasons. In this case, the lady loved to pray for others and had prayer power to exert on behalf of the man who was under a degree of spiritual assault. Those next to him seemed oblivious of the fact, but our dreamer had seen and paid attention to his need, which was revealed to her in a dream.

When a seer brings me a dream or vision which doesn't seem to fit their own life, my first question is, "Are you an intercessor?" The usual answer is, "I don't think I'm an intercessor, but I love to pray for people." This question helps us to understand when a dream or vision is calling the dreamer to pray for someone else who has appeared in the dream.

# DREAMS AND VISIONS EXERCISES EXERCISE SET 1: QUESTIONS TO UNLOCK AN INTERPRETATION

## Step One: Who or what is the dream/vision about?

To help you practise identifying who or what a dream or vision is about:

- Look at the context of each dream or vision story. Read the information about the real lives of the seers. The context will help you understand the meaning in the story.

- As you consider who or what the dream is about, remember: if the person having the revelation is observing a story, then it is about someone or something else; if the dreamer plays the key role in the story, it is about them; if the dreamer has a small part in the story, it is about something in which they are involved that concerns them.

Apply these two steps to the following three dreams and vision exercises, to decide who or what these dreams are about. (The answers to the questions – along with the full interpretations for your interest, are at the end of the chapter.)

## Exercise 1.1: Hannah's fireplace vision

### The context

Hannah, who has a Christian worldview, had this vision while praying for her neighbour. The neighbour is Angela, mum of a six-year-old boy with considerable special needs; both she and her husband John run their own businesses. They are also part of a busy community.

### The vision

"I saw John going on trips to and from their home in his car, patiently bringing logs and putting them in the fireplace. The fire was Angela –

the heart of the home. I saw a huge hand come down from above and it reached in and separated Angela from out of the fire, dusted her off and put her in an armchair – where she sat and rested. Then later Angela reached back into the fire and lit sticks from the fireplace, like torches, and gave them to different people."

Answer this question – Who or what is this vision about:

- Hannah,

- Angela, or

- John?

## Exercise 1.2: Jenny's dream: "Have grace"

### The context

Jenny is married with five children aged between three and thirteen. Sam is a gentle, loving, pastoral man on the staff of her church.

### The dream

"This was a beautiful dream. I was sitting at our dining table for a family meal. Sam was with us. My children and husband were at the table, doing things like nearly spilling drinks and dropping the food dish because of carelessness. I was about to reprimand them quickly and sharply to be more careful.

"Sam jumped in gently, before I did. And only I could hear him speaking to me: 'Have grace, Jen.' So I addressed it lovingly and gently and sorted it out in peace."

Who or what is this dream about?

- Jenny,

- Sam, or

- the family?

## Exercise 1.3 – Shannon's diving dream

### The context

Shannon is a New Age practitioner. She runs a local centre for meditation and complementary therapies. She had heard about our church dream interpretation teams and came to us to interpret her dream.

### The dream

"I was standing beside a pool with a young girl. She was my friend's child. Then I dived into the pool and swam down. I had no oxygen tank on but I could dive deeply in the clear water. I swam down to the bottom of the pool where there was the most beautiful coral. The child followed me. I broke off a piece and brought it back to the surface."

Answer this question:

Who or what is this dream about?

- The child,

- the pool, or

- Shannon?

## Step Two: What type of revelation is this?

Once we have discovered who and what the dream or vision is about, we can move on to step two: determining what type of revelation it is and what is its source.

Each different type of dream or vision has a specific purpose. In order to interpret it well and to understand why it is sent, we need to know what type it is. In this section we will look at the categories of revelation using real-life stories and exercises.

Read through the initial teaching points in a relaxed manner and then let the exercises guide you. You are on a journey of discovery as you go through the exercises; your growing experience will gradually identify more and more information about each dream. You will steadily gain clarity.

While we could be very sophisticated and break down types of dreams and visions into multiple detailed categories, for the purpose of this book and ease of interpretation we will stick to three main categories.

- Life-processing dreams and visions: these are dreams and visions from the soul, expressing our thoughts, experiences, and emotions.

- God's revelation in dreams and visions: these are dreams and visions with a specific, identifiable message from God.

- Dark dreams and visions: these are from a negative spiritual source.

Life-processing dreams are a part of our lives; they help us deal with events, relationships, and situations in a healthy way. They are messages from our own souls, asking us to pay attention to important issues we are going through or overlooking.

Revelation from God is sent to bring light and understanding. As we interpret the dream or vision, we understand what God is showing us and move into a freer, fuller, more balanced life, to pray for others or to act in the way that God is leading us.

Dark revelation needs to be discerned and balanced with truth and life. Its messages don't need to be interpreted; they are sent to intimidate or distract. They simply need to be recognized and countered.

Identifying what type of revelation you are interpreting will help you understand the meaning and the purpose for which it is sent. It will also teach you how to weigh the source of the vision or dream.

## Life-processing dreams and visions

Life-processing dreams and visions have been called "God's status reports", because although they do not contain divine instructions, they reveal the nature of a situation. The seer's subconscious is processing their feelings, needs, and circumstances. This processing, especially during dreaming, is vital for good mental health and well-being. It brings to the fore issues that may need to be dealt with.

## Stuart's surfing dream – a life-processing dream

### The context

Stuart is a kind, professional man in his early thirties. He is married, has his own business, and has two small children with whom he is very involved. The children are home-schooled and the family unit is very strong.

### The dream

"I have a recurring dream. It's always about surfing. There is always good surf. Either I can see it and not get to the beach, or I am at the beach and can't go for a surf – either because I don't have a board (or sometimes a wetsuit) or because I have something else to do."

### The interpretation

This is a life-processing dream from Stuart's own soul, about his own life. Stuart's subconscious mind is processing his feelings and needs. Many of our dreams and visions have elements of processing, even if they also contain other revelation.

Stuart loves the sea and the fun of surfing, but more than that – he finds refreshment there. He may be feeling some frustration at not being able to get away, however valid and genuine the obstacles may be. He faces the age-old dilemma of the demands of duty over his own needs. This dilemma at first affects the quality of our lives, and then goes on to affect the quality of who we are.

On a deeper level, this recurring dream carries a meaning, so the dreams are unlikely to stop until the meaning has been understood. As a busy man, Stuart has little time for himself, and his soul is showing some stress. Because this is a recurring dream, that stress is pronounced. The dream suggests that Stuart desperately needs some leisure, an opportunity for relaxation – the chance to play. It would be helpful for him to focus on the sense of his own needs coming up in the dream.

The dreams will stop when Stuart listens to the validity of his own need of rest, recreation, and refreshment. But just because we, as interpreters, understand and deliver the message of the dream, it doesn't give us a right to tell Stuart what to do. Our part is simply to help the dream achieve its purpose by explaining that it expresses an area of stress and that the recurrences might not stop until that is properly addressed.

## God's revelation in dreams and visions

Life-processing dreams bring to our attention messages from our soul; they help us understand ourselves better. But there are some dreams, just like those in the Bible, where we can identify a message or revelation from God, where He is speaking to us directly about something He wants us to do or understand, or a change He wants us to make. These messages in our dreams and visions are like the gently guiding hand of a loving father, reaching down to help us to thrive in our lives. It is priceless wisdom.

The category of God's revelation in visions and dreams can be simplified into six main types, though in practice there may be more than one of these elements in each dream or vision:

- edification, encouragement, and comfort;[51]

- calling revelation: to reveal something of a person's calling or role in life;

- prayer/prayer ministry revelation: dreams and visions given as a prompt for prayer;

- foretelling: snapshots of the future;

---

51      1 Corinthians 14:3: "But the one who prophesies speaks to people for their strengthening, encouraging and comfort."

- warning: interventions so the dreamer can prevent or prepare for something;

- direction or correction (cleansing): containing information about what we should or shouldn't do.

## Edification, encouragement, and comfort

## Nell's surfing vision: A revelation of comfort and encouragement

Nell's vision also uses the imagery of surfing, but, unlike Stuart's life-processing dream, it was a vision bringing a message from God.

### The context

Nell had had a tough year. First she had lost her job, then an important relationship had ended. Sitting in a New Year's Eve watchnight service, Nell was afraid of facing another year. She was apprehensive of what it might bring.

### The vision

"I had this vision of me holding a surfboard. I was holding it upright like a shield, to protect me as I braced myself against the coming wave of the New Year.

"The vision changed and I saw myself put the surfboard down, and confidently ride the wave on the surfboard, going easily over the rough pebbles and stones on the sea bed."

### The interpretation

There are some elements of how Nell is feeling in her life, which seem like a life-processing vision. But in the middle of the vision there is a shift, speaking the answer to how she is feeling. It doesn't just process how she is feeling; it brings answers. This is a revelation vision from God.

This vision is about Nell's own life; she is the main focus of the story. In the story we see Nell's concern about the year ahead, with an encouraging revelation which shows that she will be able to "ride the wave" of the coming year, and be carried over any difficulties or hindrances. She can relax and rely on God's help as she moves forward into the future.

If you know the Bible well, you will notice the biblical symbolism in this vision. Faith appears like a shield, held tightly to protect Nell – until she realizes she can let go and rest her weight on God's help, stand on His promises, and enjoy her life.

Nell's vision is very different from Stuart's dream. Her vision moves from simple self-expression to addressing her need and showing her a better way, with a revelation of God's power and goodness. This answer to how she is feeling is given so she can relax, trust God, and experience rest. It raises faith. It fits in with that dynamic we've seen operating in Isaiah 55, where God speaks revelation into a situation to bring peace and wellbeing.

> *"My thoughts are not your thoughts…*
> *my ways [are] higher than your ways*
> *and my thoughts than your thoughts.*
> *As the rain and the snow*
> *come down from heaven…*
> *watering the earth…*
> *so is my word that goes out from my mouth…*
> *You will go out in joy and*
> *be led forth in peace…*
> *instead of the thorn-bush will grow the juniper,*
> *and instead of the briers the myrtle will grow."[52]*

The NIV text note on this passage says, "The last verse refers to the reverse of the desolation Isaiah had prophesied about earlier" (5:6) where briars and thistles covered the land. It speaks of the recovery of the land by the release of God's word.

We see this same process of redemption happening in our own lives as God's revelation is made known through dreams and visions. Where there was disorder, peace is sown. Even desolation is reversed by the power and purity of God's word. Our eyes are lifted to the presence and promises of God's provision and we begin to live in that climate where new things grow, life streams down, and the season of singing returns to our land.

---

52    Isaiah 55:8, 12, 13.

When interpreting revelation like this to the dreamer or seer, it's important to use words that work with the vision or dream's purpose to lift burdens and release faith. It's better to avoid describing Nell's feelings with such words as "anxiety... fear... terror... dread". It's time for her to put down those fears. Instead, acknowledge the real struggle she has endured with soft words like "concerned about". It will help to raise her faith if we choose words such as "confident... pass over effortlessly... let go", perhaps saying, "Standing on His strength, you have total certainty."

Put well, an interpretation can bring into effect the dynamic of releasing power into the situation: "[My revelation] will achieve the purpose for which I sent it."[53]

In Nell's case, the vision and interpretation lifted her fears away, and she relaxed about the coming year, with a revelation of God's help and goodness. The interpreter's skill and use of positive words and tone helped Nell find that new hope and peace, which was the purpose of the vision, as her heavenly Father enabled her to receive the gift of the New Year with faith.

## Calling revelation

Every now and then, God calls us to a new sphere of service. Recently I was driving to a nearby city, when I saw a vision of a poster saying, "It's time to get married."

This vision was clearly symbolic, but I was puzzled about its meaning. When I reached the venue where city church leaders were meeting, an international prophet was saying, "It's time for you to marry the land." He then went on to talk about making a dedicated commitment to that city, where God had plans to bring about city transformation. It is only the second time I have had such a dramatic calling experience in my life.

Calling dreams and visions also speak into areas of how you may function/what you may be good at. You may even find that opportunities open up in that area, if this is where you excel.

---

53        Isaiah 55:11.

## Steve's calling dream

### The context

In his everyday life, Steve was a manager in a software company. He used to be very active in his local church, where he was part of a flourishing counselling and inner healing ministry. His loving and caring nature and his ability to think strategically meant that he was a great asset. Steve put aside this ministry when he suffered a deep personal loss, and took time out for several years to come to terms with what had happened, until he had a dream.

### The dream

"I was head-hunted and asked to go to the head office of a company dealing in medical technology. When I was there I saw people from church I used to work with. I left after meeting the boss of the company and went to find my car in the car park underneath a supermarket. I couldn't find my car at first – I had lost it. But after some time I found my car and drove away."

### The interpretation

This dream is giving Steve an invitation to reconsider his call to the area of inner healing. His car represents his vocation. It's interesting that Steve has parked his car and forgotten it. The message of the dream is that the boss at the head office (God) is inviting him to re-engage with his healing vocation. The dream carries an inherent recognition of his valued ability in the area of healing and in the team in which he was working.

### Real-life story

Steve took his time, but then engaged again with his old team at his church, picking up his counselling and prayer ministry. His gentleness and acceptance of people came into their own, and many people found comfort and healing. The encouragement in the dream gave Steve confidence and motivation, which had been stolen by his recent personal journey.

Calling dreams and visions are very scriptural, calling us either to a specific people group or to an area of work or ministry. But it's important to interpret them wisely and in general terms. This is a vital skill, because it gives the seer room to consider the possibilities that appear in the dream or vision, without directing what is to come.

As interpreters, we see part of the story, and our interpretations need to reflect that degree of insight using general phrases like, "You may like to explore this area with someone who knows you well." This avoids raising false expectations, lifts pressure, and allows a relaxed consideration of the areas suggested in the dream.

## Prayer/prayer ministry revelation

Prayer ministry dreams and visions reveal places and hurts in people's lives and situations, that need prayer for inner healing or deliverance. They often contain crucial information or bring feelings to the surface, to help us pray effectively.

## A short dream about a brother

### The context

John is a man in his forties who came from a very broken home and family. He had recently become a Christian when he had this brief dream.

### The dream

"I dreamt I was angry with my brother."

### The interpretation

This dream differs from a life-processing dream because the wounds of John's past are being addressed and healed. The dream specifically reveals areas of forgiveness for prayer ministry.

### Real-life story

This dream was the beginning of a season of prayer counselling. It took time for John to come to terms with his past and to begin to live in the present.

## Foretelling

Dreams and visions don't only reveal the things of the past, so that they can be processed and healed. They can also speak powerfully into the future.

As we collect dreams to interpret from the general public, we've found that a surprising number of people of all worldviews have foretelling dreams and visions. They are sometimes very unnerved when the event they saw really happens, especially if the event they dreamed or saw was disturbing, distressing, and came to pass.

In my own life I've found that the foretelling of events, sometimes years in advance, both comforts me and reassures me that God knows what is going on, and instructs me in handling a present situation effectively. I am forewarned and prepared. Because foretelling can help the dreamer prepare for what is to come, the difference between a foretelling and a warning can be finely nuanced. A dream or vision may contain elements of both foretelling and warning.

## A foretelling dream with a warning element

About ten years ago, I had a dream showing me I would be offered a new professional role. It gave me a timeline, using the age of my son: it would happen when Jonathan was thirteen. The dream gave a lot of specific detail about what I was to do at that stage and what I would be sent to pastor and care for. I understood the foretelling nature of the dream and put it on one side for future reference. In due course the events happened, exactly as the dream had said and at exactly that time. It was then I remembered one small sentence from the dream: "Be careful to shut and lock the door."

As it came back to me, I began to ask myself what it meant, realizing it must be an important instruction. I needed to be careful to apply that revelation. What did locking the door mean?

Some months before, a friend had given me a book by Corey Russell about speaking in tongues as a source of strength, hope, and spiritual weaponry. Though I'd had neither time nor impulse to read it, I had kept it to explore when I felt ready. As I wondered what locking the door could have meant in my dream, I picked up the beautiful little book. I opened it at random, to find that Corey was speaking about the use of tongues in locking the door against warfare or defeat, and in transforming the spiritual atmosphere around us.[54]

---

54     Corey Russell, *The Glory Within*, Destiny Image Publishers Inc, 2012, p. 135.

On the strength of what I read, I started a prayer campaign, taking time to speak in tongues each day without fail. After a week or so, AnnaElouise came down to breakfast one morning and said, "I had a dream last night – we had a massive new lock on our front door. It was huge and so safe."

We had locked the door.

You will notice that my original dream had a brief warning in it, "Be careful to... lock the door." Nonetheless, it could be identified as *primarily* a foretelling dream. In the same way, a warning dream or vision may have elements of foretelling. The differences are not always clear cut, and dreams or visions may include aspects from more than one category, but the distinctions are helpful for us in weighing, understanding, and applying the message. If I understand what a dream or vision is for, I can use it effectively.

## Warning

These differ from foretelling dreams in that they are intervention dreams, raising awareness of a coming situation not just for information but also so that the dreamer can prevent or be ready for the situation. The sentence about locking the door in my foretelling dream introduced an element of warning so that I could take action.

We have discovered that warning dreams require anointed and experienced interpretation. A high degree of revelation and considerable wisdom are needed to interpret and apply them precisely, because they often deal with things that, as yet, we know nothing about.

## Alison's dream: A warning of personal danger

### The context

We met Alison when she came to have her dream interpreted at a car boot sale where we had a stall. She came to see us with her blind infant daughter, and her mother came along to hold the baby. In some cases, having someone sitting in on interpretation conversations can cause awkwardness or embarrassment. Interpretation of dreams by definition brings hidden or coded things of real significance to the surface. So it's important to be sure before you begin that the dreamer is comfortable about the presence of anyone sitting in on the session. In this case it was clear Alison wanted her mother along and trusted her completely.

Alison had a New Age worldview, and had been reading a New Age book about psychics and prophets and the whole topic fascinated her. Interestingly, she had had an insistent thought the day before that, in her own words, "I would meet a prophet today, who would give me a message."

### The dream

"I was watching myself standing in my bedroom at the window, when I was grabbed by my hair and swung onto the floor. A light lit up the scene as if it was a spotlight."

### The interpretation

Alison was both observing the story and playing a part in it. The dream was processing her situation and also had elements of revelation from God, who demonstrated His care for her safety.

### Real-life story

As we prayed for the interpretation of Alison's dream, it became clear to my team that she was in physical danger. This is very unusual – it is the only dream we have ever interpreted like this.

Gently, I asked Alison if all her relationships were kind and safe relationships, to which she replied, "Yes." Her mother, however – a rather forthright and strong character – leaned over to me to say that the baby's father, Alison's ex-partner, had punched Alison in the face while she had been driving in the car two weeks previously.

I was able to tell them both that, in order to help her stay safe, the dream spoke of a growing concern with Alison's safety. It alerted them to what could have been a developing situation.

Alison's mother provided the context we needed to understand the situation the dream intended to address, so the warning was safely delivered. We kept in contact for many months and all was well with the family.

Alison's warning dream interpretation was specific and helpful, and was given in a productive and kind way. I have lost count, though, of the number of times people have come to me because a careless and inaccurate interpretation delivered a vague warning, leaving them with a generalized sense of impending doom and causing unnecessary fear. This is one of the reasons we suggest that, while you are in the learning stage, it's important to stick to offering interpretation on positive dreams and visions and to keep building the expertise and awareness to deal with other kinds of revelation.

We run an accreditation programme on our courses, which trains people to a competent level in interpretation, delivery, and protocol, and creates a pool of available accredited interpreters for opportunities arising in church or secular venues, including conferences. These interpreters are specifically trained to use the "behind-the-counter" medications – correction, direction, foretelling, and warning – in a measure appropriate to the context of any given interpretation.

## Direction

The phrase, Enjoy the journey is easily said, but less easily done if we have decisions to make, or if we feel lost and alone, without direction.

Directional revelation is the type of revelation most people are seeking, sometimes even without caution or common sense! This makes them very vulnerable, and they sometimes say to us, "Whatever the dream or vision tells me to do, I will do it." I have learnt never to underestimate people's need for us to be wise with them.

This is a time when our wisdom and protocol comes in to cover anybody who asks us to make decisions for them or give them directional revelation. But there is no doubt that, scripturally and anecdotally, directional revelation is very powerful, especially when it speaks straight to our hearts or contains a confirmation about a situation.

In one real-life example, a young missionary nurse in Africa was walking up a road, feeling slightly more than disgruntled because her bus driver had refused to stop the bus at her junction, giving her a journey on foot of several extra miles at the end of a long clinic. But Emma soon realized that God's purposes were unfolding in front of her, because she came upon a young woman with a baby who had a severe eye infection. The stranger greeted the nurse with great joy and told her that in a dream the night before, "a man in white" told her to walk down this road where she would meet an English nurse who would cure her son's sight.

Emma had a supply of antibiotic ointment with her to treat the baby's swollen, weeping eyes, and just as quickly the mother's spiritual eyes were opened to the love of God and His Son Jesus, who had visited her in the dream to bring direction and healing.

## Correction and cleansing

Correctional revelation speaks into areas which need change to improve our lives or bring them into order. It is not a carte blanche to judge others or to interfere in their lives, but is part of God's redemptive voice. "God's kindness leads you to repentance."[55]

### A gentle correction vision

At the end of a meeting during a prayer time, I was asked to chat to a young woman who was crying as if her heart was breaking. As we talked together, the story emerged of a negative and abusive relationship which had been outside of marriage and which had recently ended, leaving the young woman grieving and lost. Jocelyn sobbed her story and her heartbreak, and the tenderness of God rose up within me for this lovely young woman.

### The vision

I saw a picture from the Old Testament story of Ruth. Ruth was in the harvest fields of Boaz, gleaning wheat in safety under his protection.

In the Bible story, Boaz said to Ruth, "My daughter, listen to me, don't go and glean in another field and don't go away from here. Watch the field where the men are harvesting and follow along with the girls. I have told the men not to touch you, and whenever you are thirsty, go and get drink from the water jars."

Ruth was secure and provided for in the fields of Boaz. As I watched the picture unfold, it changed and I saw Jocelyn in another field, exposed and vulnerable, in stark contrast to the security of the first picture. And words spoke over the vision in a voice of achingly tender love, almost like a caress of a question, into Jocelyn's pain: "Whose field have you been sowing in, that you have been false to Me?"

---

55     Romans 2:4 (BSB).

There was no condemnation in the words. It was the concern of a loving Father about the pain that His child had suffered. The biblical imagery used in the vision confirmed the message of redemption and restoration and new life, which came after Ruth's loss and sadness, after the death of her husband. Jocelyn was being gently corrected and given hope and a future.

It was a gentle, cleansing dream to bring healthy order and life back into her situation. Correction and condemnation are totally different things. Correction comes in the context of God's loving care. It is used within pastoral and relational situations in line with our levels of responsibility for people. It comes to bring life and healing.

As Jocelyn heard the question and its gentle concern, she reconnected with God and with His plans for her life.

God had reached out to hold His child and to guide her into His green pastures. He led her in paths of righteousness, He restored her soul.[56] Cleansing came. "If someone denies that correction is needed or enjoys doing what God is trying to correct, God will persevere in His longsuffering love to bring that person around... however there will come a time when His patience will be balanced by His action to address the issue."[57]

Both correction and direction connect and reconnect us with the plans of God for our future. They come to help us fulfil our destiny and partner with Him through life's complexities, but they do need to be carefully and wisely handled.

## Steve's dream story: A case of mistaken correctional interpretation

Steve was one of the most loving men you could hope to meet, but after ten years of marriage his wife had a relationship with a mutual friend and left home, leaving the children behind. Steve forgave and welcomed her home, only for the cycle to begin again. He was left to care for their daughters, and the whole family was in pain.

From the sidelines, a church member – who didn't know the family personally – came to the leader of their church with a short snippet of a

---

56      Psalm 23:1–3 (ESV UK).
57      Adam F. Thompson and Adrian Beale, *Divinity Code*, Destiny Image Publishers Inc, 2011, p. 55.

dream in which Steve's wife was crying. Her interpretation of what she had seen was, "God is saying that they must not divorce and Steve must repent of his harsh treatment of his wife, which led her to leave."

The church leader, who had just moved to the town and taken up his post, without knowing the people involved, sent the dreamer to Steve to deliver the message. At this point Steve became confused because his church leader seemed to think he had been abusive to his wife.

We helped to unpick the tangle and talked to the dreamer. It became apparent that she had been through an abusive relationship herself and was projecting that pain and experience on to Steve's situation. Her interpretation dealt not with Steve's problems but her own issues. The correction was not helpful or accurate because neither the seer nor the leader had sufficient interpretation experience or understanding of the real-life context to discern the real meaning of the dream.

## Dark revelation

This section deals with those dreams and visions that some understandably find troubling, to help you be effective and relaxed when you interpret dark revelation. This section takes the time to defuse the unease surrounding these interpretations.

We need to sort our dreams and visions like we sort our post, in order to identify which of the three sources of revelation the dream or vision comes from. As one interpreter put it, junk mail goes into the bin or the fire. Its self-serving messages are picked up and burnt. Once sorted they receive no more of our time or attention.

Life-processing dreams and visions are a healthy part of our life, processing the situations we've been through.

Revelation, dreams and visions come from God: "Your sons and daughters will prophesy, your old men will dream dreams, your young men will see visions."[58] But some dreams, visions, and nightmares can come from other influences having an impact on our thought life that day.[59]

"Dear friends, do not believe every spirit, but test the spirits to see whether they are from God."[60] As a friend of mine put it, "Untested

---

58      Joel 2:28 (see also Acts 2:17).
59      Ephesians 6:16: "the flaming arrows of the evil one".
60      1 John 4:1.

wisdom is deception." This brings us back to Paul's biblical instruction[61] to weigh – to discriminate, interpret, make a distinction – to recognize the source of what is presented to us as revelation. Paul himself did this in the case of the slave girl who had a spirit by which she predicted the future.[62]

Asking yourself how you feel about a dream or vision can help you discern the source. It is also useful to ask about the quality of light and colour in the revelation. Dark dreams and visions are often exactly that – weather can be stormy or gloomy, colours can be muted or non-existent.[63] It's helpful to ask the seer how they felt about the dream or vision, whether it brought peace or fear, clarity or confusion. Test the messages contained in the revelation against the loving standards of Scripture in tone and content.

If you have an acknowledged gift of discernment you will instinctively recognize revelation from a dark source. But if your gift is not matched with security, wisdom, and maturity in you as the interpreter, it can operate in fear and suspicion. Dark revelation needs to be dealt with confidently and calmly, in the light of God's wisdom.

## Tercia's vision story: An immature interpretation

"I saw a line of angels, full of light, on the mountains around Bergen. My immediate reaction was, 'Oh no! If those are God's angels, we are going to be involved in a war.'"

Tercia's reaction to the revelation of spiritual things was fear, even dread. Her own feelings about life became a lens through which she interpreted this very positive vision of angels surrounding the city. Tercia's interpretation reveals a pastoral need to see things in the light of the loving provision of her heavenly Father.

When you are reading this section, it is possible that you, like Tercia, sometimes use a lens of fear as you engage with revelation. We've seen many people begin to walk out from a life rooted in fear as they begin to test, question, and bring down to size the lies of the enemy in dark

---

61      1 Corinthians 14:29.
62      Acts 16:16–18.
63      It's important to note, however, that one study has found that those who regularly watch black and white television or films tend to dream more in black and white. Study by Eva Mrzyn, University of Dundee, UK, cited in "It's Black and White: TV Influences Your Dreams", 17 October 2008, available at newscientist.com (accessed 23 August 2017).

revelation. As they do so, they discover the safety and security of God, and become quietly confident about life and spirituality.

It may be time for you to go on a journey to find His abundant and life-giving truth, as it comes through revelation, to set you free. And to search out some wise counsel from someone mature enough to know both the security of God's power and love and His compassion toward those who are on a journey into security and faith.

Elisha, the Old Testament prophet, had a similar issue with his servant Gehazi, who woke up one morning to find the enemy army surrounding their camp. Until his eyes were opened, he totally failed to see the many angels that God had sent to address the situation. "And Elisha prayed, 'Open his eyes, Lord, so that he may see.' Then the Lord opened the servant's eyes, and he looked and saw the hills full of horses and chariots of fire all round Elisha."[64]

Our team has appreciated the power of God at a totally new level when we have met with darkness in interpretation situations. The issue is to bring light, not to battle the darkness. "And God said, 'Let there be light,' and there was light."[65] God has not finished creating. It's His nature as the Creator God. Our joy, as interpreters, is to encounter people in their darkness and to speak, "Let there be light." In the words of author and pastor Bill Johnson:

> *Light drives away darkness without a fight. I can't*
> *afford to live in reaction to darkness. If I do, darkness*
> *has a role in setting the agenda for my life... Jesus lived*
> *in response to the Father. I must learn to do the same...*
>
> *Our actions come from one of two basic emotions –*
> *fear or love. Jesus did everything from love. So much of*
> *what is called "warfare" comes out of fear...*
>
> *But it's a place of weakness. God calls us into a place of*
> *strength... walking with Him.*[66]

It requires peaceful wisdom and a developing maturity to test dark revelation, discern the enemy, and in its place plant the counsel and

---

64      2 Kings 6:17
65      Genesis 1:3.
66      Bill Johnson, *Hosting the Presence*, Destiny Image Publishers Inc, 2012, p. 35.

peace of the living God so that the people involved can flourish. When they come across an instance of dark revelation, some interpreters are tempted to share personal experiences of the demonic. It's not helpful. That raises fear or fascination with the darkness. The aim is to communicate the sense of God's love.

## Fiona's dream story: Dealing with nightmares

*He will cover you with his feathers,*
*and under his wings you will find refuge;*
*his faithfulness will be your shield and rampart.*[67]

### The context

Fiona is a young university student who came into our café to have her dream interpreted. She is one of a number of people who have approached us for help after having nightmares. She could not shake off this recurring dream, which began when she moved into her current bedroom. As she confided in us I could sense the fear and darkness it invoked.

### The dream

"This is a recurring dream. I was sleeping and had my eyes closed in the dream, but I felt a ghost walk up to me from behind and touch my cheek. A voice said, 'Who are you?' The speaker had a black hoodie, shaggy hair, a long beard, and a red jacket.

"Then I asked in turn, 'Who are you?'

"It replied, 'I live in your room.'

"It walked away and lightly touched my lower calf. Then suddenly it was in my face. I screamed and woke up."

### The interpretation

In this dream story, we are dealing with two things: the simple request to explain the dream and a very frightened young woman.

As you consider how to deal with interpreting a troubling dream or nightmare, and discern how to bring light into this dark dream, these questions will help you:

---

67      Psalm 91:4.

- Is this a recurring dream? (In this case we know it is.)

- When did it begin? (In this case it began only after Fiona began living in the current bedroom. Nothing else had happened in that room. It was in general a good place for Fiona.)

The literal interpretation of the dream was that there was a spiritual presence in Fiona's bedroom. The dream was more than a mental image of a scary story; it was an "encounter dream". The dark spiritual presence was hidden, intimidating, and powerful, and it was manifesting as she slept. It manifested again as she relayed the dream.

Encountering spiritual beings through dreams and visions is clearly described in Scripture in the story around the birth of Jesus. This time of heightened spiritual activity draws back a curtain into the spiritual realm and teaches us a lot. Encounters with angels seemed to be firing off all over the place. Zachariah, Mary, Joseph, and the shepherds all had visitations from an angel of the Lord.

The angel Gabriel was sent from God to Nazareth for a literal encounter with Mary.[68] Secondly, "an angel of the Lord appeared to [Joseph] in a dream".[69] Visitations like these are more unusual than our dream and vision stories but they are very impactful, either beautifully or scarily, depending on the source. They are identifiable because of the sheer power of their content and their lasting impact.

Had we told Fiona this literal interpretation of her dream, it is highly unlikely that she would have been able to go home that night. Instead, she needed our help, so the conversation with Fiona went something like this:

"That's an unpleasant dream. I think you might be quite spiritually aware, because in the dream you mention that you sensed, not saw, the things you dreamt about. It's a lovely thing, to be spiritually aware. Can you tell me, do you sometimes sense atmospheres in places – sometimes harmonious and peaceful; sometimes not quite as nice? Yes, you're spiritually aware, that's great. But it's even better when things are all settled around you. So this dream started when you moved into your bedroom? It sounds to me like your bedroom needs to be a more

---

68      Luke 1:26.
69      Matthew 1:20.

peaceful place for you. And we can give you some ways to settle that down if you're interested."

We gave Fiona a copy of the Compline prayer (an ancient night-time blessing to bring calm and peace, given in Appendix 1) to use at bedtime, asking God to come into her sleeping space to bring light and peace. We also explained that she could ask God to look after her whole life, and as we did, she met Him at the point of her need. His power brought cleansing and peace to her bedroom, and when we met her again, Fiona was happy and relaxed, and the nightmares were a thing of the past.

Nightmares usually occur for one of three reasons. To deal with them effectively, you need to establish the root.

- Life-processing dreams: something unpleasant and stressful is going on in the present which is being expressed in the dream.

- Spiritual nightmares – an intimidating set of thoughts and images introduced by a negative spiritual force.

- Recurring past trauma dreams: the soul is trying to process and express pain or hurt from the past.

To evaluate this scenario, you can ask two simple questions: "Is this a recurring dream or vision?" and, "Is it a difficult dream or vision that reminds you of something?" (It's important not to ask what those events are, and don't guess! Simply listen well to anything they want to tell you until they have finished.) If the answer is yes, don't interpret the dream. Instead you can, for example say, "That's a tough dream. It may be that you have been living with this for a long time. Some of these feelings can be very raw and it might be that your dreams are expressing these emotions. It can be good to find someone who can help us process these feelings, and then the dreams will begin to fade away. You might like to consider doing that."

You can finish the session by gently moving on, while continuing to show care for and interest in the person. This is far from changing the subject; rather, you are providing a bridge away from the upsetting dream content by your calm demeanour and simple friendliness. As you round off the conversation, your loving attention reclothes the dreamer in a sense of peace, so they can be settled again. It's important to do this, because they have shared something very deep with you.

During interpretation you may encounter and uncover seriously traumatic situations. We once interpreted a dream that uncovered family ritual witchcraft abuse from a man's childhood on a level that was almost impossible to comprehend.[70] We were the first people he had ever been able to tell. At this point we needed to stop and listen without displaying shock or fear, although in such a situation I prefer to remove any young or vulnerable interpreters fast.

Because you have uncovered past trauma, this should be your priority here. Ask yourself:

- How do we cover the person in this conversation by listening and caring?

- To whom do we refer them for the right help?


This can of course be upsetting, and it's important to talk to your team leader about what happened in your interpretation encounter, so that you can be supported and so that the safeguarding lead in your ministry can be aware of the situation in case further action is needed.

If the person talking to you is an adult, unless you are concerned that they might harm themselves or someone else, you carry no legal responsibility. I do, however, like to gently check that the person with the dream has someone in mind that they can talk to, before they leave us.

In our outreach work we have trained listeners available in case they are needed. This shows the beauty and importance of teamwork. Interpretation is a prophetic function. Prophetic ministry is best undertaken in teams, with the covering of pastoral leadership completing a thought-through competence and accountability structure to ensure the most effective and responsible ministry.

## Spiritual nightmares

These can be associated with any of three things:

- previous involvement in occult/New Age/witchcraft activity,

---

70      Ritual abuse is not primarily a matter for deliverance but for inner healing, which of course may in turn bring about the deliverance needed. See Francis MacNutt, *Deliverance from Evil Spirits*, Chosen Books. 2009, p. 89.

either personally or through the family line;

- sleeping in a place that is spiritually unsettled;

- an occasional part of our life experience.

This is something to be explored very gently. Words like "unsettled, annoying, settling it all down" are very helpful, recasting a frightening experience as merely an annoying event which is part of life experience and can easily be dealt with.

If the person is part of the Christian community, we have adopted the traditional practice of the Church of England and the Catholic Church of celebrating communion in a spiritually unsettled place to bring peace. We hold a simple communion service in the bedroom of the person who has been experiencing the nightmares, declaring "the death and resurrection of Jesus Christ in this place". It has a peaceful effect. In our experience it settles the issue if the nightmares were spiritually rooted.

Walking with assurance of Christ's power and supremacy helps us to reverse the flow of spirituality from heaven to earth, as God establishes His rule and order. "You, dear children, are from God and have overcome them, because the one who is in you is greater than the one who is in the world."[71]

> *In the name of the Protecting Father,*
> *In the name of the Conquering Son,*
> *And in the name of the liberating Spirit.*
> *Amen.*
>
> *I rise today through a mighty strength,*
> *The invocation of the Trinity.*
> *I call all heaven to witness today that I have put on Christ.*
> *I choose no other Lord than the Maker of heaven and earth.*
> *This day I walk with Him and He will walk with me.*[72]

---

71      1 John 4:4.
72      *Celtic Daily Prayer Book Two: Farther Up and Farther In*, Harper Collins Publishing, 2015, p. 1102.

# DREAMS AND VISIONS EXERCISES
# EXERCISE SET 2: QUESTIONS TO UNLOCK AN INTERPRETATION

## Step Two: What type of dream/vision is this and what is its source?

To help you practise identifying the three main different types of revelations simply identify whether each of the four dreams and visions are life-processing revelation, dark revelation, or revelation from God.

The answers to the questions, along with the full interpretations for your interest, are at the end of the chapter.

## Exercise 2.1: A pharmacist dreams about catching a train

### The context

The dreamer was a pharmacist who is a very detailed person with a strong sense of responsibility and concern about getting things right.

### The dream

"I was at the train station with a girl. We were going to Brisbane, Australia. We went to the ticket counter. She got her ticket. But I got the PIN wrong on the card machine and the train left with her and without me."

What type of dream is this and what is its source?

- life processing;

- dark dream;

- revelation dream from God.

## Exercise 2.2: A dream about prayer meetings

### The context

A young minister was organizing prayer meetings to pray for physical healings in the locality.

### The dream

"I dreamt a man came into my bedroom and he said, 'I hear you are asking God to heal people. If you do this…'" (There followed a threat which we will not dignify by repeating, even in this exercise.)

What type of dream is this and what is its source?

- life-processing dream,

- dark dream, or

- revelation dream from God?

## Exercise 2.3: A vision of a visit to a grave site

### The context

An intercessor with a praying heart for Israel had this vision one night. Later the next day, Yitzhak Rabin was assassinated.

### The vision

"I was looking at the gravestone of Yitzhak Rabin, a former prime minister of Israel, who played a significant role in the Middle East peace deal."

What type of vision is this and what is its source?

- life-processing vision,

- dark vision, or

- revelation vision from God?

## Exercise 2.4: Sea of Galilee vision

### The context

A senior manager had been made redundant and was in transition while being interviewed for several other posts. During some family difficulties she had this dream.

### The vision

"In my vision I was in a storm in high waves. I was aware of the terrible danger I was in, when suddenly a figure walked by the boat. I knew it was Jesus. He got into the boat and calmed the storm. Suddenly I was aware of the beach we had left and all the good things we had left behind. Then immediately I saw the impression of the coast ahead of us. It was green and lush and peaceful, and we were en route to some really good things. I relaxed."

What type of vision is this and what is its source?

- life-processing vision,

- dark vision, or

- revelation vision from God?

## Step Three: What protocol should I apply?

Once you have carried out Step One (understanding who and what the dream or vision is about), Step Two (determining what type of revelation it is), you can move on to Step Three – deciding the right protocol to apply.

"Wisdom and revelation are often paired together in Scripture: "For there is a proper time and procedure for every matter."[73]

The safe practice in the rest of this chapter will help you to work in wisdom, humility, and love – all the hallmarks of a Christlike, Spirit-led ministry.

> *Love is patient, love is kind… it is not proud. It does not dishonour others, it is not self-seeking… Love does not delight in evil but rejoices with the truth. It always protects."*[74]

Protocol is the trellis on which the gift of interpretation is trained to produce good fruit. Revelation and interpretation are powerful guns in a ministry arsenal. The safe measures we put around their use bring security and peace to the "family".

"God is not a God of disorder but of peace",[75] wrote Paul to the Corinthian church when he was correcting the misuse of the spiritual gifts.

I've heard countless examples of revelation that has been misinterpreted and misapplied; so much so that I have some sympathy with those who put aside the prophetic gifts because of the disorder that has resulted from misuse. Their answer is to keep the gifts on one side, because it is too risky to use them. In this way the protocols are never taught and the church never matures in wisdom for their use. The gifts are inevitably taken out again by immature people who operate without guidance, and people can be hurt through misinterpretation and misapplication.

I met one young pastor who was serving on the staff of a church under a minister who told him that he had received a revelation from

---

73    Ecclesiastes 8:6.
74    1 Corinthians 13:2, 4–7.
75    1 Corinthians 14:33 (ESV).

God about whom the young man should marry. The young pastor, impressionable and trusting, duly began to pursue his supposed bride, and he was very hurt when she wanted nothing to do with him. Devastated, he returned to his minister who came up with the preposterous statement, "God has changed his mind." Another person had been hurt by a blatant lack of wisdom, guidelines, and safe practice. I wish that I could say this was an isolated event.

There is a useful and pithy little piece of protocol which is commonly used: "No dates, mates, or babies." These three areas – when things will happen, who someone will marry, and if they will have children – are sensitive and deeply emotional issues which can cause considerable devastation if they are interpreted wrongly. They are foretelling and directional issues which should be handled in a highly mature and general way. Those who are learning need to be taught safe guidelines from the birth of their gifts. When gifted people grow up in mature families, the guidelines by which they need to operate safely are naturally passed on. Right use beats dis-use as a source of safety.

My family have a farm in a beautiful part of Dorset on the south coast of England. For as long as I can remember, my grandfather had a double-barrelled shotgun to shoot pests; it was casually laid up against the wall in the corner of the farmhouse study. Nowadays, the law requires that even unloaded guns are locked away in a cabinet. But when I was a child, the family protocol was so strong that neither I nor the other children in our family ever touched the gun. We were taught one piece of protocol: dis-use: "Don't touch the gun," and we never did. The boys in the family were gradually initiated into the rites and rules of gun safety. As a girl, I never had any further instruction until, as a young teen, I came across my brothers and cousins practising shooting clay saucers, and they offered me a turn. As I picked up the double-barrelled shotgun, my lack of protocol was about to become very dangerous indeed.

After some simple instructions about how to hold the gun, to counter its kick, I shot my first clay saucer, leaving one more cartridge in one barrel of the gun. I was so excited that I wheeled round in a circle with whoop of jubilation. All the boys in my firing line hit the ground except for my brother Murray, who, with both hands in classic "surrender" position, said calmly, "Liz, put the gun down." The problem with "dis-use" as a piece of protocol is that untutored people will pick up the gift and begin to experiment.

We need corporate, thought-through learning communities where accountability and love surround the use of the gifts to bring peace and order with biblical teaching to bring safety to the area of interpretation.

"Right use" is the safest answer, through training and practice. As you read this book, I'd like you to become an ambassador for order and safety, for maturity and good practice. All before you interpret a single dream or vision fully!

We interpret dreams and visions into the context of a community. Appendix 2 contains a good practice summary for you to photocopy and give to a wise member of your community or church leader, who can help to hold you accountable for your wise and safe practice. A peer group working together to mature in using wise principles is also invaluable while we are practising in the community.

Appendix 2 also contains a brief set of guidelines for you to give to people for whom you interpret dreams and visions. My own experience is that we should never take for granted that people know these guidelines, especially when they are stressed. They need reminding of their own safe practice.

The protocol to follow is, of course, determined by the nature of the dream or vision.

| Type of dream or vision | Protocol to apply |
|---|---|
| **Over-the-counter meds** | |
| Encouraging revelation | Interpret and encourage |
| Calling revelation | Be general not directive. "You may find you are good at…" / "You may find opportunities in the area of…" |

| Type of dream or vision | Protocol to apply |
| --- | --- |
| Prayer/prayer ministry revelation | Be general about the area for prayer. Simply suggest that their attention is being drawn to this area for prayer and that they might like to talk to a trusted friend about it. |
| Dark revelations and nightmares | Don't interpret the content. Instead, deal with the person, if they are afraid, by bringing in peace, light, and reassurance. |
| **Behind-the-counter meds** | |
| Direction, correction, foretelling, and warning | Unless you are responsible for the dreamer or seer's discipleship or well-being in some way (parent, counsellor, pastor), be very general about the areas that the dream speaks of "The dream speaks about issues of…" |
| Moving into ministry/counselling based on a dream or vision | Deeper issues need ministry from experienced people in a safe, often ongoing, relationship |

We consider direction and correction, foretelling, warnings, and using dreams and visions for ministry/counselling, along with interpreting dark revelation and nightmares, as our "behind-the-counter medications", to be given and applied by those with expertise and some level of responsibility.

Easily purchasable "medications" compare to the types of revelation that bring edification, encouragement, and comfort. These are readily available to all and can be used freely according to the "manufacturer's guidelines": love, tact, and gentleness, embracing the cultural norms of good manners and behaviour. Humbly offer up your positive interpretation without being dogmatic or presumptuous.

With "behind-the-counter medications", expertise works hand in hand with having the relationship or authority to speak into the person's life and situation. To continue the medical analogy, just because I'm a qualified doctor doesn't mean I can prescribe for anyone in whom I notice disease. If you're sick, you consult your own GP and follow an appropriate chain of referral.

To work with someone in interpretation, I need to be qualified – that is, I need to have the relevant expertise in interpretation – and I need to have the relationship and position to do so.

The chosen "doctor" or consultant figure (parent/best friend/pastor/spouse/counsellor/youth leader) will ideally have knowledge about the dreamer's life and context; they will know the way that person hears and responds to input, and know what practical care to take when relaying sensitive information. This familiarity with the individual allows them to help the seer with the outworking of their dream or vision. Love covers the interpretation process.

The safeguards for "behind-the-counter" revelation suggest that you should:

- ensure you have the people skills to deliver this humbly, kindly, and wisely. These people skills include the ability to recognize when you are dealing with a vulnerable adult. With a vulnerable adult, just as with a child, who asks for a dream interpretation or vision reading, it's our practice to ensure that a carer/parent is present and to edit the content and give only light-hearted, encouraging, positive messages.

- work in a team.

- work with those who know the detail of the life context: does what you are saying line up with the real-life story?

- ensure that what you are saying lines up with other pieces of corroborating revelation that have come independently.

- ensure that the interpretation lines up with Scripture – in love as well as truth – and that the receiver understands how to weigh the message of the vision or interpretation. Record your interpretation and keep a copy for future reference, in case the receiver has questions about what was said.

The ideal is to practise with someone who is experienced until we have internalized the guidelines, which then become an automatic filter.

Training helps us to become wise in our interpretation. Working in a team supports us during the learning phase, and continues to cover our blind spots. If this is not possible, restrict your interpretations to encouraging and very general interpretations.

Following the protocol will protect us from falling prey to our own prejudices and from jumping to conclusions. Our protocols line up with biblical guidelines that ensure we have been thorough and responsible in weighing the material presented to us.

In our own family, before we respond to revelation, we have a worked-through weighing approach. My attitude is, "If I've heard God correctly then this is going to happen." And then I privately ask God for several pieces of confirmation: an independent piece of revelation which backs up what I've heard, independent confirming circumstances – like provision of any necessary resources – and then wise and trusted counsel. This formula has stood us in good stead when God has sometimes led us to step way out of our comfort zones into exciting new pastures.

Perhaps our clearest application of this weighing process was when my husband and I were newly married. I had a health problem which led to a significant level of pain and limitation. So we assumed it wasn't time for us to have children, and had talked about adopting later in life.

But one day God spoke to me clearly as I was reading the Bible, and I felt strongly that He had told me that I would have children of my own. Instead of telling anyone what I had heard, I prayed about it and asked God for our three levels of confirmation: an unsolicited, independent and confirming circumstance – in this case a significant sum of money to help with childcare; I also asked for independent medical advice, and for a wise counsellor who would weigh the revelation with us.

The three things happened very quickly, before I had even told Dave what I had felt. Within two weeks an unexpected cheque literally fell on our doormat by post for £24,000. I had a routine consultant's appointment two weeks later, at which my consultant asked me if I had any children. I simply replied that I couldn't see how we could have children with my health situation. He looked at me and said, "I can get you through the pregnancy if you'll compromise on drug relief, and if you can find help afterward." It was time to talk to Dave. We sought out some wise and trusted counsel, and the person whom we asked said, "It sounds like God's leading." And we had the blessing of two wonderful little people who have added joy to our lives.

This checking and weighing process is very scriptural: "Suppose one of you wants to build a tower. Won't you first sit down and estimate the cost to see if you have enough money to complete it?"[76]

Working in revelation doesn't mean you suppress or suspend your brain function. Common sense is also part of wisdom. Wisdom and revelation work together to bring success. Immaturity and super-spirituality honour no one, but well-weighed, theologically sound actions following God's leadings through dreams and visions bring glory to His Name, because His goodness is seen on the earth. In his book, *Faith to Live By*, Derek Prince explains, "It's important to evaluate carefully the evidence of our own senses. God does not ask us to close our eyes and ears and walk about as though the physical, material world does not exist. Faith is not mysticism."[77]

I once had a rookie dream interpreter say to me, "It's not my fault if a dream tells a woman to leave her husband. It's in the dream!"

Let's consider how carefully applying our protocols to a dream apparently encouraging a woman to leave her husband could have prevented such a careless statement.

## Protocol One: Be general in your interpretation

You might say, for example, "That's an interesting dream. I'd imagine it's speaking about the issues of marriage. You may like to go with that and talk to someone you trust about that issue if it's coming up in your dreams, because it seems to be something you are concerned about."

Being "general" applies when you are asked to interpret a dream or vision when you have no knowledge about the seer's life, or you have no relational or positional responsibility connecting you with the seer.

With no overview of the person's life, no relationship with them, and no other pieces of reliable independent revelation to back up what you personally see, it is imperative that you are cautious and general in your response. This is especially true if you are interpreting dreams

---

76      Luke 14:28.
77      Derek Prince, *Faith to Live By*, Kingsway Publications, 1984.

and visions on your own, and if the dream or vision belongs to the direction, correction, foretelling, or warning revelation categories.

## Protocol Two: Work in a team

It is clear throughout the New Testament that ministry is best undertaken as part of a team. Those ministering often operate in pairs, rarely alone, and as part of an accountability structure: "Two or three prophets should speak, and the others should weigh carefully what is said."[78]

That corporate weighing is especially important when the dream or vision involves one of the "behind-the-counter" categories of dreams or visions. Telling the dreamer to follow a course of action would be highly directional. If a woman had a dream about leaving her husband, and it was considered by the team, the more mature among them would quickly identify the problem with the rookie interpreter's assessment that the dream was telling the woman to leave her husband. They would remind the rookie to consider what type of revelation this is before deciding what course of action to apply. If it is a life-processing dream, then the dream is not an instruction to be acted on but an exploration of how the dreamer feels about her life circumstances. If it is a revelation from God about the dreamer's marriage, then it is vital to understand and interpret the message wisely. Mature weighing may in fact pick up that the rookie dream interpreter was entirely mistaken in their interpretation. It would certainly pick up that they were entirely inappropriate in their proposed course of action.

## Protocol Three: Work with those who know the detail of the life context

Does what you are saying line up with the real-life story? Is there corroborating information or revelation that has come independently?

If the team has a trusted relationship with the dreamer, the more mature members can check how the dream story fits into the life context of the dreamer, and how the message of the dream harmonizes with what God is saying specifically into the woman's life.

---

78    1 Corinthians 14:29.

They would explore who has a knowledge and an overview of this woman's life. Those individuals will know the relevant facts that need to be taken into consideration. For example, the dream will be a matter of pastoral concern if she's being beaten or abused. Or if it's a life-processing dream, she may be processing any number of feelings about her marriage. But the interpreter cannot possibly know this, while those with overview of the context of the dreamer's life will have an informed perspective and may or may not be interested in the experience and message of her dream.

When interpreters work with practitioners in pastoral settings, the dream or vision gives light to the pastoral situation, and in return, the pastoral situation gives light to the dream or vision.

## Protocol Four: Ensure you have the people skills to deliver your interpretation humbly, kindly, and wisely

A dream such as this flags up the likelihood of marital difficulties. This must be considered with tact and compassion. The attitude expressed in the remark, "It's not my fault if a dream tells a woman to leave her husband," shows that the interpreter has some considerable way to go before handling such delicate and serious relational issues.

## Protocol Five: Ensure that the interpretation lines up with Scripture – in love as well as truth

In matters of such importance, it's vital that the interpretation lines up with Scripture when it is tested by scriptural principles. In every situation the guideline is, "Follow the way of love."[79] The interpretation of the dream should be characterized by loving concern for the woman herself and her choices. Any interpretation that is given to the woman needs to leave her with freedom of choice. The woman herself must weigh any interpretation carefully.

- Does the message of the interpretation you have received line up with Scripture?

- What do wise people who know you say about it?

---

79      1 Corinthians 14:1.

- Is there any independent confirmation of this message from God through others?

If these five relevant protocols for "behind-the-counter" dream interpretation are carefully followed, the damage that could have otherwise resulted from the rookie interpreter's careless and inexperienced interpretation will be avoided.

# DREAMS AND VISIONS EXERCISES
# EXERCISE SET 3: QUESTIONS TO UNLOCK AN INTERPRETATION

## Step One: Who or what is the dream/vision about?
## Step Two: What type of dream/vision is this?
## Step Three: What protocol should I apply?

In this exercise set, you will be asked to answer all three questions. The answers to the questions and the full interpretation for each dream or vision are given at the very end of the chapter, so you can compare your conclusions with those of our team.

Please note: these dreams and visions may contain symbolism included in the interpretations at the end of the chapter. A full introduction to, and discussion of, the validity of symbolism is the subject of the next chapter. So put your questions on hold and answer only the three questions given, for the purpose of this exercise set.

After each of the dreams and visions in this section you will find our three questions to help you identify the type of revelation and how to handle it well.

- Who or what is the dream or vision about?

- What type of revelation is it and what is the source of the dream or vision?

- What protocol should I apply when interpreting this type of revelation?

Answer the questions for each exercise.

Every dream you do will teach you something, especially if you get it wrong. Assess and calibrate your answer with the correct answers from the end of the chapter.

## Recap tips to help you

You may like to photocopy this brief recap to have it next to you as you interpret each dream or vision.

Types and sources of revelation – a quick reminder.

- How does the person feel about this dream or vision?

- Are the lighting and colours clear and bright, or dark and dingy?

Revelation dreams and visions from God, bring a higher perspective:

- edifying, comforting, and encouraging;

- calling dreams and visions;

- prayer/prayer ministry dreams.

Particular care is needed with dreams and visions which carry:

- direction, correction (cleansing), foretelling or warning, and those which are used for ministry;

- encounter dreams and visions contain an encounter with God or a spiritual being;

- healthy life-processing dreams and visions.

Source – the soul (mind, will, and emotions)

Nightmares – sources:

- dark dreams with negative spiritual revelation;

- soul dreams processing daily stresses;

- recurring trauma dreams – processing traumatic past events which need to be healed.

Dark visions – intimidating or negative visions.

Hallucinations caused by an imbalance in levels of brain chemicals owing to medical conditions, prescription drugs, or drug or alcohol abuse.

Protocol: "There is a proper time and procedure for every matter"(Ecclesiastes 8:6).

- Edification, encouragement, and comfort revelation: interpret and encourage.

- Calling revelation: be general not directive. This speaks of areas the seer may be good at and where they may even find opportunities opening up.

- Prayer/prayer ministry revelation

- Be general about the area for prayer, without being dramatic or raising fear.

Direction, correction, foretelling, warning, and dreams for ministry: be very general about the areas that the dream speaks of: "The dream speaks about issues of…"

- Work in a team and record your interpretation for future reference.

- You are given a little part of a person's life as a jigsaw puzzle piece.

- If the person is known to you, work with those who know the detail of the person's life context. Does what you are seeing line up with the real-life story?

- Ensure that what you are seeing lines up with the other pieces of revelation from independent sources, and with what God has already shown the person.

- Ensure each person understands their own weighing process.

We check out significant revelation for our own lives with three guidelines:

- Does it line up with the loving values of Scripture?
- What do the trusted counsellors in our life say about it?
- Does God confirm it independently?

Nightmares/dark visions: don't interpret the content; deal with the fear:

- Bring a sense of peace and space into stressful times.
- Bring light into dark dreams.
- Bring a place of general calm and care into trauma dreams. Don't discuss the content of the dream, although if someone appears to be telling you a dream containing a traumatic memory and they are giving a clear rendition of the dream, it's important to listen until they have finished. Don't comment, don't display shock, just listen sympathetically. We suggest something along the lines of, "These sorts of dreams can be difficult; we always leave them with the experts to deal with. You may like to find someone to talk to. If you do, your doctor could help you with that."

## Exercise 3.1: Two dreams

Compare these two dreams.

## Eleanor's bumblebee sting dream

### The context

A leading intercessor came to us with this dream.

### The dream

"My nine-year-old daughter, Eleanor, is having a recurring nightmare in which she is being stung by a bumblebee. She wakes up terrified and we can't seem to stop it."

Answer these questions:

- Who or what is the dream about?

- What type of revelation is it? What is the source of the revelation?

Tip:

- How does the mother describe the dream?

- How does Eleanor feel?

- What protocol do I need to apply when interpreting this type of dream?

## Gerry's trapped bumblebee dream

### The context

A university student had this dream in his hall of residence.

### The dream

"I had this dream in my hall of residence at university. I dreamed about a bumblebee in my room. When I woke up, I pulled the curtains and there was a big bumblebee trying to find a way out of the window."

Answer these questions:

- Who or what is the dream about?

- What type of revelation is it? What is the source of the revelation?

- What protocol do I need to apply when interpreting this type of dream?

## Exercise 3.2: A car crash dream

### The context

The dreamer was a father of four who was making some important decisions.

### The dream

"I was driving with my wife and family on a motorway in the left-hand slow lane. I wanted to go faster, so I moved into the fast lane and overtook the other cars. As I moved into the fast lane a lorry suddenly

came toward us and crashed into our car – it was a horrendous crash."
Answer these questions:

- Who or what is the dream about?

- What type of revelation is it? What is the source of the revelation?

- What protocol do I need to apply when interpreting this type of dream?

## Exercise 3.3: Tony's vision about a gear change

### The context

Tony is a mature business man with a sizeable property and business.

### The vision

"I was driving down a steep, steep hill. I was aware how steep it was and felt concerned whether I should stay in second gear, or shift down to first."
Answer these questions:

- Who or what is the vision about?

- What type of revelation is it? What is the source of the revelation?

Tip:

- How is Tony feeling?

- Is there a reassurance in the vision?

- What protocol do I need to apply when interpreting this type of vision?

## Exercise 3.4: A student's Snapchat dream

### The context

Alex was a second-year university student. Sophie was on a parallel course, and they joined together for some lectures.

### The dream

"I dreamed Sophie was in America, and because of the time difference we couldn't always Snapchat.[80] I was frustrated, because she would be asleep when I was awake. When we could, we did Snapchat."

Answer these questions:

- Who or what is the dream about?

- What type of revelation is it? What is the source of the revelation?

- What protocol do I need to apply when interpreting this type of dream?

## Exercise 3.5: John's gorilla dream

### The context

A young man, John, who has notable pastoral gifts, had been praying about what God wanted him to do with his life. He had just been invited to be involved with prison ministry.

### The dream

"In my dream I was in a huge room. I was looking up at two landings, which went along the wall opposite me. Each landing looked like a horizontal line and was about one metre deep with a guard rail. There were lots of doors leading off behind the landings. Stairs went up from the ground floor at either side of the room – to the first landing and then to the second floor. It was very bleak.

"Men were being lined up on the landings by gorillas with guns. I was looking at the scene, seeing how hopeless the men seemed. I was holding an open book in my right hand. The chief gorilla turned his gun on me, but he couldn't shoot me or control me because of the book that I was holding and reading from. I had no fear; I felt calm and powerful in the situation."

Answer these questions:

- Who or what is the dream about?

---

80      A mobile app allowing you to send images and videos that self-destruct within seconds of viewing; also used for messaging.

- What type of revelation is it? What is the source of the revelation?

Tip:

- Note that in this intimidating environment, John feels calm and powerful.

- What protocol do I need to apply when interpreting this type of dream?

## Exercise 3.6: Bobby's shark vision

### The context

An established prophet had this vision. He gave it to a young minister in training.

### The vision

"I see a clear blue wave breaking on to a beach. There is a shark in the water. If the wave breaks and the shark is still there, the shark will be washed up on to the beach with the wave in full view. The wave is bright and white and blue."

Answer these questions:

- Who or what is the vision about?

- What type of revelation is it? What is the source of the revelation?

Tip:

- The waves here speak of cleansing.

- Sharks are hidden below the surface.

- What protocol do I need to apply when interpreting this type of vision?

## Exercise 3.7: Ben's writing on the wall dream

### The context

The dreamer was part of a large organization with offices in one building.

### The dream

"We were in a hotel and needed somewhere to work. I was with three colleagues. A random person who worked there said we could use her bedroom. We were busy planning and used the wall of her room to write on. It was a really constructive time. When we left, she was upset that we had written on the wall. We were surprised that she hadn't understood the importance of what we were doing."

Answer these questions:

- Who or what is the dream about?

- What type of revelation is it? What is the source of the revelation?

Tip:

- How sensitive was the dreamer to the person who gladly offered help?

- What protocol do I need to apply when interpreting this type of dream?

# TWO LESS COMMON DREAMS AND VISIONS PHENOMENA

## Open visions

Open visions happen in front of you when your eyes are open. They present in two ways:

They can sometimes seem real, as in this example in which the seer was driving along a country road when,

> a "thundercloud"… appeared in the sky above him,
> then he saw that it wasn't a cloud at all – it was a
> huge honeycomb in the sky. He pulled the car off the
> road and watched it. It was dripping honey on all the
> people under the cloud and some were gathering it
> up in an effort to save it, while others were joyfully
> catching the dripping honey in their hands and eating
> it. The seer heard a voice saying, "It's My grace, John.
> It's for everyone. You don't have to beg Me for what I'm
> already pouring out on everybody."[81]

Other visions are obviously in the spiritual realm:

> As I was going up the stair,
> I met a man who wasn't there.
> He wasn't there again today,
> Oh how I wish he'd go away.[82]

This stanza illustrates the experience of spiritual sight as it interacts with our real, daily environment; in this case – the real staircase and the vision of the unwelcome spiritual figure. The physical and spiritual are blended together in one vision story.

### Open vision – The knife

One day when I was teaching a prophecy class, a woman I had never

---

81      Carol Wimber, *John Wimber: The Way It Was*, Hodder and Stoughton, 1999, p.135.
82      From the poem "Antigonish" by William Hughes Mearns, originally published 1922.

met before came to introduce herself to me. She was all smiles, but in her hand I saw a vision of a dagger with a curved and serrated blade that was pointed toward my side.

Important parts of the vision:

**Knife** (negative symbol): insult, sharp tongue, gossip, hidden attack.

**The woman** (literal): the real-life woman who was holding the symbolic knife.

**The seer** (literal): me.

### The interpretation

The woman is carrying something which will cause damage.

The woman joined one of our prophetic classes. Over time, we realized that a constant stream of judgment flowed from her tongue, which began to affect the people around her. It was a real puzzle because her intentions were so good. As we walked with her, we saw disappointment and lack of self-awareness that were joined to her spiritual gifting, and we had many conversations to help her come into a place of peace.

In this case, seeing the negative symbol of the knife in her hand allowed us to be prepared to deal with a situation which needed to come into order. It allowed us to help the woman with both awareness and compassion.

One night, about ten years ago, I had a terrifying nightmare. It impacted me so deeply that I switched on the light, which woke my husband. When Dave saw how scared I was and that a "there, there" wasn't going to help, he went into the spare room to pray for me, figuring that that would be the best way for us to get some sleep.

I kept the light on, and suddenly, in the right-hand corner of the room, three men appeared who were about thirty years old, all wearing Roman Centurion uniforms. They were holding short swords. They had dark brown short hair. The second I saw them, something inside me recognized that they were bodyguards, and I relaxed. I remember saying, "Oh, if you're here, I can go back to sleep." I instantly lay down, feeling totally safe, and slept like a baby.

The next morning, Dave told me that he had asked God to send angels, and when he came back after praying, I was fast asleep.

Spiritual sight is often paired with the gift to discern spirits, to be able to instinctively recognize whether a revelatory encounter is from God, dark spirituality, or someone's own thoughts.

> *Now to each one the manifestation of the Spirit is given*
> *for the common good... to another distinguishing*
> *between spirits, to another speaking in different kinds*
> *of tongues, and to still another the interpretation of*
> *tongues. All these are the work of one and the same*
> *Spirit, and he distributes them to each one, just as he*
> *determines.*[83]

During a prophetic seminar, a very nice man started to prophesy during an exercise. I was listening in. His prophecy to the pastor's wife seemed entirely reasonable and theologically correct, and was put both politely and with care. But there was something about it that didn't ring true, and my sense of discernment was uneasy. So I asked him to tell me about his prophecy. He did so, explaining that he'd been talking to the pastor that morning and telling him the same thing. His prophecy was really an idea from his own mind.

If you feel uneasy about an encounter or a prophetic revelation, it won't necessarily be because there is an evil spirit at work. Visions and prophecy can simply come from a person's soul or imagination. Discernment is key.

One acquaintance, who had an illness which gave her disturbed episodes, would occasionally report somewhat bizarre "visions". Her behaviour and thinking grew increasingly erratic, to the point where it was time to consult her doctor.

A mature and balanced approach is vital. A well-travelled, wise, and experienced seer with a gift of discernment and plenty of common sense is a gift to a revelatory community. If you add in a lively sense of humour, you have the perfect balance.

It is vital to make sure we don't believe, focus on, communicate, or interact with false revelation. The gift of discernment is to help with an accurate weighing process. If you have that gift, you will know it. But until we teach people to use it well, it can often be unsettling to pick up the varied spiritual climate around. (We will specifically explore living at ease with spiritual gifting in chapter 3.)

Seeing visions from God in the context of our everyday life can help us to work with God and what He's doing in any given situation.

---

83    1 Corinthians 12:7, 10–11.

## Exercise 3.8: Seeing Jesus

This exercise, suggested by Jim Driscoll, a North American minister and author, helps us to discern the presence of Jesus and to partner with what He is doing in a particular time and place. "For where two or three gather in my name, there am I with them" (Matthew 18:20).

You may like to do this exercise and write down what God shows you. If what you see impacts you deeply during a vision exercise, it's important to share what you see with a close friend, or someone who will listen wisely.

**Step 1**: Ask the Lord to show you a sense or a picture of where Jesus is in the room you are in. Describe what you see.

**Step 2**: Describe what Jesus is doing. Is He sitting or standing? Which way is He facing?

**Step 3**: Describe what He is wearing. Take note if His clothes seem to be vocational or task related.

**Step 4**: Ask Jesus why He is there. Describe what you hear. Make note of any noticeable tone or emotion.

**Step 5**: Ask Jesus how you can cooperate with what He is doing. Describe your impressions. This might not just be about actions but about attitudes and beliefs.

**Step 6**: Ask Jesus how He feels about the person He is standing closest to. This might be you. Describe what you hear. Make sure you express in an edifying way any emotions that might be perceived as negative. If there seem to be negative emotions, ask Jesus what He wants to do with that.

**Step 7**: Ask Jesus how you can have the same heart He does for this person, possibly you. Describe what you hear. Try to use descriptive language that as much as possible expresses the depth of Jesus' heart.

**Step 8**: Weigh what you feel Jesus said to you against the loving values and Jesus' teaching in Scripture. If you don't have a proven background in scriptural understanding, weigh your vision with a friend who is familiar with the Scriptures and can help you use a scriptural filter for your impressions.

Developing the habit of weighing our own visions brings safety and integrity to our life as a seer. It also helps us discern the source of the vision, whether it is from God, whether it is a product of our own soul, or whether it is from a negative source.

## Lucid dreaming

As you engage with dreams you will meet a minority of dreamers who dream in a really interesting way. Lucid dreaming is not a separate category of revelation, but a way some people experience dreams. Even though they are asleep, lucid dreamers are aware that they are dreaming. They may be having a beautiful dream, or be caught up in a nightmare, aware that they are stuck in an unpleasant dream. The dreamer can sometimes have a measure of influence on the dream, just as if they were playing a computer game, deciding how to respond to the events occurring around them in the dream story.

Alan Hobson, a neuroscientist at Harvard Medical School, says of lucid dreaming, "It has huge entertainment value."[84]

One dreamer, John, said, "I often dream that I'm flying through a lush tropical rainforest. I can choose how I fly – fast or slow, above or through the canopy of the trees. I have never yet been able to land, but I have total freedom of choice about how and where to fly."

Flying dreams are among the top twenty most common dreams. In a lucid flying dream, the dreamer can enjoy the sensation of "letting go of the earth" and feeling free to fly wherever they would like to.

Lucid dreamers experience different levels of choice and freedom. Studies by neuropsychologists have shown that brain activity while lucid dreaming is quite distinct from a non-lucid dreaming state, or from being awake. It is closer to REM (Rapid Eye Movement) sleep, when the action of the neurons of the brain becomes quite intense, much like that during wakefulness.

Those who dream lucidly experience dreams very vividly and often ask for help to bring God's *shalom* into this type of dream. The suggestions in this section also have general application for creating healthy dream space, calming fears, and restoring peace. Method two,

---

84      "Lucid dreaming: Rise of a nocturnal hobby", BBC News Magazine, 31 May 2012, available at http://www.bbc.co.uk/news/magazine-18277074 (last accessed 12 August 2017).

the Compline exercise, can be used to prepare anyone's mind for sleep, inviting the presence of God into our dreams, whatever they may be.

My husband Dave and our children are all lucid dreamers. As they talk about their lucid dreams I listen and am amazed because I am a very conventional dreamer. While the children were still very young, Dave taught them to use their capacity to dream lucidly to their advantage, telling them if they were having a nightmare to say in the dream, "Jesus, stop the dream." Then they would instantly wake up.

As a teenager, our daughter began to handle her dreams differently. She would think about and decide how to take charge of the dream story. If she was being chased, she would decide how to outwit her pursuer – so instead of being at the mercy of the dream story, she would write a new ending where she was safe. This gave her a healthy sense of empowerment in her dream life.

Lucid dreaming is a fascinating and attractive prospect, and groups of people exploring this form of dreaming are springing up in surprisingly large numbers. The BBC reports between forty and fifty groups in London alone. One regular attendee says, "I've come to understand a lot of my fears now because I'm able to confront them in dreams."[85]

When interpreting people's lucid dreams, it's helpful if we encourage them to celebrate this interesting ability and help them engage with God in that experience, especially if they're having nightmares. He can help them at their point of need, and it's often then the beginning of building a relationship with Him.

Sleep should be a restorative, safe, and restful time. Our nights are when we need to be safest and at ease, to be able to be at our most vulnerable. When our sleep is good, our physical and mental health blossom, and the impact on our relationships and quality of life is huge. We all need that safe, protected, healthy space.

You can prevent disturbed dreams by creating a time of inner and outer quiet before sleep. This simple exercise appears on our website,[86] to help dreamers of all worldviews enjoy a safe and settled dream life:

• Find a quiet, private space (a warm bathroom is ideal).

---

85      "Lucid dreaming", BBC News Magazine, 31 May 2012.
86      www.lovehasavoice.org (last accessed 10 August 2017).

- Begin by consciously emptying out all the tensions and concerns of the past day. Let cares and defences drop. Be still. Relax. Be quiet. Shift the focus of your attention to God – a loving, caring, strong, Higher Power, who, in this exercise, comes to shelter and protect you.

- Breathe deeply and slowly before and between each section. Slow your breathing down and say aloud:

> *May God shield me,*
> *May God fill me,*
> *May God keep me,*
> *May God watch me,*
> *May God bring me this night to the nearness of His love.*
> *Circle me, Lord,*
> *Keep protection near*
> *And danger afar.*
> *Circle me, Lord,*
> *Keep light near*
> *And darkness afar.*
> *Circle me, Lord,*
> *Keep peace within,*
> *Keep evil out.*
> *The peace of all peace*
> *Be mine this night,*
> *In the name of the Father*
> *And of the Son*
> *And of the Holy Spirit,*
> *Amen.*[87]

Sleep well.

---

87    Assembled from *Celtic Daily Prayer: Inspirational Prayer and Readings from the Northumbria Community*, Marshall Pickering Collins, 1996.

## Teaching points from Chapter 2

In this chapter you have been learning and applying the following points:

- Good interpretation is a mix of gifting, revelation from God, practical training, and growing experience. Your journey begins in the place of prayer.

- Knowing the context of the person's life situation will help you to interpret their dream or vision. It's like putting a jigsaw piece in a partly formed picture.

- There are questions you can ask when looking at a dream or vision which help you to interpret it:

    – Who or what is the revelation about?

    – Are you in the dream or vision? It's about you or what you are part of. Up to 95 per cent of our dreams and visions are about our own lives.

    – Are you observing? It's about what you are observing.

    – What type of revelation is it, and what is the source?

Recognizing the type of revelation we are dealing with will help us to interpret the dream or vision and understand its purpose.

## Types of revelation

- Revelation dreams and visions from God bring a perspective beyond the seer's own perspective:

    – edifying, comforting and encouragement;

    – calling dreams and visions;

    – prayer/prayer ministry dreams.

- Particular care is needed with dreams and visions which carry:

    – Direction, correction (cleansing), foretelling or warning; a counselling/ministry agenda or dark revelation.

- Encounter dreams and visions contain an encounter with God or a spiritual being.

- Healthy life-processing dreams and visions:

  – Source: the soul (mind, will, and emotions)

- Nightmares: sources:

  – dark dreams with negative spiritual revelation;

  – dreams processing daily stresses.

  – a recurring trauma dream: processing a traumatic past event which needs to be healed.

- Dark vision – an intimidating or negative vision..

- Hallucinations caused by an imbalance in levels of brain chemicals owing to medical conditions, prescription drugs, or drug or alcohol abuse.

## Protocol

We interpret dreams and visions into real-life situations, so it's necessary to be sensitive and wise and to apply the correct protocol for each interpretation. There are safeguards for handling "behind-the-counter" interpretations:

- Be general in your interpretation.

- Work in a team.

- Work with those who know the detail of the subject's life context. Ensure that what you are saying lines up with their real story.

- Ensure that there is independent confirmation of what you are seeing, in real life or in other pieces of revelation.

- Develop the expertise to deliver these interpretations humbly, wisely, and kindly.

- Ensure that what you are saying lines up with Scripture in truth and love. It is the interpreter's responsibility to take time to ensure the person they are interpreting revelation for understands the weighing process:

– Does the message of the interpretation line up with Scripture?

– What does wise counsel say about it?

– Is there independent confirmation from God?

Record the bullet points of the interpretation and keep a copy for future reference.

When you are presented with nightmares or dark revelations, don't interpret the content; deal with the fear

Recurring dreams and visions carry a repeating message. They will stop once that message has been heard, understood, or acted upon.

- People experiencing recurring trauma dreams should be referred to qualified counsellors and not be dealt with by interpreters. This should be done within a calm and accepting conversation – with an emphasis on listening, not asking questions.

- From time to time you may meet people who are having hallucinations caused by an imbalance in the levels of brain chemicals, because of a medical condition, or because they have been using certain legal or illegal drugs. If this is something you suspect, it may be helpful to suggest the person tells a close friend or relative about their visions in case they are in need of medical assistance.

- By the skill of the interpreter and the language we use, we can help the dream or vision to achieve the purpose for which it is sent.

- You can ask the person telling you the dream or vision questions to give you helpful information:

    – How did you feel about the dream or vision?

    – What were the lighting and colours like?

    – Is this a recurring dream? When did it start? Are you still having it?

    – Is this something you normally do in real life, or is it unusual?

If you get exercises wrong, you learn more than if you get them right, especially if you take time to look at why you misunderstood.

Open visions happen in front of you when your eyes are open. Sometimes they can seem real. At other times you are aware that they are a spiritual symbol. They come from the three usual sources of revelation:

- God may be showing the seer something.

- The seer may be perceiving something negative which is spiritually present.

- People who have a mental health issue may be experiencing something as part of their illness, in which case they may need medical attention. Simply suggest that they share what they are seeing with a close friend or relative.

As with all revelation, it is important to discern what the source is and then deal with it appropriately:

- Spiritual matters need wisdom and good practice.

- Medical matters need proper medical attention.

- If we know and care about the dreamer we can subconsciously add our hopes or opinions into the interpretation.

- Team interpretation will always be more accurate and comprehensive.

Lucid dreams are a way of dreaming experienced by a minority of dreamers. They are aware that they are dreaming and can sometimes make decisions on how they act in the dream.

# CHAPTER 2: ANSWERS AND INTERPRETATIONS

## Exercise Set 1

### Exercise 1.1: Hannah's fireplace vision

#### The vision

"I saw John going on trips to and from their home in his car, patiently bringing logs and putting them in the fireplace. The fire was Angela – the heart of the home. I saw a huge hand come down from above and it reached in and separated Angela from out of the fire, dusted her off and put her in an armchair – where she sat and rested. Then later Angela reached back into the fire and lit sticks from the fireplace, like torches, and gave them to different people."

#### The interpretation

This vision is about Angela. Hannah is observing a symbolic story about Angela's life.

The interpretation is expressed in neutral language to be relevant for Angela's worldview. The interpreter might say, "You seem to be at the heart of everything – keeping everything surrounding you going. John helps you a lot. The vision speaks of there being quite a demand on you and that you need time to come apart from that role sometimes to rest. In my worldview – and it may not be your worldview – I would say God has seen all you do for everyone. He wants to reach down to care for you, and then give you some resources from outside yourself with which you can continue to fulfil everything you do for others, without drawing on your own strength."

### Exercise 1.2: Jenny's dream: "Have grace"

#### The dream

"This was a beautiful dream. I was sitting at our dining table for a family meal. Sam was with us. My children and husband were at the table, doing things like nearly spilling drinks and dropping the food dish because of carelessness. I was about to reprimand them quickly and sharply to be more careful.

"Sam jumped in gently, before I did. And only I could hear him speaking to me: 'Have grace, Jen.' So I addressed it lovingly and gently and sorted it out in peace."

### The interpretation

This dream story is about Jenny and how she relates to her family. The dream story is described as "beautiful" – ending in peace, with everything being sorted out lovingly.

The interpretation must match the dream in feel as well as content, so the interpreter might say, "It seems to me that you have a lovely family who spend time together, but this can sometimes get stressful for you. It may even be there's a bit of thoughtlessness in the melée of family life. This dream recognizes that you need some help to address this, to reduce the stresses you feel and to resolve the problems without spoiling the feeling of family time together. Your dream shows God cares about how hard you have found family life sometimes.

"Sam represents Jesus in your dream. He is gently coming to help you to have grace with your family. The dream points out that His grace solves the problems, relieves you of stress, and keeps the peace of the family unit. You may even want to go with that and ask the Lord to help you with His grace because He seems to have noticed you struggling and wants to help you."

## Exercise 1.3: Shannon's diving dream

### The dream

"I was standing beside a pool with a young girl. She was my friend's child. Then I dived into the pool and swam down. I had no oxygen tank on but I could dive deeply in the clear water. I swam down to the bottom of the pool where there was the most beautiful coral. The child followed me. I broke off a piece and brought it back to the surface."

### The interpretation

This dream is about Shannon and the pool. Although the child is in the dream, if we take the child out the dream still works fine and carries nearly all of the same message. The dream isn't about the child.

We asked Shannon a question: "Have you ever seen this pool before, in your dreams, in meditation, or been in that pool?" Her answer was, "No".

The interpretation can be put in spiritual language as the dreamer has a spiritual worldview.

My interpretation to the dreamer was, "There is something new in the Spirit, which you have yet to explore and experience, and it's right in front of you. It's a place of purity, depth, and supernatural beauty. When you do, you will find a sense of freedom and ability and clarity. You will be able to go to new depths of revelation and see new and beautiful things, which you will bring back to your daily life. The dream suggests that where you go others will follow in a very relational environment. The pool is the key to this dream for you because when coral is taken from the water, it dies. The water is life-giving.

"It may be that you want to go with that, and ask the giver of the dream – I would say that's God – to help you access this new place of revelation."

Along with the interpretation, there followed a discussion about a new dimension of revelation in the depths of God's Spirit and that He wanted to invite her to experience His freedom.

## Exercise Set 2

### Exercise 2.1: A pharmacist dreams about catching a train

#### The dream

"I was at the train station with a girl. We were going to Brisbane, Australia. We went to the ticket counter. She got her ticket. But I got the PIN wrong on the card machine and the train left with her and without me."

#### The interpretation

About: the dreamer
Type: life-processing
Source: dreamer

An interpreter might say, "This dream is processing some of your feelings. I imagine you may be good with details and like to get things right. This dream shows some pressure you sometimes put on yourself – if you don't get everything right, you won't get where you want to go – or that around the area of relationships things won't work out.

"There's a lot of pressure indicated. But the dream story has some natural checks and balances. At a train station there's usually another train along shortly. The right person would wait for you at the other end. This may even be a good test of the faithfulness needed for any relationship to succeed, and you can let go of your stress."

## Exercise 2.2: A dream about prayer meetings

### The dream

"I dreamt a man came into my bedroom and he said, 'I hear you are asking God to heal people. If you do this…'" (There followed a threat which we will not dignify by repeating, even in this exercise.)

### The interpretation

About: the dreamer
Type: intimidating dark dream
Source: a dark spiritual source

This is a dark dream, bringing intimidation to prevent prayer for healing. Mahesh Chavda[88] once said that the difference between a threat and promise is the cross. Interpreters lacking the security of knowledge of God and His power will struggle to bring light and to dispel the shadows cast by dark revelation.

## Exercise 2.3: A vision of a visit to a grave site

### The vision

"I was looking at the gravestone of Yitzhak Rabin, a former prime minister of Israel, who played a significant role in the Middle East peace deal."

---

88      Mahesh Chavda and his wife Bonnie lead Chavda Ministries International, a worldwide apostolic ministry based in America.

### The interpretation

About: Yitzhak Rabin
Type: foretelling/prayer dream
Source: God

This is a revelation vision from God. This particular intercessor gained quite a reputation for seeing what would happen before it happened. He frequently saw snapshots of the future.

## Exercise 2.4: Sea of Galilee vision

### The vision

"In my vision I was in a storm in high waves. I was aware of the terrible danger I was in, when suddenly a figure walked by the boat. I knew it was Jesus. He got into the boat and calmed the storm. Suddenly I was aware of the beach we had left and all the good things we had left behind. Then immediately I saw the impression of the coast ahead of us. It was green and lush and peaceful, and we were en route to some really good things. I relaxed."

### The interpretation

About: the dreamer
Type: encouraging vision
Source: God

This vision has life-processing elements. The seer is afraid and facing stormy circumstances during a transition in her life. But it is a revelation vision from God to reassure her that Jesus is with her to deal with the difficult situation she finds herself in. There is also a recognition that she might feel in the middle of nowhere, having left good things in her past. But the future ahead is equally bright.

## Exercise Set 3

### Exercise 3.1: Two dreams

Compare these two dreams.

### Eleanor's bumblebee sting dream

#### *The dream*

"My nine-year-old daughter, Eleanor, is having a recurring nightmare in which she is being stung by a bumblebee. She wakes up terrified and we can't seem to stop it."

#### *The interpretation*

About: Eleanor
Type: negative spiritual dream
Source: dark

Protocol: lift fear and be relaxed. This is a common and annoying type of dream. In my experience, dreaming of being stung or attacked by an external negative source (like a bumblebee or scorpion) may suggest a level of spiritual attack at night. However, I would first ask the mother if Eleanor had a particular fear of bumblebees, to rule out a life-processing dream, which could simply be processing those fears. In fact, Eleanor quite liked bees, and this dream indicated a level of spiritual harassment at night, but that's not helpful for a mother to be told. Using the biblical language of Ephesians 6,[89] a reference to the "flaming arrows" will give a helpful context to talk to Christian parents. The important thing to communicate is the solution.

The interpreter might say, "This dream seems to suggest there's a 'fiery dart' coming into Eleanor's dream life, unsettling her sleep. It's often easily solved by taking communion in the bedroom, declaring the death and resurrection of Jesus Christ (she needn't be there). You might also like to share Compline together to make bedtime nice and peaceful." (Compline can be found in Appendix 1.)

---

89    Ephesians 6.16: "In addition to all this, take up the shield of faith, with which you can extinguish all the flaming arrows of the evil one."

The family took communion in the bedroom without telling the child why, and without mentioning the nightmare. The nights returned to peace.

## Gerry's trapped bumblebee dream

### The dream

"I had this dream in my hall of residence at university. I dreamed about a bumblebee in my room. When I woke up, I pulled the curtains and there was a big bumblebee trying to find a way out of the window."

### The interpretation

About: a real-life bumblebee. (It's important to notice that the student was not stung or "attacked" by the bee. The bee was simply present.)
Type: life-processing dream
Source: the soul (mind, will, and emotions)
Protocol: simply explain life-processing dreams freely, unless there is anything sensitive, in which case employ normal manners and tact.

The interpreter might say, "Your mind was picking up the drone of the bumblebee and you were aware of it even while you were in your dream. Your dream was simply processing what you were hearing."

## Exercise 3.2: A car crash dream

### The dream

"I was driving with my wife and family on a motorway in the left-hand slow lane. I wanted to go faster, so I moved into the fast lane and overtook the other cars. As I moved into the fast lane a lorry suddenly came toward us and crashed into our car – it was a horrendous crash."

### The interpretation

About: the family
Type: warning dream
Source: God
Protocol:

- record your interpretation for future reference

- work in team
- ensure the seer knows the weighing procedure for weighing your interpretation
- be general, not directive.

The interpreter might say, "This dream could suggest that there may be a decision to move quickly in a situation, but the dream story contains an indication that this might have a very real consequence for your family."

The husband persisted in his decision, despite the interpretation of the dream. He persuaded his wife that the decision would be advantageous financially. The whole family was put under great strain, and the wife had a suspected heart attack as a result of the stress on the family and spent a short time in hospital. Thankfully, apart from the financial impact, no lasting damage was done. The couple learnt from the experience, decided to take greater care in their decision-making process and in considering their dreams in the future. It was a sobering learning curve.

## Exercise 3.4: A student's Snapchat dream

### The dream

"I dreamed Sophie was in America, and because of the time difference we couldn't always Snapchat. I was frustrated, because she would be asleep when I was awake. When we could, we did Snapchat."

### The interpretation

About: Alex (the student) and his interest in Sophie

Type: life-processing dream

Source: the soul

Protocol: be sensitive as you interpret this. Alex is in love! It shows Alex's feelings. Don't interpret in front of his friends or others. Be general. You might say, "This dream is processing some feelings. It looks to me as if you and Sophie are in contact but not really connecting on a deeper or more personal level. The dream may suggest that can be frustrating or not quite how you'd like it to be."

## Exercise 3.5: John's gorilla dream

### The dream

"In my dream I was in a huge room. I was looking up at two landings, which went along the wall opposite me. Each landing looked like a horizontal line and was about one metre deep with a guard rail. There were lots of doors leading off behind the landings. Stairs went up from the ground floor at either side of the room – to the first landing and then to the second floor. It was very bleak.

"Men were being lined up on the landings by gorillas with guns. I was looking at the scene, seeing how hopeless the men seemed. I was holding an open book in my right hand. The chief gorilla turned his gun on me, but he couldn't shoot me or control me because of the book that I was holding and reading from. I had no fear, I felt calm and powerful in the situation."

### The interpretation

About: John and the context he's seeing

Type: calling dream

Source: God

Protocol:

- record your interpretation for future reference

- work in a team

- ensure the seer knows the procedure for weighing your interpretation

- be general, not directive

The interpreter might say, "This dream speaks about you and the power you have to affect a very difficult situation. The dream speaks about men who are hopeless and held captive. There is also a degree of intimidation and control against them from authority figures. You are carrying the Word of God into the situation, which gives you the power and a peace to deal with it confidently and calmly."

## Exercise 3.6: Bobby's shark vision

### The vision

"I see a clear blue wave breaking on to a beach. There is a shark in the water. If the wave breaks and the shark is still there, the shark will be washed up on to the beach with the wave in full view. The wave is bright and white and blue."

### The interpretation

About: the young minister

Type: correction/warning/revelation dream

Source: God

Protocol: because of the established relationship between the overseeing prophet and the minister, the protocol for this vision is very different. He was able to speak directly and strongly to correct the minister. An observer to the young minster's life, who lacked that relationship and authority, would have used the standard protocol to:

- Record the interpretation.

- Work in team.

- Ensure the seer knows the procedure for weighing your interpretation.

- Be general, not directive.

In this case, the following interpretation was given: "I see a picture as I look at you… This kind of symbolism speaks to me about a hidden issue which will come into full view during a public time of cleansing. This vision has been given to encourage you to sort this situation out in private before that time comes, and everybody is aware of that hidden issue."

The young minister initially responded well, saying that he knew what the issue was and he was working with accountability to deal with it. In actual fact, he did everything he could to evade accountability and was asked to step down from his official position in ministry when the situation came to light.

## Exercise 3.7: Ben's writing on the wall dream

### The dream

"We were in a hotel and needed somewhere to work. I was with three colleagues. A random person who worked there said we could use her bedroom. We were busy planning and used the wall of her room to write on. It was a really constructive time. When we left, she was upset that we had written on the wall. We were surprised that she hadn't understood the importance of what we were doing."

### The interpretation

About: Ben's work situation

Type: revelation and correction

Source: God

Protocol:

- record your interpretation for future reference

- work in a team

- ensure the seer knows the procedure for weighing your interpretation

- be general, not directive.


It could be put like this, "This dream speaks about people who share your space and how you interact with them. You have a busy and constructive work life, and that seems interesting. But the dream seems to suggest there may be a need to relate to people in that environment with a degree of awareness, sensitivity, and care – so everyone can get on well and be relaxed – beyond your immediate team. I don't know if that could fit anywhere in your life?"

# Chapter 3

# SYMBOLISM: NOT MISUSE, NOT DISUSE, BUT RIGHT USE

*"...Let the wise listen and add to their learning*
*and let the discerning get guidance –*
*for understanding proverbs and parables."*[90]

This chapter contains a number of dreams and visions exercises so that you can practise and develop your core skills and learn to recognize and interpret the way symbols are used in dreams and visions.

Take each section slowly; there is no hurry. Your skills will develop as you do the exercises and gradually begin to see the way dreams and visions work. A quote that is sometimes attributed to Benjamin Franklin says, "Tell me and I forget. Teach me and I remember. Involve me and I learn."

## Symbolism: The great debate

There are two camps when it comes to the interpretation of symbols in dreams. Because I have friends in both camps, I've been able to listen closely to both sides. Those in the first camp use interpretation in the therapeutic environment with counselling and inner healing, particularly with dreams. They have a high awareness of the individuals, of their life stories and experiences. They engage in deep listening to what that person's self is saying through their dreams and visions. They value the language a person's soul uses as unique to that individual. It

---

90    Proverbs 1:5–6.

is almost an offence to this camp of interpreters that the (possibly glib) use of a universal dream dictionary be applied to such a precious voice. Dream dictionaries are simply compilations of symbols and some of their possible meanings, which various people have noticed cropping up from time to time in dreams and visions. The concern is the danger of simplistic application of generalized symbolic meanings.

Those in the second camp use interpretation in a more strictly biblical form, as I will explain below, looking into dreams and visions beyond the voice of the individual, and seeking the voice of God.

The more experienced you are as an interpreter, the less you will rely on the scrupulously prescriptive use of a dream dictionary. But, conversely, the more experienced you are, the less you can ignore the commonality in some repeating patterns of symbols in dreams. We have to remember that patterns are fluid, flexible, and open. When people try to apply these patterns as an inflexible code, they risk limiting the creativity and beauty of individuality, personality, style, and experience. God who created everything has endless imagination. He uses all kinds of things to make Himself known. He doesn't always oblige us by following the rules we have drawn up.

As you work through this chapter's dream and vision exercises and consider any repeating symbols, I suggest you reserve judgment and make up your own mind. I once heard Ian Coffey, a wise Christian leader, observe, "Somewhere between naivety and cynicism lies the place of faith."

In each exercise, the meanings of the individual symbols are given to help you understand how symbols play their part in the dream or vision story, so you can successfully interpret the exercise. Outside the exercise, in a different dream or vision, the same symbol may carry a very different meaning.

## Questions to unlock a dream or vision: Identifying the symbols

- What are the important elements in the dream or vision story? Are they literal or symbolic?

- What is their meaning in the context of this particular dream or vision?

The individual elements in the story add detail and clarity to the interpretation. Refining the dream or vision down to its key elements draws attention to the essence of the story. These important parts of the revelation might include: key statements, items, people, places, feelings, colours, names, numbers, quality of light, or weather.

The examples and exercises in this chapter will teach you to use these questions and their answers to help you to understand and interpret the individual dreams and visions.

## Section 1: Biblical, personal, cultural and universal symbols in dreams and visions

We have noticed four types of symbols present in dreams and visions:

- Biblical symbols. Interestingly, biblical symbolism occurs in revelation dreams and visions from peoples of all faiths and none, including those who have never read the Bible.

- Personal symbolism unique to the individual's own life story, arising from a person's experiences and relationships. This can extend to couples, groups, and families; they develop their own bank of shared experiences and references, which might make little sense to anyone else.

- Cultural symbols from the person's culture, subculture, or surroundings, forming part of their subconscious language.

- Universal symbols which reappear in the dreams and visions of different people groups, nations, nationalities, and ages. They are part of our common human culture and language.

In reality, these four types of symbols overlap. For example, biblical phrases have become common cultural phrases – such as, "a drop in a bucket"[91], or to escape "by the skin of my teeth"[92] – and some universal symbols have become part of a sub-group's private language, such as the rainbow having been chosen as the symbol of the LGBT Pride movement, the context giving it a new meaning in that subculture.

---

91      Isaiah 40:15.
92      Job 19:20.

### *Biblical symbolism in dreams and visions*

It's important for you to be familiar with the Bible and its symbols, because biblical symbols often occur in modern-day dreams and visions.

As I learnt about dream and vision symbolism, I became more highly aware of the rich language of symbol, metaphor, and story used in the Bible. Symbolic language conveys meaning, evoking images, feelings, associations, and a depth of understanding. The Bible uses a wealth of stories and symbols as shorthand. Dreams and visions mirror that device that Jesus often used to find the shortest distance between two points: the symbolic story.

The Hebrew language of the Old Testament has its origins in a pictographic script, much like Egyptian hieroglyphics, which has a symbol for each consonant. The Hebrew pictograph for God (Hebrew – *El*) is an ox head and a shepherd's crook. Both these symbols were deeply rooted in the culture of the Old Testament: the ox carries the image of rippling strength and muscle, a force to be reckoned with; the shepherd's staff evokes the image of a leader, a capable authority proactively protecting and providing for his flock with strength and care. Both images carry a vivid picture of the personhood of God.

Our written and spoken Western language can be abstract, and something of the richness contained in the original Hebrew imagery is lost. But in our dreams and visions, metaphor, symbols, and stories come into their own, often reflecting literal pieces of imagery from the Bible.

## Patti's dream about numbers

Helpful hint: can you recognize the New Testament Bible verse referred to in this dream?

### *The context*

Patti, a mature, committed Christian, had this dream in which she had an instinctive feeling that God was trying to tell her something. She brought the dream to us, hoping that we could explain the message that it carried for her.

### The dream

"I was in a garden where everything was radiating this brilliant light I have not seen before in the earthly realm. There was a man in a robe and he said, 'Let me show you what that means.' We walked over a small bridge and he showed me a piece of paper with the number 70,000 on with a big dot/full stop after it."

"I said to him, '100,000' (I was thinking money)."

"He said, 'No, 70, 000.'"

"I said, '90,000.'"

"He said, 'No, 70,000. It is a gift from God and you have to do nothing to earn it.'"

### The interpretation

This dream is about the dreamer, Patti. It is full of light; a revelation, encouragement, and prayer ministry dream from God. The interpretation needs to carry the clarity of that revelation and sense of light.

To unlock the message of the dream, we can ask some questions to understand the story and its symbols. First, look at the sense of the story, which is the basis of your interpretation. This dream's story headline is that Patti is being shown something by a man in a robe. There's an emphasis on it being a gift and not earned.

- What are the important elements in the dream?

- Are these elements literal or symbolic?

Use the helpful symbols list below to explore the important parts of the dream and how they add to the sense of the story. They might be: key statements, items, people, places, feelings, colours, names, numbers, quality of light, or weather.

The symbol meanings are for this context. In another context they may mean something quite different.

### Important parts of the dream

**Patti** (literal): dreamer
**Bright light** (symbol): place of revelation
**Garden** (symbol): safe place of peace and growth

**Crossing the bridge** (symbol): faith journey from one place to another
**Big full stop** (symbol): a firm emphasis that something is finished
**70,000** (symbol): perfect forgiveness
**100,000** (symbol): Law
**Man in robe** (symbol): Jesus

The picture-book symbolism of a man in a robe easily suggests to us that he represents Jesus. But in order for that to be the case, the message in the dream will have to line up with the words of Jesus recorded in Scripture in both grace and truth. The question we have to ask is whether a free gift of forgiveness lines up with Jesus' teaching.
This biblical filter safeguards an interpreter. Any teaching by a "man in a robe" who represents Jesus would line up with this Scripture:

> *One of the teachers of the law came and heard them debating. Noticing that Jesus had given them a good answer, he asked him, "Of all the commandments, which is the most important?"*
>
> *... Jesus [replied]... "Love the Lord your God with all your heart and with all your soul and with all your mind and with all your strength." The second is this: "Love your neighbour as yourself." There is no commandment greater than these."*[93]

The symbolism in the dream tells us more about its message. Here in Patti's dream, 70,000 is pointed out as important three times. A recurring message highlights its importance. Looking at the meaning of 70,000 is the key to the dream. It is also a nice example of biblical symbolism in dreams.

The zeros give the number weight. If I gave you an amount of money, it carries more weight and buying power if it has several zeros after the first number. It's the numerical equivalent of a recurring message. Interestingly, the Hebrew language of the Old Testament also uses plurals to identify quality and weight.

---

93     Mark 12:28–31.

*Western languages use the plural to identify quantity, such as two trees for instance. The Hebrew language can say "one trees", identifying its quality as being larger or stronger than the other trees.[94]*

Where in the Bible do we find the number seventy? In Matthew 18:21–22, Peter asks: "'Lord, how many times shall I forgive… seven times?' Jesus answered, 'I tell you, not seven times, but seventy-seven times.'"

### Interpretation summary

This dream contains the message of complete and perfect forgiveness as a gift from God. The full stop and crossing of the bridge extend the idea of leaving the past behind to perceive and receive a sense of total acceptance. The fact that the figure in the dream (Jesus) rejects the figure of 100,000 (ten representing the Law – the Ten Commandments), indicates that Patti is moving from an Old Covenant worldview to a New Covenant worldview, of grace.

The scriptural reference gives the interpretation added authority, which is very helpful because, although Patti has a thought-through Christian doctrinal worldview, she was evidently still struggling with receiving the gift of absolute forgiveness.

The interpreter for Patti's dream has a beautiful job: to interpret the dream in a way which helps Patti to cross the bridge of faith and receive that gift of forgiveness, leaving her fears behind.

## Exercise 4.1: Adam's Noah's Ark dream: biblical symbolism

### The context

Adam had a Catholic background but throughout the long and traumatic illness of a loved one, he pulled away from his upbringing to explore different, spiritually dark, avenues. He brought this dream to the outreach community for an interpretation on his first visit.

### The dream

"I am stood on the deck of the ark with a man with a white beard and who was wearing an oatmeal-coloured floor-length gown. I thought

---

94      Jeff A. Benner, *His Name is One: An Ancient Hebrew Perspective of the Names of God*, VirtualBookworm.com Publishing Inc, 2003, p. 40.

this was Noah. We are looking out over a desert setting. I then said to him, 'So you have to get all the animals in here then?'

"He replied, 'Yes,' and smiled."

"I then said jokingly, 'Spiders as well?'"

"He grinned broadly and said, 'Yes, spiders too.'"

"I then said, 'But no people as they're not worth it?'"

"His expression suddenly changed to a slight frown and he looked at me with disappointment."

Answer the questions which unlock the dream:

• Who or what is this dream about?

• What type of dream is it and what is its source?

• What type of protocol do I need to apply to interpret this type of dream?

First look at the sense of the story: what is the headline of the dream story?

Use the helpful symbolism list below to explore the important parts of the dream. What do they add to the sense of the story?

• What are the important parts of the dream?

• Are these elements literal or symbolic?

• They might be: key statements, items, people, places, colours, names, numbers, feelings, quality of light, or colour.

These symbol meanings are for this dream context. In another context they may mean something quite different.

### Important parts of the dream

**Adam** (literal): the dreamer

**Ark** (symbol): vessel of salvation

**Noah** (symbol): God

**Desert** (literal): setting the scene of the Bible story

**"Spiders as well"** (statement): representing inclusivity

**"But no people as they're not worth it"** (statement): conveying judgmental attitudes

**Frown of disappointment** (emotion): disappointed with that attitude

Use the sense of the story, the answers to the questions, and the symbolism list above to write an interpretation of the dream.

Compare your interpretation with the interpretation at the end of the chapter. Was there anything you missed?

## Developing as an interpreter: Anointed interpretation

To interpret Patti's dream about numbers, and Adam's Noah's Ark dream, and to achieve the purpose for which they are sent, needs far more than factual interpretation – it takes anointed interpretation. Only an encounter with the Holy Spirit's love and truth would enable Patti to receive a revelation at a heart level of being deeply accepted and forgiven. Adam needed a realization of God's mercy and love for all men and women, including himself. These are moments of epiphany.

"At the interface of the Word of God and the concrete situation stands the prophet."[95] Prophetic people are those who deal with revelation, unlocking what God is saying and releasing it into the present situation. One of the biblical words for prophet is "seer" – those who see dreams and visions.

In the Old Testament Hebrew pictographic script, the pictograph for "seer" consists of a tent and a sharp knife, representing the tabernacle of God's presence (Exodus 33:7), and the seer's ability to release that presence. An anointed seer will spend time with God in the secret place. When God speaks, His Word creates an opening in the tent of His presence, allowing the presence to stream out to minister through the interpretation.

It's easy for me to tell which dream interpreters have been spending time in God's presence in any season, because that same presence is manifestly operating through their ministry.

## A Norwegian dream: 180 degrees is peace

### The context

The Norwegian church has an unusually high number of anointed seers. When training a group of seers in one church in Norway, I used

---

95      Jenny Campbell, *Light on Prophecy*, Paternoster, 2012, p. XVII.

the following dream during the teaching. It dramatically illustrated this dynamic of anointed dream interpretation.

## The dream

"I was walking down a pathway to a day retreat centre. I was allocated a room which had a noisy worship band at the front of the hall, which was discordant and very distracting. I was disappointed and upset.

"Then an old man at the back of the hall very slowly and clearly said to them, 'Why don't you try it like this?' and he sang '180 degrees is peace, 180 degrees is peace.' Then he said, 'Even 90 degrees is a step in the right direction.'"

## The interpretation

This dream talks about disturbing influences from the church which were distracting the dreamer, taking the focus from seeking God in a place of peace and rest. Unlike Patti's dream, the number symbolism is mathematical, not biblical; it's about angles.

The father figure (God) is calling all the participants of the dream, especially the dreamer, to turn around and look at Him, away from life's distractions. It recognizes that this may be difficult to do, and encourages making a start by turning away from focusing on the specific situations that are distracting them.

In Norway, as I asked Idar, one of the delegates, to give the message of the dream which he had been interpreting, from the front of the class on the microphone. To my surprise he did it very literally and broke into song. At that point we also saw into Idar's secret prayer life, as his clear voice sang out over the room: "180 degrees is peace." The peace and presence of God fell in the room and brought everyone present into a place of rest, as eternity hung in the room. Nothing mattered. The room was perfectly still as he sang over and over again, "180 degrees is peace."

> Be still and know that I am God...
> the Lord Almighty is with us.[96]

Idar knew what it was to be still before God.

---

96      Psalm 46:10–11.

*My heart only be silent unto God,*
*for my expectation comes from Him.*[97]

As Gill's beautiful old commentary puts it:

> *The presence of God alone, could lull his heart into*
> *quietude, submission, rest and acquiescence, but when*
> *that was felt, not a word or thought broke the peaceful*
> *silence...*

> *No eloquence in the world is half so full of meaning as*
> *the patient silence of a child of God. It is an eminent*
> *work of grace that the whole mind lies before the Lord*
> *like the sea beneath the wind, ready to be moved*
> *by every breath of His mouth, free from all inward*
> *emotion as also from all power to be moved by*
> *anything other than the Divine will.*

> *Because from Him, "cometh my salvation, both*
> *terminal [the practical now] spiritual [life, power and*
> *purity of space] and eternal [forever].*[98]

There comes a time and space when all previous conversations are swept away. Their noise and contention fades. It is at these moments that we arrive home in the presence of God. This is the time God set aside for us to live in – this silence, this stillness, this home.

This is the day which Paul talks about in Hebrews 4:7–10:

> *Therefore God again set [aside] a certain day, calling it*
> *"Today"... There remains, then, a Sabbath-rest for the*
> *people of God; for anyone who enters God's rest also*
> *rests from their works.*

It's this day that David talks about in Psalm 84:10: "Better is one day in your courts than a thousand elsewhere."

---

97      Psalm 62:1 (author's paraphrase).
98      Gill's exposition of the Bible in his commentary on Psalm 62:1, available at
http://www.biblestudytools.com/commentaries/gills-exposition-of-the-bible/psalms-62-1.
html (last accessed 12 August 2017).

The day when Christ cried out from the cross, "It is finished."
He is now in charge.

As an interpreter, we need to take time to follow this truth, to quieten
down, and to spend time still before God. To do so is to follow a river
into a pool to bathe and to rest in His love.

At the age of eighteen I walked with a friend to see a waterfall. I'd
never heard of prophecy, but I was able to sense that God was speaking
to me through it. I knew nothing about interpretation and so I was
considerably frustrated because I didn't know the substance of what He
was saying to me. It rankled. The clear memory of the revelation never
went away.

Thirty-five years later, in a lull between conference sessions, God
spoke to me: "I'm about to tell you the meaning of the waterfall." I
looked up at the giant screen at the front of the auditorium to see a
waterfall on the loop system going on and on and on and on and on.
"It's my grace, Liz, it goes on and on and on."

The interpretation had taken thirty-five years, and God hadn't
finished yet! Five years later, we went as a family to Austria. We climbed
up a mountain track to get to a hidden waterfall. We followed the
tumbling river up and up and crossed over a truly terrifying bridge,
and as we rounded the corner we came upon a thundering cloud of
white water. The force of its power was immense. We entered a "today
moment" as the power of God hit us and we stood and stared at the
awesome revelation of the sheer power of Grace. Nothing could stand
in its way; nothing could fail to be removed by its might.

The revelation of the juxtaposition of the stillness of God's presence
and the might of His power was displayed in that moment as the four
of us stood together and just looked and drank it in.

> *It is when the soul is hushed in silent awe and worship*
> *before the holy presence... that the still small voice of*
> *the blessed Spirit will be heard.*[99]

This is the place from which anointed interpretation flows.

Learning a practical skill set to interpret dreams and visions with
its questions, symbolism, and growing experience of interpretation is

---

99    Andrew Murray, *Abide in Christ*, Whittaker House, 1979, p. 145.

only part of the ability to understand revelation. Interpretation is highly relational. Spending time with God will help you to discern His voice and His messages in dreams and visions. Without a relationship with and knowledge of God, we may give distant, even accurate interpretation, but we won't carry His healing and presence into the interpretation.

> *"You will seek Me and find Me when you seek Me with all your heart. I will be found by you," declares the Lord.*[100]

The next two exercises are written to help you develop a practice of drawing near to God. Find an uninterrupted place where you can work through them, at different times this week.

## A prayer for his manifest presence

Find a quiet comfortable place.

Before we built my studio, if my house was busy I would drive to a quiet layby with a view, or lock the bathroom door, with my back against the warm, cosy radiator.

Play a track from a worship album.

Just sit. Picture yourself sitting before the Lord.

And just sit.

There are times to use words, but sitting before Him is also a prayer.

Breathe deeply. See yourself waiting before Him as a prayer for His manifest presence.

Think about, be aware of this verse about Jesus:

> *The Spirit of the Lord will rest on him*
> *The Spirit of wisdom and of understanding,*
> *The Spirit of counsel and of might,*
> *the Spirit of knowledge and fear the Lord –*
> *and he will delight in the fear of the Lord.*[101]

Ask God silently that His Spirit will rest upon you.

You don't have to do, say, or hear anything. Your sitting before Him is your prayer.

---

100     Jeremiah 29:13–14.
101     Isaiah 11:2–3.

## Coming to stillness

Settle yourself into a quiet space. You may like to use this passage as a basis for meditation. Quietly or silently read these verses as a prayer to bring you to stillness. Consciously put down any great matters – things that are weighty and burdensome.

> *Lord, my heart is not proud;*
> *my eyes are not haughty.*
> *I don't concern myself with matters too great*
> *or too awesome for me to grasp.*
> *Instead, I have calmed and quieted myself,*
> *like a weaned child who no longer cries for its mother's milk.*
> *Yes, like a weaned child is my soul within me.*[102]

Be aware of your rhythmic breathing between each reading of the verses.

We've noticed that during this exercise, people sometimes cry as they feel the release of a build-up of stress.

## Personal symbolism in dreams and visions

By definition, personal symbols are difficult to interpret. There is a simple piece of protocol that will help you to interpret personal symbols: ask questions.

Kat, one of our outreach team, is an enthusiastic gardener, and her dreams and visions are often filled with gardening symbolism. "To me a tray of leggy tomato seedlings symbolizes a person being moved to a new place/season, which might initially feel slightly uncomfortable for them, but will produce tremendous growth. Whereas seeing a pile of manure means to me a time of being richly fed and nurtured."

The positive symbol of a pile of manure is probably unique to a gardener or farmer. So a useful question to ask would be, "Are you a gardener? I wonder if manure is a positive or negative symbol to you?" Asking a seer, "What does this symbol mean to you?" tells us more about the context of the dream or vision.

---

102    Psalm 131:1–2 (NLT).

If dreams and visions are about the seer's life, personal symbols may have a special meaning for them. If it's a revelation dream or vision from God for others, a symbol or statement may have a special meaning for that person, which the seer may know nothing about. In which case, it can be especially meaningful as it is evident that God is speaking to a person very intimately in their own private language.

One prophetic minister was prophesying to an elderly woman in front of a large room full of people. He knew that he was expected to give a lucid, perhaps even impressive vision, but true to his own values, he didn't bow to pressure, and simply gave what he saw: "The Lord showing me that He saw you plucking that duck!" The elderly woman fell to her knees, weeping. During World War II, she had often felt her contribution was insignificant: she had been comfortably provided for on a farm. One day she was plucking the feathers from a duck to feed the family, but felt discouraged and of little use. But she carried on with her work faithfully. It meant so much to her that God had seen her, that He valued her work, even though she herself had despised it. It was an especially meaningful affirmation, because only God could have known about that incident in her life.

## A vision of Cornwall

### The context

Some years ago, shortly before the birth of my son by planned caesarean section, my friends gave me a baby shower. Each friend brought me a gift, along with a vision, prayer, or prophecy. The experience was especially meaningful because my previous caesarean had been a rushed and unpleasant experience, which I was not keen to repeat.

At the shower, one friend gave me a vision.

### The vision

"I see a map of Cornwall for you, but I have no idea why."

### The interpretation

The vision was about me. It was a revelation vision, but it had no sense of a story.

There was only one symbol in the vision: a map of Cornwall. A question soon brought the meaning to light. They asked me, "What does Cornwall mean to you?"

My answer was that in the early years of our marriage, my husband and I would holiday with friends in Polzeath, Cornwall. The September sun was always low on the beach at about 5 p.m., when we would enjoy the vast empty sands and swim in the high rolling waves of the sea. These holidays were relaxed, spacious, sunny, and peaceful.

The answer to the question, "What does Cornwall mean to you?" turned the simple vision of the map of Cornwall into the message that everything was going to be fine. And I didn't have one qualm about that operation from that time on. The question about what the symbol meant to me evoked those beautiful memories and gave my friends an accessible prayer agenda. They prayed for me that peace, rest, and joy would surround the birth process.

And it turned out to be a beautiful experience, attended by all of those qualities.

## Exercise 4.2: Teddy bear dream – personal symbolism

### The context

A dreamer brought this dream to a dreams course. She told us that she had just started a new job as a therapist, after being a midwife for many years.

### The dream

"I was watching a young woman in her twenties whom I knew. She was walking through a bright hallway, dividing two rooms. As she did, I noticed she was carrying a teddy bear. The teddy bear suddenly changed and became covered in attached colourful little bears of different sizes, about six or seven of them. The bears were part of the fabric of the teddy bear."

Answer these questions:

- Who or what is this dream about?

- What type of dream is it and what is its source?

- Identify personal symbolism: what questions would you ask the dreamer?

133

- There is one symbol in this dream, a personal symbol, arising from the dreamer's therapeutic training. Understanding that symbol is key to this dream. In order to help you practise asking appropriate questions, your task for this dream is simply to come up with a question you could ask the dreamer to help you understand the symbolism.

- Check your answer and read the full interpretation of the dream in the answer section at the end of the chapter.

## Developing as an interpreter: Becoming aware of personal symbolism

Dreams and visions open a window for us to glimpse into the private life of the person or situation the dream or vision is about. Lives, hopes, fears, and personal symbols are projected into stories. To listen to someone's dream or vision is to hear those very personal stories, sometimes expressed in very personal language, and as we do so, we can help people to understand their own journey.

A good interpreter makes space for people to tell their dream or vision story. Sometimes these encounters take place in busy locations and in short time slots, but the quality of that encounter can stay with the seer, because there is something redemptive about listening.

In listening to the dream in which the teddy bears represented the fragmented young woman, our interpreter was able to help her access a safe place where she could talk, because she was professionally qualified to do so. Listening is part of a healing encounter, where people are truly accepted as having value, and recognized as having the right, as well as the need, to be heard.

> *Listening moves us closer, it helps us become more whole, more healthy, more holy. Not listening creates fragmentation.*[103]

Listening heals, and allows us not only to understand the dream or vision with its personal symbolism, but also to work with its purpose in whatever measure is appropriate for that encounter. It's important,

---

103    Michael Mitton, *A Heart to Listen*, The Bible Reading Fellowship, 2013.

because sometimes people fail to listen to themselves and then misunderstand the messages in their dreams and visions. It's important to learn to listen to the voice of our own soul, so that we don't confuse it with God's voice.

## Ben's dream about Alexandra's family

### *The context*

One day, Ben, a young man in his twenties, came to tell me that he was moving to another city. He was literally "following his dream".

### *The dream*

"I just walked into the dining room in the family home with Alexandra. Her mum was in the kitchen preparing a meal, where I felt like I had her approval and acceptance. Then her dad and brother were at the dining room table and it was as though she brought me home for dinner to present me to the dad and brother."

### *The interpretation*

Ben had strong feelings for, and hopes for a relationship with, Alexandra, whom he had seen and chatted to at several worship gatherings.

Good questions to ask Ben about his dream, would be, "How did you feel about being part of that family?" "What did it mean to you to be there?"

On finding out that he would really like a relationship with Alexandra, a good listener could have asked some gentle questions to help Ben listen to his own soul: "I wonder whose voice is talking in this dream?" "Have you had any other guidance about moving city?"

Asking questions about our own dreams and visions and the dreams and visions of others is part of listening deeply. Listening deeply means we listen with wisdom and compassion to understand and discern what is really going on in the dreams and visions we interpret. It takes us beyond shallow, presumptuous interpretation, which can lead to misunderstanding.

Because it is easy to jump to conclusions and to misunderstand personal symbolism, it's important to ask the questions we need to ask, to learn to listen well to the dream or vision and to those who share them with us. There's a listening that goes beyond what our eyes see or our ears hear. We need to listen so we see what is really going on. The humility to ask questions keeps us from occupying the territory of the "know-it-all expert". It keeps us dependent on God.

## Cultural references in dreams and visions

In modern-day revelation and in biblical dreams and visions, contemporary culture pops up time and again. It's included in the language of our thought life, and the different cultures and subcultures in which we live are clearly visible.

John's vision in the book of Revelation contains a direct cultural reference to the way the various national rulers of the subject territories of the Roman empire responded when Rome came to call. The local ruler would come to meet the emperor or his representative outside the city, and literally take off their crown and lay it down in front them as a symbol of their own rule being submitted to Roman rule.

John's vision picks up on this cultural reference and uses it to symbolize the twenty-four elders giving honour and precedence to Jesus Christ.

> *Before me was a throne in heaven with someone*
> *sitting on it... Whenever the living creatures give glory,*
> *honour and thanks to him who sits on the throne...*
> *the twenty-four elders... lay their crowns before the*
> *throne.*[104]

In the same way, our own dreams and visions draw on the symbolism of our cultures and sub-cultures.

## A dream about roasting a brother

### The context

The dreamer, a middle-aged Christian man, came into our community café for a dream interpretation. He was quite agitated in his manner and it took considerable gentleness to settle him down.

---

104     Revelation 4:2, 9–10.

### The dream

"In my dream, I was taking something in a roasting tray out of the oven. When I looked – it was my brother. He was roasted like a piece of meat, the edges burned by the heat. It frightened me."

### The interpretation

This dream uses a piece of cultural symbolism, referring to criticizing someone as giving them a good roasting.

This dream is about the dreamer. It's a life processing dream with elements of revelation from God.

This dream reveals to the dreamer the harmful effects of his words on a person he has been criticizing. It also suggests that, on reflection, he may not have wanted to cause real damage to the person concerned.

## Exercise 4.3: Tick dream

### The context

This dreamer is a compassionate prophetic minister. There was a very difficult member in the extended family, involved in negative spirituality, whose anger problems had a very corrosive effect on the family.

### The dream

"I dreamed I was in a hospital setting – I was visiting the hospital. I found a tick in my right ear. I got it out and I made sure I had the head of the tick.

"I was really annoyed in the dream that the tick had dared to be there. My response to it was, 'How dare you!' My right ear was really important in the dream. Strangely the dream felt good, and once I'd got rid of the tick I felt happier.

"The tick's body was green with red legs, to try and attach itself."

Helpful hint: Has anyone ever got under your skin, been green with envy, or "seen red" as a sign of aggression or anger?

Answer the questions which unlock the dream:

- Who or what is this dream about?
- What type of dream is it and what is its source?
- What type of protocol do I need to apply to interpret this type of dream?

First look at the sense of the story: what is the headline of the dream story?

Use the helpful symbolism list below to explore the important parts of the dream. What do they add to the sense of the story?

- What are the important parts of the dream?

- Are these elements literal or symbolic?

- They might be: key statements, items, people, places, colours, names, numbers, feelings, quality of light, or colour.

These symbol meanings are for this dream context. In another context they may mean something quite different.

### Important parts of the dream:

**Hospital** (symbol): place of healing

**Tick** (symbol): parasite, hidden unclean spirit

**Head** (symbol): authority

**Right ear** (symbol): creative, prophetic, relational side, faith, and obedience to God

**Green** (symbol): jealousy

**Red** (symbol): anger, war, suffering

Use the sense of the story, the answers to the questions, and the helpful symbolism list above to write an interpretation of the dream.

Compare your interpretation with the interpretation at the end of the chapter. Was there anything you missed?

## Developing as an interpreter: Interpreting dreams and visions for people with different cultural values and beliefs

Living in a diverse society gives us the rich experience of interpreting dreams and visions for people from different subcultures. This diversity of culture and language gives our world the equivalent of the different plumage and songs of the birds, which give our countryside colour and life. This means that we will often interpret dreams and visions from groups with beliefs, interests, or behaviour which will be different from our own.

I have some hilarious meetings with my missional and theology students who are in their early twenties. They often translate my middle-class, middle-aged language into more culturally relevant prose for our website or for our tweets. They inform me that it is no longer "hip" to use the word "hip", that on my tweets I can no longer use the character-saving abbreviated text talk that was current years ago.

It is a skill to relate well to people from different subcultures who bring their dreams and visions to us. Their dreams will contain cultural symbolism which may be foreign to you. There is a real chance that you may not understand, or that you may disagree with their worldview.

If we are so caught up in our own culture that we cannot compassionately listen to others and discern what God is doing with them in that moment, then we are not yet ready to interpret dreams on a scale wider than our own community. It's important not to assume that dreams revealing issues that we don't agree with are necessarily correctional dreams.

Asking the question, "Why has this dream or vision been sent?" is the way to stay open to the purpose of the interpretation encounter and true to your own views, and to be the good news of God to them at that moment. In this way people meet the body of Christ and another brick in the wall of segregation is removed. When the walls come down, conversations can take place. God can speak and the Holy Spirit can do what He does best, and restore order where there may be chaos, and show people what the truth is for their life and what goodness looks like through revelation.

> *So let me be a peacemaker,*
> *A bridge builder.*
> *Teach me to lay down my life.*
> *So let me be a breach-repairer,*
> *A new-way maker,*
> *Relationship-broker.*
> *May I be heaven's message,*
> *Present and earthed.*[105]

---

105    *Celtic Daily Prayer Book Two*, HarperCollins, 2015, p. 1135.

## Universal symbolism in dreams and visions

Universal symbols relate to people of all cultures and worldviews. We share common experiences: night and day, the earth and sky, relationships, and family dynamics. Some of the most frequently occurring dreams and visions worldwide concern our bodies or our personal habits: washing, going to the toilet, cleaning our teeth, or having them fall out or become loose. Spiders, snakes, dogs, and crocodiles can appear in our dreams, whether we have them in our immediate environments or not. But universal symbols are always interpreted in the light of the individual dream or vision story, as well as from or into the context of the seer's life. This contextual interpretation will prevent us from making rash assumptions about the meanings of universal symbols.

## Sophie's bag dream

### The context

Bags of some type or other are used the world over, as part of our universal experience. Sophie sent us this dream when she was nearing the end of her degree in Manchester, because she was considering where she would live next. She was wondering if the dream had anything to say into her situation (which straight away makes us very cautious about how we put the interpretation of this dream, because we don't want to tell Sophie what to do).

Sophie ran the children's group at her church. Esther ran the youth programme at the same church and the girls had been working together to put on the youth and children's programme. Sophie's uncle had been one of the elders at the church, but he had sadly died a few months previously.

### The dream

"I was at church and the meetings had finished. People were standing around and I was looking everywhere for my soft green leather handbag, which had all my cards, my driving licence, and my money in it. (In real life, I don't have one like this.)

"Eventually I found it, or I thought I had, but when I looked inside, I realized that it was Esther's bag. It had her purse and belongings in it."

### The interpretation

This dream is about the dreamer, Sophie. It has elements of a life-processing dream, and a revelation from God. The interpretation needs to be put carefully as Sophie is seeking direction and could otherwise make a decision based on this small piece of revelation.

The protocol needed is to interpret the dream to help Sophie get her bearings at this difficult juncture of her life, especially as her confidence is low.

In the dream story, a meeting has finished. Sophie has lost her bag and can only find Esther's bag, which is very similar. The loss of Sophie's handbag represents the sense of the loss of her identity and favour relationally at church, following the death of her uncle. It also represents the loss of her sense of purpose in where she is going in her life at this juncture. Esther's bag symbolizes that Esther still has favour and identity at church. Its green colour may suggest some rivalry or jealousy between the girls.

This dream carries a sense that Sophie is in transition, both at church and in her life. It suggests that she may have been feeling a little displaced recently, especially at church. She may also be feeling that Esther has more favour than she does, which can be a difficult feeling for Sophie to navigate. The interpreter can suggest that these are difficult feelings, and she may like to seek some support at this time. In actual fact, shortly after Sophie had her dream, Esther was put in charge of the whole of the children's and youth work at church. But by that time, Sophie had acted on the suggestion that had been made, and the support that she was receiving helped her during her transition back to her home town following her degree.

## Exercise 4.4: Isaac's spider dream – universal symbolism

This exercise contains the universal symbolism of spiders. Spiders are present everywhere, from the Arctic to the Equator. But it is important not to take for granted what they mean in a particular dream or vision.

The purpose of this exercise is to help you focus on whether a symbol is positive or negative.

There is a traditional Western nursery rhyme which portrays most people's reaction to spiders:

*Little Miss Muffet sat on her tuffet,*
*Eating her curds and whey,*
*There came a big spider,*
*Which sat down beside her,*
*And frightened Miss Muffet away.*

Fear is a common reaction to spiders. Add to that the use of cobwebs and spiders for spooky theatre sets or Halloween costumes, and we have a general cultural frame of reference which is far from positive. A quick look into many dream glossary suggestions finds exclusively negative meanings, including "set a trap" or "occult and demonic attack".

It's no surprise, then, that when the mother mentioned Isaac's dream to her close friends, they all raised concerns about the spiders.

Isaac's context: this symbol appears in Isaac's dream story. We are not looking at our own phobias or dream glossaries. We are looking at Isaac's life and dream story. What does the story say about spiders?

## The context

Isaac is a six-year-old boy who has lots of dreams. Some of the dream experiences are dark and some are beautiful places of encounter with God. His mother is highly prophetic and sent me the dream because she wanted to know if she needed to be concerned about Isaac. The family used to live in Australia.

## The dream

"I went to Australia with school and my class. It was a trip. I was excited. I was there for ten days. God was there. The whole reason for the trip was to look for spiders. On the last day before we went home, I was looking for redback spiders. But instead I found a spider under my bed. I was not frightened; it was not scary. The spider I found was green and big. It had gold legs and the spider had a crown on his head. We left it under the bed."

Answer the questions which unlock the dream:

- Who or what is this dream about?
- What type of dream is it and what is its source?
- What type of protocol do I need to apply to interpret this type of dream?

First, look at the sense of the story: what is the headline of the dream story?

Use the helpful symbolism list below to explore the important parts of the dream. What do they add to the sense of the story?

- What are the important parts of the dream?
- Are these elements literal or symbolic, positive or negative?
  They might be: key statements, items, people, places, colours, names, numbers, feelings, quality of light, or colour.

These symbol meanings are for this dream context. In another context they may mean something quite different.

I have left the meaning of the spiders blank, to give you space to explore the place and meaning of the spiders in Isaac's dream.

To help you, you may like to google redback spiders, which is information that Isaac takes for granted, because he used to live in Australia.

### Important parts of the dream

**Isaac** (literal): the dreamer
**Australia** (literal): where Isaac used to live; a symbol which Isaac's dream uses to explore its message about spiders
**School/class** (symbol): safe place of learning
**Excited** (feeling): excited
**God** (literal and symbol): God, safety
**Ten** (symbol): unfinished, journey, to weigh, authority
**Redback spiders** (symbol):
**Bed** (symbol): place of rest and refreshment
**Spider under my bed** (symbol):
**Crown** (symbol): the crown is a cultural sign of authority and rule
**Green** (symbol): growth, life, shepherd (green pastures)
**Gold** (symbol): kingship, the glory of God

Use the sense of the story, the answers to the questions, and the helpful symbolism list above to write an interpretation of the dream.

Compare your interpretation with the interpretation at the end of the chapter. Was there anything you missed?

A few months later, Isaac had another dream.

### The dream

"I was being chased by angry wolves. I did not like them. They had red eyes. I looked around and found a tree. I made and carved a sword out of the tree. I killed the main wolf with this sword. Jesus was there."

This second dream carries the same mix of negative and positive symbols about spirituality. But there is a difference here. Isaac is not looking for wolves in the safety of a school party – he is being chased. But there is a positive shift at the end of the dream. He deals with the situation with the classic biblical symbolism of the sword – the Word of God. Jesus is still right there with him.

### The interpretation

This second dream shows the mother that the spirituality around Isaac is unsettled at this point in time, and that he has a need for help and covering. It carries the suggestion that Isaac is ready to be gently led through how to use "the sword of the Spirit, which is the word of God"[106] when he is challenged.

The wolf symbolism in Isaac's dream is very common, it also appears in Rose's dream in chapter 1, although Isaac and Rose are in different countries and have never met. They are both spiritually aware children and are processing the atmosphere around them.

## Developing as an interpreter: Walking in peace and authority as a seer

Seers, be they children or adults, need to learn to settle their spiritual space and enjoy life. At first the gift of spiritual sight can be a challenge, but as we mature, our giftedness becomes a source of God's light and power for our lives. That switch is a learning curve.

Learning to live in victory is a process. Once, when I was in my twenties, during a time of prayer, I had three visions, one after the other:

In the first, I was being pounded by hard cricket balls which were being thrown at my head. They all hit me.

Then I saw a second vision in which I had learned how to duck and weave skilfully so that the balls could not hit me.

---

106   Ephesians 6:17.

In the third scene, I saw myself again, but this time I was standing confidently holding a purple cricket ball. I saw myself casually throwing it up and catching it in my right hand. And then I said threateningly, "Now YOU run." And I moved as if to throw the ball hard at whatever I was seeing.

These three scenes represent three stages of spiritual growth. The first: becoming aware of spiritual attack. The second phase of learning was how to handle that within the context of daily life. And then the mature stage was reached: the power had shifted, and I had the ball which was purple (the colour of royalty and authority), as a child of God.

This progression is one which we grow into, as we become aware of God's proactive loving care, of the power and strength of His word to overcome the enemy, and stand in the authority of Christ. As we do, we begin to live differently.

Some years later, I had another vision about the cricket ball. This time I was at the cricket crease playing cricket and batting. I concentrated hard on the ball and gave it my full attention to keep the ball from knocking down the wicket.

Then the scene quickly changed. I was lying on a sunny day on a sunbed, relaxing and at peace with a drink in one hand and a cricket bat held loosely in the other hand and with a book next to me. Every now and then a ball would fly in toward me from the cricket game and I easily put up my cricket bat to deflect it and stop the ball. And then I carried on with my drink and my book.

In my vision, faith had become an automatic shield, so that I was no longer focusing on the enemy, his distractions and attacks, but living my life with peace and ease in the goodness of God. This place of assurance is where Jesus drew the eyes of the seventy-two disciples after they had discovered the power to overcome demons.

> *The seventy-two returned with joy and said, "Lord,*
> *even the demons submit to us in your name."*
>
> *He replied, "I saw Satan fall like lightning from heaven.*
> *I have given you authority to trample on snakes and*
> *scorpions and to overcome all the power of the enemy;*

*nothing will harm you. However, do not rejoice that the*
*spirits submit to you, but rejoice that your names are*
*written in heaven."*[107]

As well as going on our own journey of maturing into authority and peace, many of us are bringing up children who are spiritually aware. It's an important job for the parents of gifted families.

## Courtyard vision story

### The context

My sister and I were talking about bringing up her two small children in the ways of God. Before I went to bed, I asked God what He had to say about that.

### The vision

"I was watching a small, square, walled garden. It was a restful scene. It had garden beds in a rectangle around the walls, a rectangular path, and a grass area with a well in the middle. The adults were relaxed and gardening at the beds around the walls, and every now and then they went to the well and took a cup and had a drink. Then they returned to the work. The children who were playing in the garden watched the adults, and they too began to drink when they were thirsty."

### The interpretation

This simple vision shows that our children learn and copy what is happening around them. If we are living with God as our source, in an effective and natural way, they will find that life-giving supply.

The fact that our own faith and victory needs to be a model to our children occurred to me forcefully when we were on holiday a few years ago. We went on the highest cable car we could find. It was at this point I discovered a fear of cable cars! I also discovered that my family had no such fear, because they were enjoying making the cable car rock from side to side. Fortunately we had a car to ourselves because I realized that if I sat in the middle of the floor, I couldn't see out of the windows.

It came to me that my reactions weren't good parenting or good

---

107    Luke 10:17–20.

discipleship. So I sat up on the seat again and said, "In the name of Jesus Christ of Nazareth, the Son of the living God, I bind the fear of cable cars."

From that moment I enjoyed the view and saw the river that the family had been raving about, and we had fun at the top of the mountain – until the journey back down, when I said, tongue in cheek, "Oh good, another cable car." At this point my then twelve-year-old son came over, put an arm around my shoulders, and said, "In the name of Jesus Christ of Nazareth, the Son of the Living God, I bind the fear of cable cars." And the fear stopped again.

We teach what we live during our challenges.

It's also important to learn to guard our family's spiritual space by sorting out discord as quickly as is realistic. "How good and pleasant it is when God's people live together in unity!... For there the Lord bestows His blessing, even life for evermore."[108]

Sharing your space with someone else is inherently stressful. But we have seen a change come over the peace of children and the quality of their dream and seer life when the parents set their hearts to love and honour one another and place the peace of their home as a top priority. It changes the spiritual atmosphere. Everyone thrives.

> *The fruit of that righteousness will be peace;*
> *its effect will be quietness and confidence for ever.*[109]

Peace between the parents, an emphasis on fun and laughter, and a firm and relaxed victory at the point of battle is the remit of the prophetic home. We won't get everything right, but that never was the deal. We don't have to: that's what grace is about.

I'd like to suggest that you plan something fun this week or weekend for you and those who live in your household. The joy of the Lord is your strength.[110] Gifted children need this balance and help, because they notice things. Isaac is a well-adjusted, happy little boy who loves cars and his many friends; he is also a seer. When he went into his school he noticed things about the other children. He would see darkness over

---

108      Psalm 133:1, 3.
109      Isaiah 32:17.
110      Nehemiah 8:10.

certain children; he would see angels standing next to others. He would sense any inner pain.

Isaac began to leave the classroom, asking the teachers if he could go to the bathroom or get a drink. The teacher began to question whether he had diabetes. We talked to Isaac and lightened the whole concept by just teaching him to sing, "Somebody needs a smile, somebody needs a smile" to Jesus, or, if he was really concerned, to mention his worries to the teacher. As we taught him to sing the light-hearted prayer, the false responsibility that he was carrying lifted, and he began to enjoy school again. We had taken away the intensity of what he was seeing.

This teaching and discipling process is essential for our children.

In Isaac's wolf dream he killed the wolf with his sword. It reminded me of the story pastor Bill Johnson told about his son Brian. As a child, Brian, today a leading prophetic worship leader and recording artist, had seen things in his room at night.

A couple of years earlier, Bill's wife Benni had told me how some nights, Bill would lay nose to nose with a very young Brian on his bed, worshipping God to calm his fears.

So I was interested to hear Bill's side of the story about the night he had said to Brian, "You can come in and get me any time, but first, why don't you try to pray for yourself?" The next morning Brian had reported that he prayed and anything unpleasant that he was seeing had gone away. Bill's voice broke as, through tears, this committed and caring father said, "That night, he got his own sword."

As we mature, we begin to notice that the spiritual climate doesn't affect us as much, and we maintain our balance automatically, like a cat using her tail to balance when climbing. We travel successfully through the spiritual melée of our environment, and, when we need to, we can stop and restore order.

During one church visit, we were asked to stop off at an old church building and pray for it before we had lunch. The team agreed; we were happy to bless their building. But when we stopped off at the church we were told more about the reason for the prayer: the church had a resident spirit. Something that was not of God was interacting with the people there with very specific manifestations. They had even given it a name, as if it were a pet. Strange things had been happening, which stopped entirely after we prayed and cleansed the building.

Learning how to interpret dreams and visions is a very successful way to begin to understand what is happening around you. What is God, what is not, and how to deal appropriately with what you see.

One of our main tasks with spiritual people of all walks of life is to help them to understand what they are seeing and sensing, and to rightly handle their own giftedness within their environment so they are at peace, powerfully praying, "Thy kingdom come, Thy will be done on earth as it is in heaven."

## Section 2: Identifying figures in dreams and visions

## Luke's "Nikita" dream story

### The context

This dream was given to our outreach ministry by a gifted member of the team. At the same time, although he didn't know it, a friend who was home on sabbatical from the International House of Prayer in Kansas City, USA, had offered to run a prayer set for our ministry. She happened to be a young black woman. Interestingly, her real name was not "Nikita".

### The dream

"We were sent on a government mission in Asia under cover. The country was controlled by enemy soldiers and we were spies. A girl called Nikita, a young black woman, was spending time in prayer with some other girls whom I didn't recognize, in a very holy place, interceding with God. The rest of us stood around in a circle having fun. I noticed the guy who plays Alfie Moon from *EastEnders* dressed up as a Buddhist monk with huge teeth and a big beard. He came to attack the girls in the prayer space. I saw him and attacked him because he was trying to curse the innocent girls and he was full of anger."

### The interpretation

This dream is about the girls who pray for the ministry, particularly the new prayer set leader. It is a revelation prayer dream from God.

The protocol is to interpret with clarity in an atmosphere of faith, for the core leaders of the ministry, before asking the team to pray and support the girls.

The sense of the story is simply that there is a level of attack on the girls who are praying.

The characters in this dream story are:

- Nikita: representing our prayer set leader. Nikita means "victorious one"

- the girls in the prayer room: our intercessors

- the rest of the outreach community: the community circled around them

- the dreamer, Luke: representing leadership

- Alfie Moon: Alfie Moon is a deceitful character with a criminal record from a UK soap opera. His big teeth represent false wisdom.

This is an intercession dream, sent to raise prayer covering on behalf of the prayer leader, whom God esteems highly and has called "the victorious one". Those with her will also come under a level of hidden attack. The big teeth draw attention to the ferocity of that attack and that it will come as false wisdom affecting the girls' thoughts, and bringing confusion and discord around them.

There are some simple questions which help you to interpret figures in dreams and visions.

Questions to ask yourself:

- Do I know the person?

- Are they literal (themselves in the story) or do they represent someone/thing else?

- Does their name mean something?

- What is the sense of their part in the story?

- Are they a positive or negative figure in the story?

## Developing as an interpreter: Recognizing the Trinity in dreams and visions

In the first vision in the Bible, in Genesis 15:1, God revealed himself to Abram:

> *Some time later, a message came from the Lord to*
> *Abram in a vision. "Stop being afraid, Abram." he said.*
> *"I myself – your shield – am your very great reward."*[111]

---

111    ISV.

In our modern-day dreams and visions, God sometimes appears, quite predictably, using our cultural symbols of father/boss/head teacher/ kind authoritative figure. If we weigh this symbolism against Scripture and think of the parable of the prodigal son, God appears in the story as the father to welcome the son (symbolizing us) home with loving arms.

That piece of symbolism fits well with us.

But we've already seen that at other times, biblically, Jesus talked about Himself as the Bread of Life,[112] actually causing offence. The symbolic message about bread from heaven was a recurring theme from Scripture which began with manna from heaven. The Jews in this passage failed to be reassured by the progressive scriptural explanation which Jesus used to introduce His metaphor.

I once saw my grandfather wrestling with an interpretation of a symbol about Jesus. Kenneth White was a famer and an ardent evangelist. He was known simply as "Grandad" to many hundreds of people who came to stay at the farm. As I grew up I saw the fields being used for Christian camps for people who came year after year to the beautiful costal location in Dorset. Sometimes uninvited families or groups would turn up and ask for permission to stay on the land. And Grandad, being Grandad, always said yes.

I remember two young men who were invited to the little chapel with us on a Sunday after staying in one of the fields and being welcomed into the farmhouse for breakfast. They heard and responded to the simple gospel message before moving on.

This was a frequent pattern, both for those who visited the farm and for the students who came to work there. It was a pattern which continued until the end of my grandfather's life. At his hundredth birthday party, he took the hand of one young girl and pointed her toward Jesus. Shortly afterward both she and her partner became Christians.

The patriarch of our family, Grandad was the one around whom we all orbited and to whom we all returned. I've never met anyone with a more profound respect for God. But this very reverence made it a challenge when he encountered symbolism.

One summer a young preacher and translator from the Wycliffe Bible Translators came to the little chapel. He talked about the

---

112     John 6:35.

challenges of translating the Bible into the culture and unwritten languages of the South American jungle tribes. He used the example of Jesus "the Lamb of God". These tribes had no sheep, no books, no awareness of Jewish heritage, and needless to say no internet. But in their culture they had a prized and precious possession: their pigs.

While searching for a way to translate the gift of God's Son to the world, the Wycliffe translators settled on the piece of cultural symbolism to describe Jesus – the "pig of God". Grandad listened and, over lunch, in the sunlit dining room that overlooked the sea, shook his head in bewilderment. "I don't know, Lizzie, Jesus being the 'pig of God'. I'm not sure about that." That's all he said, but I could see that this farmer and Englishman had been troubled and puzzled by the idea.

I've come to realize that unusual symbolism can be part of dream or vision stories, but the orthodoxy and safety comes as we weigh and measure the message and values of the vision or dream against the message and values of Scripture. Does it line up, once it has been biblically filtered?

In order to do this, a mature interpreter will have biblical literacy, developing prophetic literacy, and increasing interpretation experience. In this book we layer biblical teaching, prophetic understanding, and exercises to enable you to develop that experience in a guided and safe way, so that you can grow a measured and developed trustworthy gift.

In this section, we are looking at the variety of ways in which the Trinity appears symbolically in dreams and visions.

## Victoria's dream story

### The context

Victoria was a young woman in her twenties who had been a Christian for three months. She'd come with a church from Latvia to Norway for a Prophetic Mentoring school. As we spoke, it became apparent that Victoria had a very busy thought life which God was gradually bringing to peace. Christa and Lara were two young but mature Christian women in her church. The girls did not attend college together.

### The dream

"I was in a classroom with Lara and Christa. There was a random man who was making lots of noise annoying and distracting me. Christa went to deal with him and made him leave. Lara came to comfort me and I felt calm again.

"Lara made me a cup of tea but I was worried about giving her my honey (to sweeten the tea) and I thought, "I won't have any left." But then Lara told me there was still some left.

"Christa was making bread. She had pink, blue, and white flour and it suddenly became a dark chocolate brown bread (traditional Latvian bread). I thought, I can't do it like that. I'll never be able to be like that."

### Interpreting the figures in Victoria's dream

Questions to ask:

- Does Victoria know the people? Lara and Christa, yes; the man, no.

- Are they literal (themselves) in the story, or do they represent someone else? Victoria is clearly literal. The dream is about her.

As you interpret dreams and visions and begin to identify the figures in them, you will begin to be alert to biblical keywords. There are two in the dream:

- The name "Christa" (named after Christ).

- The role Lara played: Victoria was comforted by Lara.

Tip: who is the comforter?

- The identity of the unknown man lies in what he represented – he is symbolic of insistent, consistent, annoying thoughts, so that Victoria couldn't settle and learn. The dream suggests these thoughts may be spiritual in origin.

Before we interpret this unorthodox dream, let's run its symbolism through a biblical filter. If this dream has a symbolic level, it uses two positive, kind, and faith-filled figures in Victoria's life to portray the role of Jesus and the Holy Spirit.

The authoritative role that Christa takes up in the making of the "Bread of Life"[113] fits well scripturally, as does the role of Lara bringing comfort and peace.[114]

Symbolism is not literal; it's an image which portrays and conveys something to the hearer about God in their life. However, this imagery used may initially cause some raised eyebrows, because unusually the figures used symbolically are women. So let's run that through a scriptural filter.

I researched whether there is any symbolism in Scripture using something feminine to portray an aspect of God's character or function. As I traced this question back, I found several places containing a feminine symbol reflecting part of the nature of God:

- The woman was made in the image of God. Genesis 1:27:
  "So God created mankind in his own image, in the image of
  God he created them; male and female he created them." She
  portrayed something of His image.

- Matthew 3:16–17 portrays the Trinity:

  > *As soon as Jesus was baptized, he went up out of the water. At
  > that moment heaven was opened, and he saw the Spirit of God
  > descending like a dove and alighting on him. And a voice from
  > heaven said, "This is my Son, whom I love; with him I am well
  > pleased."*

God is the Father affirming the Son. Jesus is in human form – a young man. The Holy Spirit is represented in the form of a dove (*peristera*) which, interestingly, is the feminine form of the Greek word. A female rock dove is representing the Holy Spirit.

- In the Old Testament, the Hebrew word for the "wind of the
  Holy Spirit" is *Ruach*, which is the feminine rather than the
  masculine form of the word.

---

113    "Jesus declared, 'I am the bread of life. Whoever comes to me will never go hungry" (John 6:35).
114    "But the Comforter, which is the Holy Ghost, whom the Father will send in my name, he shall teach you all things" (John 14:26, KJV).

- In Genesis 17:1, one of the names of God reveals part of His nature: "… the Lord appeared to [Abram] and said, "I am God Almighty [*El Shaddai*]; walk before me…""

There is an ongoing debate as to the meaning of *El Shaddai*. Just as the Wycliffe Bible translators translated the "Lamb of God" symbol into the ancient cultural language of the tribes of the Amazon, Old Testament Bible translators have the task of translating the ancient Hebrew script into modern Western cultural language for us. Something of a richness of the imagery of the original Hebrew gets lost in translation.

*El Shaddai* is translated as "God Almighty". It is suggested by scholars that the Greek translators of the Hebrew Old Testament, the Septuagint, thought that the word *Shaddai* came from the Hebrew root word *Shadad*, meaning "to overpower", giving us the Western translation of "Almighty".

Scholars are divided on the root of the word *Shaddai*. Some consider that it comes from the root word *Shad* meaning "breast". As we take the time to look further back into the ancient Hebrew origins of the words, it is rather fun and more than a little unusual. The Hebraic pictographs present a challenge to our Western thinking.

At this point it's good to state again that symbols convey meaning. Their purpose is not to be controversial, but to convey an image which displays a truth to make it accessible to us. The study of the original ancient pictographic Hebrew script "can sometimes yield an insight into the underlying meaning (etymology) of Biblical Hebrew words".[115]

The ancient pictographic Hebrew has pictures for each consonant. At the beginning of this chapter we looked at the pictograph for God (*El*): an ox head and a shepherd's crook.

## Shaddai

In his book, *His Name Is One: An Ancient Hebrew Perspective of the Name of God*, Jeff A. Benner gives an insight into the potential ancient original meaning of this symbolism, examining the ancient pictographs which make up the word *Shaddai*.

115    John J. Parsons, "Hebrew Pictograms", available at http://www. hebrew4christians.com/Grammar/Unit_One/Pictograms/pictograms.html (last accessed 12 August 2017).

The *Sh* is a picture of two front teeth, meaning "eat" or "consume".

The *d* is a picture of a tent door with the meaning "hang" or "dangle". As the door is hung, it dangles down from the tip of the tent. The combined meaning would be "two danglers".

When a young goat needs milk, it presses on one of the two teats that dangle underneath the udder of the parent goat. The milk provides everything that the kid needs. It's a picture of provision, nourishment, and protection. This is unconditional care by a mother for a young goat, who can ceaselessly and easily turn to its mother for consistent supply.

> God promised the nation of Israel that He would bring them into a land flowing with milk and honey. God as "El Shaddai", the "mighty teat" will supply His children with life sustaining milk.[116]

This angle on the root of the Hebrew word certainly sounds strange to our Western way of thinking!

In Victoria's dream, a female, named Christa – Christ's own name – represents Jesus. Jesus is more frequently shown in a robe, as a carpenter, or as a pastoral authoritative young man. The Holy Spirit's role in dreams and visions seems to be more symbolic, using symbols such as water, wind, fire, a dove, a grey-coloured bird, and sometimes that of a woman, often with blond hair, giving direction and assistance, or silver hair, giving comfort. The symbols are used to convey an aspect of God's activity.

But again, put these frequently-noticed patterns to one side and see what you find as you interpret revelation. The interpretation of frequently seen symbols has to be weighed and balanced with a deliberate weighing of any messages the dream or vision may carry. If a symbol seems to represent God, Jesus, or the Holy Spirit, as we discussed in Patti's dream interpretation, the message of the dream will align with the plumb line of Scripture.

### The interpretation of Victoria's dream

"I was in a classroom with Lara and Christa. There was a random man who was making lots of noise, annoying and distracting me. Christa

---

116        Jeff A. Benner, *His Name Is One: An Ancient Hebrew Perspective of the Name of God*, virtualbookworm.com publishing Inc, 2003, p. 48.

went to deal with him and made him leave. Lara came to comfort me and I felt calm again.

"Lara made me a cup of tea but I was worried about giving her my honey (to sweeten the tea) and I thought, 'I won't have any left.' But then Lara told me there was still some left.

"Christa was making bread. She had pink, blue, and white flour, and it suddenly became a dark chocolate brown bread (traditional Latvian bread). I thought, I can't do it like that. I'll never be able to be like that."

The dream is about Victoria. It's a revelation from God with some life-processing elements revealing how Victoria is feeling.

The symbol meanings (in this dream context) help us toward an interpretation:

### Important parts of the dream

**Classroom** (positive symbol): place of learning
**Victoria** (literal): name meaning "victorious"
**Lara** (literal): Lara; (positive symbol): Holy Spirit
**Christa** (literal); (positive symbol): Christ
**Annoying man** (negative symbol): distracting thoughts
**Bread** (positive symbol): words of life
**Pink flour** (positive symbol): love
**Blue flour** (positive symbol): revelation
**White flour** (positive symbol): purity
**"I won't have any left"** (negative statement): feeling concerned about provision
**"I can't do it like that"** (negative statement): feeling negative about herself

### The interpretation

This lovely dream shows Victoria in a time of learning and growing, with caring friends to help her. She has been distracted by annoying thoughts, but this dream uses the symbolism of Lara and Christa to express Christ's authority to remove harassment from her, and to help her to sort that out. Lara represents the Holy Spirit who is close by to give her comfort and peace. The dream explains that Jesus will give her everything she needs, and that everything's OK. She can relax and learn all the things that God has to teach her about His provision, love, revelation, and purity.

If the interpreter also had a discipling role in Victoria's life, it would be good to weigh Victoria's negative statements in the dream about lack and inadequacy. But in the context of the truths contained in the dreams, as the old song says, "accentuate the positive, eliminate the negative, that's how you get to the affirmative". Victoria will have a particular need to accentuate the positive and play down the negatives during this conversation, which would need to take place in an ongoing pastoral and teaching context.

## Exercise 4.5: Jesus and the wagon dream

In this exercise you will decide whether the figures in the dream are literal or symbolic, positive or negative. Fill in this information on the helpful symbolism list.

### The context

Emma is a strong, forceful, humorous, independent, resourceful person who came to faith after exploring other spiritual avenues.

### The dream

"Jesus and Emma are sat on a wagon, like the ones you see in Westerns. There are two white horses pulling this wagon and they're walking calmly along a long road. All around is just desert.

"Jesus has hold of the reins for the horses. He looks at Emma and says, 'I have the reins, don't I, Emma?' Emma nods in agreement.

"Jesus then asks, 'Have I ever let you have these reins, Emma?'

"Emma replies, 'No.'

"Jesus then says, 'Nor will I ever let you hold these reins, Emma, because I am in control.'

"Suddenly, a rumbling comes from the distance, and it's cowboys on horseback. There are many of them, and they all gallop round the wagon, shooting their guns off and shouting, 'Yee ha!'

"Jesus then calmly looks at Emma and says, 'Pay no attention to them; it's just a distraction.' The wagon is still moving through this.

"Jesus and Emma end up in a town. They are both near a saloon. The wind is blowing, and little bits of paper are being tossed around.

"Jesus points to a poster pinned to a post. They both look at it: it is a 'Wanted' poster and it has Emma's face on it. Jesus says, 'Read it.'

"It says, 'Wanted everywhere I am.'"

Answer the questions which unlock the dream:

- Who or what is this dream about?

- What type of dream is it and what is its source?

- What type of protocol do I need to apply to interpret this type of dream?

- First look at the sense of the story: what is the headline of the dream story?

Use the helpful symbolism list below to explore the important parts of the dream. What do they add to the sense of the story?

- What are the important parts of the dream?

- Are these elements literal or symbolic, positive or negative?

- They might be: key statements, items, people, places, colours, names, numbers, feelings, quality of light, or colour.

These symbol meanings are for this dream context. In another context they may mean something quite different.

### Important parts of the dream

**Emma**

**Jesus**

**Cowboys**

**Wagon** (positive symbol): pioneer vehicle

**Desert** (negative symbol): barren terrain

**Reins** (positive symbol): in control

**"Pay no attention to them"** (positive statement): instructions about focussing on being led with Jesus on the peaceful journey

**Town** (positive symbol): community

**Saloon** (positive symbol): place of provision

**Poster** (positive symbol): revelation of a message

**Wanted** (positive symbol): affirmation of love and value

Use the sense of the story, the answers to the questions, and the helpful symbolism list above to write an interpretation of the dream.

## Exercise 4.6: The palace awards ceremony

### The context

The dreamer was a capable administrator who worked in a parish with three churches under the charge of one vicar. At the time of the dream all was well, but some dispute arose later in the form of a power struggle between the administrator and the church warden. She felt that she was being unfairly treated when responsibility was lifted from her as a result.

### The dream

"I was arriving at an awards ceremony in the king's castle. I was wearing a long, gold, beautiful dress. I expected as I was arriving that the prince would be invited as well, though I didn't see him in the room.

"We sat in a large studio with blue seats, almost like a lecture hall. I was sitting toward the left side, halfway back. There were about fifty people in the room.

"As people's names were called, they came forward to collect their awards. On the awards were written their names and what they were being awarded for doing. I didn't see or know any of the people in the ceremony or in the audience. I was called forward and received my award, but my name was wrong and it wasn't for what I had done. In the dream I was upset. On my way to the awards dinner, I stopped off at a beautiful palace sitting room. It had a high marble mantelpiece, and on the mantelpiece was a package wrapped like a gift in blue and silver paper. The duchess was there and she was crying. She was grieved that I had been wrongly named. Then she reached up and undid the package, which was a beautiful, airy, light shawl in silver and blue, which she gave to me to put on."

Four specific people are mentioned in this dream:

- the dreamer

- the king

- the prince

- the duchess.

Answer the questions which unlock the dream:

- Who or what is this dream about?

- What type of dream is it and what is its source?

- What type of protocol do I need to apply to interpret this type of dream?

First look at the sense of the story: what is the headline of the dream story?

Use the helpful symbolism list below to explore the important parts of the dream. What do they add to the sense of the story?

- What are the important parts of the dream?

- Are these elements literal or symbolic, positive or negative?

- They might be: key statements, items, people, places, colours, names, numbers, feelings, quality of light, or colour.

These symbol meanings are for this dream context. In another context they may mean something quite different.

### *Important parts of the dream*

**King's castle** (positive symbol): God's home

**Prince** (positive symbol): Jesus

**Large studio** (positive symbol): church

**Award** (positive symbol): recognition of work done, affirmation and thanks

**Incorrect label** (negative symbol): lack of understanding/care

**Package** (positive symbol): gift

**Duchess** (positive symbol): Holy Spirit

**Shawl** (positive symbol): anointing

**Blue** (positive symbol): divine revelation, prophetic communion, Holy Spirit

**Silver** (positive symbol): redemption, strength, grace, purification

Use the sense of the story, the answers to the questions, and the helpful symbolism list above to write an interpretation of the dream.

Compare your interpretation with the interpretation at the end of the chapter. Was there anything you missed?

## Exercise 4.7: Mel's dream

In this exercise you will decide whether the grandmother is literal or symbolic. Fill that information in on the helpful symbolism list.

### The dream

"I was sitting at the table with my family. My father was at the head of the table. He was shouting at me, as usual, criticizing me again and again about something I had done. My mother sat silently. But my grandmother, who doesn't usually eat with us, was sitting at the foot of the table and she was crying and crying because my father was berating me."

Answer the questions which unlock the dream:

- Who or what is this dream about?

- What type of dream is it and what is its source?

- What type of protocol do I need to apply to interpret this type of dream?

First look at the sense of the story: what is the headline of the dream story?

Use the helpful symbolism list below to explore the important parts of the dream. What do they add to the sense of the story?

- What are the important parts of the dream?

- Are these elements literal or symbolic, positive or negative?

- They might be: key statements, items, people, places, colours, names, numbers, feelings, quality of light, or colour.

These symbol meanings are for this dream context. In another context they may mean something quite different.

### Important parts of the dream

**Table** (negative symbol): place of unhappy community/family

**Father** (literal): harsh father

**Mother** (literal): passive mother

**Grandmother**

Use the sense of the story, the answers to the questions and the helpful symbolism list above to write an interpretation of the dream.

Compare your interpretation with the interpretation at the end of the chapter. Was there anything you missed?

For the next exercise, and those which follow, I would like you to move on from "explaining" the interpretation and write the interpretation as if you were speaking to the seer of the dream or vision. This will help you begin to develop language to use in real-life interpretation situations.

## Exercise 4.8 – Hannah's dream

### The context

Hannah has been married to Alan for nine years. Their relationship is unsettled and difficult. Josh was her old boyfriend when she was in the army. He was strong and kind. Hannah has a Christian worldview. Your task in this exercise is to decide and discern who the character of Josh represents. Fill that information in on the symbol list below before you interpret the dream.

### The dream

"I'm walking along a road with Alan and suddenly a car pulls up to offer us a lift. As I get into the back I see that the driver is Josh and I'm amazed to see him. Josh has blond hair.

"Then we (myself and Josh) are on a bus. Josh is sat on the right side, and I'm sat on the left but a seat down from him. He then gets up and comes over to the left side and stands two seats in front of me, but he's not looking at me. All this time I cannot take my eyes off him and I think to myself, how gorgeous he is! I then hear him mentally say, 'I have to go back Thursday.'"

*Hint:* Is Josh staying around?

Answer the questions which unlock the dream:

- Who or what is this dream about?
- What type of dream is it and what is its source?
- What type of protocol do I need to apply to interpret this type of dream?

First look at the sense of the story: what is the headline of the dream story?

Use the helpful symbolism list below to explore the important parts of the dream. What do they add to the sense of the story?

- What are the important parts of the dream?
- Are these elements literal or symbolic, positive or negative?
- They might be: key statements, items, people, places, colours, names, numbers, feelings, quality of light, or colour.

These symbol meanings are for this dream context. In another context they may mean something quite different.

### Important parts of the dream

**Alan** (literal): Alan

**Josh**

**Driving** (positive symbol): in charge

**Car** (positive symbol): Josh's life call as a "pastoral" person

**Bus** (positive symbol): ministry/vehicle to your destiny

**Looking past me** (negative symbol): distant – it was a long time ago

**"I have to leave"** (negative symbol): distant/going/gone

**"How gorgeous he is"** (feeling): longing for safety, kindness and love

Use the sense of the story, the answers to the questions, and the helpful symbolism list above to write an interpretation of the dream that you would give to the dreamer.

Compare your interpretation with the interpretation at the end of the chapter. Was there anything you missed?

## Section 3: Numbers in dreams and visions

Understanding the numbers in dreams and visions often adds meaning and depth to an interpretation. Numbers can be interpreted in different ways, depending on the context of the dream or vision.

Earlier in this chapter we looked at two dreams with numbers:

- Patti's dream, using the biblical symbolism of Matthew 18:22,

- and "180 degrees is peace", using angles as a piece of mathematical cultural symbolism.

From these two dreams you've noticed that both scriptural number symbolism and mathematical symbolism can have meaning in dreams.

One night, when I was speaking into a particular church, I had a dream. Fractions – ¼ ¼ ¼ ¼ – were dancing across the screen of my dream. As I watched, a well-known male prophet appeared in the dream story, representing Jesus, and said, "My body is fractured."

Using a play on words, my dream had pointed out God's compassion for the brokenness of the people that I was dealing with. The central issue I had to address was their disunity and fragmentation, in order to lead the people into forgiveness and healing.

The number symbolism in the dream used fractions as a piece of mathematical cultural symbolism. Mathematically, these fractions symbolize the whole number divided into four pieces. The numbers in the fractions dream also used word play. The word "fractions" evoked the meaning "fractured".

We see God using a play on words to speak to Jeremiah. Jeremiah saw the "branch of an almond tree", and God replied, "I am watching to see that my word is fulfilled."[117] In Hebrew, "almond tree" is *shaqued*. The word for "watching" is *shoqued*. The words sound similar.

Word play crops up from time to time in dreams and visions, and it's one option to keep in mind when interpreting numbers.

---

117     Jeremiah 1:11–12.

## Exercise 4.9: Penelope's "28" dreams

### The context

Penelope, a dynamic and highly capable woman, was in a time of thinking about what her future was, when she had two dreams within a two-week period.

### Dream 1

"I had a dream about the letters W-A-I-T in big black letters, bigger than me; they were on the left side of the path I was walking down."

### Dream 2 (two weeks later)

"I was walking down the same path again and the number '28' was in big black digits on the other side of the same path."

Answer the questions which unlock the dream:

- Who or what is this dream about?

- What type of dream is it and what is its source?

- What type of protocol do I need to apply to interpret this type of dream?

First look at the sense of the story: what is the headline of the dream story?

Use the helpful symbolism list below to explore the important parts of the dream. What do they add to the sense of the story?

- What are the important parts of the dream?

- Are these elements literal or symbolic, positive or negative?

- They might be: key statements, items, people, places, colours, names, numbers, feelings, quality of light, or colour.

These symbol meanings are for this dream context. In another context they may mean something quite different.

**I** (literal): Penelope

**The path** (positive symbol): journey of life, transition

**Right and left** (positive symbol): two sides of the path and two possible directions

**W-A-I-T** (literal): wait

**28** (positive symbol)

Your task is to decide whether this number is used as a:

- frequently noticed number symbol, meaning eternal life;

- a mathematical symbol;

- a "sounds like" symbol;

- a biblical numerical symbol (a reference or from a Scripture text).

Use the sense of the story, the answers to the questions, and the helpful symbolism list above to write an interpretation of the dream that you would give to the dreamer.

Compare your interpretation with the interpretation at the end of the chapter. Was there anything you missed?

## Developing as an interpreter: Using a bank of recurring number symbol meanings in a balanced way

So far we have looked at numbers using word play, mathematical symbols, biblical symbols, and cultural symbols. But in addition to these four ways that numbers appear in dreams and visions, there are some repeating number meanings that people have noticed, patterns that people have observed from their own dreams and visions and the dreams and visions of others. They are based in personal symbolism, biblical symbolism, cultural symbolism, or universal symbolism.

For example, if we were to write our own symbol bank to go with this chapter, we would now include the possibility that "twenty-eight" in a dream or vision may mean "to wait".

The problem with introducing you to the idea of a symbol bank comes when an interpreter is inexperienced and "drowning" in a sea of confusion when approaching a dream. There is a risk of taking hold of any lifebuoy available and holding on to it for dear life, and the symbol bank fits the bill perfectly. Our call as interpreters is to move past that, to a place where we are confident that God understands the dream perfectly and that He is capable of communicating the individual meaning of the symbol as well as the interpretation to us.

In this development section we will look at dreams and visions which seem to use some of the commonly occurring number interpretations that people have noticed.

Your task is to hold in tension different ways in which numbers can be interpreted, alongside using a number symbol dictionary.

It's important to interpret numbers in dreams and visions carefully. The dream story below contains the number of the dreamer's home, which was wrongly interpreted. The dream story involved two members of one of our communities, Paul and Lucy, who were renting a beautiful house, which suited their artistic and hospitable lifestyle. Their house was number four.

When their home was unexpectedly put up for sale, Lucy had a dream which also contained the number four. We don't have the whole dream recorded; the number four was interpreted by one of their friends to mean that the house was definitely not going to be sold and that they needed to engage in a prayer campaign. Game on.

They prayed, but some months later the house was sold, and new accommodation was reluctantly found. Paul and Lucy moved into a cute little cottage a few roads away.

By the time they brought the dream to me, the misinterpretation had added confusion to the many emotions being experienced and processed at this unsettling time. The obvious personal meaning of the number of their house had been chosen over a commonly occurring piece of cultural symbolism: four seasons. The number four can signify a change of season.

Good protocol would have been very helpful to cover the interpreter and Paul and Lucy, especially as the friend who interpreted the dream was personally involved with the couple and had strong feelings about them wanting to stay in their home. When we are personally involved with the dream or vision story, the desired interpretation can come from our own soul.

Paul's instruction in 1 Corinthians 14:29 contains the advice that both revelation and weighing are a corporate activity: "Two or three prophets should speak, and the others should weigh carefully what is said."

If the dream had been weighed and interpreted by a team, and balanced or confirmed by other revelation about the house move, it could have been a real blessing. Paul and Lucy would have realized from the context of the wider revelation that the number symbolism referred to a change of season. The dream could have helped them move toward accepting the fact that the season was changing and they were moving on.

Presumptuous interpretation is immature interpretation. It's important to ask the question, "What type of symbol is this?" because that question prepares people to look in the right place for the answers. In the case of personal symbolism, we look into what the symbol means for the seer of the dream or vision; for biblical symbolism, we look to Scripture for meaning; for cultural and universal symbolism, we can consider the symbols which other people have noticed in dreams and visions and collated into what becomes their own bank of frequently noticed dream and vision meanings. The real issue isn't whether we sometimes explore a bank of symbol ideas to see if they can bring understanding, but the discernment with which we use them to interpret symbol meanings.

As people have interpreted dreams and visions, certain number patterns have been noticed. Just like any other "language", they began in an oral tradition, being passed from one person to another. These became simple lists of meanings which people have noticed while interpreting revelation. As we look at frequently occurring number meanings, one may stand out and be a perfect match for the story and its context. Or it may not.

Different schools of interpreters translate numbers, colours, and symbols differently. Don't worry about trying to calibrate the whole world of interpretation. There is no definitive list of meanings. There is rather a broader overlapping symbolic language, which you can begin to recognize in some revelation. Our own souls will continue to draw symbols from our own subconscious library, and from the world around us. Make up your own mind about whether you think or feel the lists are useful resources for you to draw on as you develop as an interpreter.

The following dream stories and exercises use number symbolism, some of which are clearly identifiable as rooted in biblical, mathematical, cultural, or universal symbolism. The logical origin of the occasionally recurring meaning of others is a complete mystery to me: I find it fascinating that they still seem to reappear from time to time in different pieces of revelation.

### An exercise using frequently noticed number meanings

Your task for the next exercise is to see if you can identify the correlation between the numbers used in this dream and the frequently noticed number meanings for that number. I have given you the number meanings you will need in this dream context. Keep an open mind as you go through the exercises and assess whether the number meanings apply or not.

## Exercise 4.10: Stuck in Leicester dream

### The context

This highly capable, professional woman went on a course in Leicester. That is her only connection with the city. In her life she had been through several difficult transitions, including being involved in a particularly nasty church split.

### The dream

This is a recurring dream.

"I was trying to get home from Leicester. I had to get home as I have children and pets. There was a train crash at Leicester station. I took another train but I was being hunted by other beings and they were hindering me. They shot me.

"I had no handbag, no money – I needed £76 to get the ticket. I found a car to drive, but I wasn't in control of it."

### The interpretation

This dream is about the dreamer. It is has elements of life-processing and elements of revelation from God.

The protocol is to kindly recognize the difficulty of the journey and how well the woman has done to cope. And to bring in the message of the dream. The sense of the story is, "I'm blocked and stressed; I can't find home, even though I'm really trying."

## Important parts of the dream

**Leicester** (negative symbol): separation and pressure

**Children** (literal): a sense of responsibility

**Home** (positive symbol): place of rest, peace, and belonging

**Train** (negative symbol): a church which was supposed to carry her home, but it crashed and caused hurt

**Other beings** (negative symbol): spiritual attack – sense of things being spiritually unsettled around her. She was doing her best to cope with that.

**Missing handbag** (negative symbol): lack of sense of identity

**Lack of money** (negative symbol): lack of provision and favour

**Car** (positive symbol): deciding to go it alone but life seemed out of control

**Ticket** (positive symbol): the means by which to get home

## The interpretation

"The dream suggests you're a person who works really hard and takes care of what's been given to you. It shows that you may have been let down by an organization you expected to help you. You may have felt alone and perhaps lacking a sense of ease in life. The dream seems somewhat spiritually unsettled, and that can be tough to handle.

"But there's a sense here of trying to find your true identity and a way to complete your journey, to a place of love and belonging. The money speaks of you being given favour and provision. It's the means to achieve an end – homecoming."

Interpreting the significance of the number seventy-six adds detail and meaning to the dream. In dream dictionaries there is no number seventy-six, so we will look at seventy, seven and six to see whether or not there is something there which will help us.

The underlined meanings resonate with the dream story.

|   | Frequently noticed positive meanings | Frequently noticed negative meanings |
|---|---|---|
| 6 | Man, image, secular perfection, man's willingness | flesh, man's disobedience and unwillingness to submit to Holy Spirit, People not yet in rest of God |
| 7 | Completeness, perfection, finished, rest of God, God's will, deliverance and redemption, temporary perfection | |
| 70 | Increase, perfected ministry, absolutely acceptable | absolutely unacceptable |

The interpreter might say, "The number seventy-six speaks about two things coming into line: knowing you are completely loved and accepted and coming into a sense of rest and peace. There are also two other positive and almost contrasting truths, suggested by the number symbolism that God's will is to rescue, justify, retrieve, and recover your situation, but when you are ready, from a place of rest, for Him to do that.

The fact that the number seventy-six was seventy-six pounds, brings in the message that "you need favour and provision in order to help you do this".

Interestingly, there may be an inherent suggestion in the dream that this will happen when the dreamer connects with another "train", an organization involved at some stage to carry her to that place of home, where acceptance will be personified, and she will find rest.

NB, if, as an interpreter, you've been spending time with God, His peace and anointing will come in, and bring a sense of what home is like.

## Exercise 4.11: Vision exercise using a list of frequently occurring number options in seer revelation

Use the frequently recurring number and colour charts in the following pages to help you begin to think about the numbers in your vision. These lists were compiled over time by one of the trainers on our courses. Your task is to see if they are relevant. Stay open to other personal meanings taking precedent over any pre-written ones.

Having visions isn't hard; it's impossible! So you may as well relax and enjoy the journey.

I once heard a teacher tell the story of a visit to a farm with her class. At the end of the day, the children sat around on straw bales and the teacher quizzed them on what they had seen. The farmer was watching at the back as, one after another, the children put up their hands and gave answers, all except one little child with additional needs. So he moved to crouch down beside her and whispered the answers into her ear. That's a picture of us – the child with additional needs, with God, the compassionate father whispering in our ears.

> *"I am the good shepherd; I know my sheep and my*
> *sheep know me... My sheep listen to my voice; I know*
> *them, and they follow me."*[118]

It may be that you are learning how you experience His voice, how you hear, see, and sense Him speaking to you. This is the place where we will give you that experience. In this simple vision exercise, I will ask you to be quiet, shut your eyes, and see a picture. We will then go through the usual weighing and interpreting process so we can see if it's "just me".

In our courses and schools, the bonus of having mentors around is that we can give you confidence and confirm when it is "God" and when it is "just me". With that outside help, you can grow in confidence.

But to encourage you, I had no one to teach me when I started seeing pictures and hearing God. This journey is real and the Good Shepherd is as present as that farmer with the child with additional needs: you are simply stepping into God's grace.

**Step One**: Take some paper or a journal.

**Step Two**: Find a comfortable, still place. Pray that the Holy Spirit will gently draw you into this activation and that you will see clearly and simply. It's that easy. It's a two-way thing.

**Step Three**: Close your eyes and look at your internal television screen. Depending on how you are "wired", you will either see a

---

118    John 10:14, 27.

picture in your mind's eye, or get an idea or a memory. I get faint impressions which become a clear moving story. You may get one still picture.

**Step Four**: Ask the Lord to show you a door. Take your time; let it emerge. I'd like you to write down what you see.

**Step Five**: Ask the Lord to show you what colour it is.

**Step Six**: Ask God what number is on the door? Write it down.

**Step Seven**: Those of you who are well travelled in the prophetic will be seeing a story around your door. Go with it; see what is happening in your vision. Write down what you see.

### Interpreting your door vision

What number and colour was on your door? Look at the following number and colour charts to see if they help you with your vision. Again, this is not a definitive list of meanings, but suggestions which have been frequently noticed.

Recap:

- Zeros add weight and importance to a number.

- When using these number and colour charts, you are not looking for rote interpretation, but for the witness of the Holy Spirit confirming any suggestions that are on the page. It may be that none of the suggestions is appropriate.

- You can mix and match digits to get the number you're looking for.

- Remember: the number meaning may be a personal piece of symbolism that means something only to the dreamer.

- It may be a scriptural reference, a mathematical symbol, a "sounds like" symbol, or a cultural symbol.

- Stay open-minded and don't be prescriptive with any of these suggestions.

- Check your number interpretation by sharing it with a close friend who knows the context of your life, and the loving messages and good boundaries of Scripture. Where might your heart be speaking? What might God be showing you?

Checking what you see and hear against Scripture is an important habit to get into, although it's important not to take individual verses out of context.

| | Example of a number chart with possible meanings |
|---|---|
| 1 | God as source, new beginnings, unity, independent, first in time, rank, order or importance, power of God |
| 10 | Law, order, test, journey, pastor, wilderness, government, authority, restoration, fulfilment, to weigh |
| 100 | Fullness, full measure, full reward, God's election of grace, children of promise |
| 11 | Prophet, transition, end, stop, last |
| 111 | "My beloved Son" (Mark 1:11), 3 x 37 |
| 12 | Apostle, divine or apostolic government, apostolic fullness, joined, everlasting perfection, unity, review |
| 120 | End of flesh, beginning of life in Spirit, divine period of probation |
| 13 | A reflection of God's blessing in your life, change |
| 14 | A reflection of God's blessing in your life, change |
| 15 | Mercy, free, honour, grace, frankness, redemption, to cover sins with blood |
| 16 | Established beginnings, free spirited, without boundaries/law/ sin, salvation, love, spirit |
| 17 | Election of elect, perfection in the area of spiritual maturity |
| 18 | Established blessing/judgment, victory, the beginning of God's order |
| 19 | Without self-righteousness, faith, to confess, to know have received righteousness in Christ |
| 2 | Multiplication, witness, testimony, to agree, unity, discern, Christ, prophetic, partnership |
| 20 | Holy, tested, and well tried and found to be faithful, expectation, divine order, redemption |

| | Example of a number chart with possible meanings |
|---|---|
| 21 | To enter into the perfect rest (7 x 3) |
| 22 | Light |
| 23 | Psalm 23:4, comfort, sustaining, reassurance in difficulty |
| 24 | Complete counsel of God, close to the throne, established order, heavenly worship, priestly behaviour, achieve perfection, to rule over earth, full authority, time, day, 1,000 years |
| 25 | Begin ministry training, forgiveness of sins, training in pastoral ministry |
| 26 | The gospel of Christ |
| 27 | Preaching the gospel |
| 28 | Eternal life |
| 29 | Departure |
| 3 | Godhead, trinity, divine completeness, conform, divine abundance, one accord, solid, real, harmony |
| 30 | Begin ministry, maturing in ministry |
| 32 | Covenant |
| 33 | Promise |
| 34 | Naming of a son |
| 35 | Hope, highway of holiness |
| 37 | Firstborn, (37 x 3 = 111 "My beloved Son"), Word of God |
| 4 | God's creative works, worldwide, universal, earth, creation, winds, seasons, reign, perfection, revival, abundance of material possessions, the natural, to govern the earth |
| 40 | Completed rule, generation, testing, trial, acceptable authority |
| 5 | God's grace to man, responsibility to man, redemption, cross, atonement, serve (to be of service); fertility, five-fold ministry |
| 50 | Freedom, liberty, Pentecost, jubilee, deliverance, year of grace and favour, restoring of blessings, mature service revealing fruit of spirit |
| 51 | Divine revelation |
| 6 | Man, image, secular perfection, man's willingness |
| 7 | Completeness, perfection, finished, rest of God, God's will, deliverance and redemption, temporary perfection |

| | Example of a number chart with possible meanings |
|---|---|
| 70 | Increase, perfected ministry, absolutely acceptable |
| 8 | Sanctify, new beginning, teacher, deliverance, put off sinful nature, to fatten in the spirit ("ate"), shape = eternal |
| 80 | Double preparation, training and testing, sinful nature laid down |
| 9 | Evangelist, finality, nine gifts and fruits, fullness of the Spirit, perfection, worship and praise, harvest, fruit, fertility, deeper with God, exhorting |

| | Example of a colour chart with possible meanings |
|---|---|
| Blue | Divine revelation, prophetic, masculine, spirit of revelation and knowledge, communion with God |
| Brown | Pastor, compassion, humility, repentance |
| Gold | Kingship, kingdom glory, God, being refined, holiness, precious, glory of God |
| Green | Life, conscience, shepherd, growth, prosperity |
| Grey | Maturity, honour |
| Pink | Femininity, love, romance, affection, soft, innocence, vulnerability, compassion |
| Red | Anointing, wisdom, power, passion, wisdom, zeal, strength, blood of Jesus Christ |
| Bright Red | Freed from sin |
| Purple | Royalty, wealth, intercession, kingship, prophetic |
| Silver | Purification, redemption, grace, strength, seven times, God's word tested in your life |
| White | Purity, light, righteousness, Holy Spirit, teaching, priestly, to pray, Spirit of the Lord, holy power |
| Yellow | Welcoming, mind, hope |
| Turquoise | Will, perseverance |
| Orange | Get ready/pay attention (traffic light), perseverance |

## Section 4: Vehicles in dreams and visions

These dreams and visions carry some classic symbolism. Revelation about vehicles is another one of the top twenty most frequently occurring revelation.

Cars and vehicles are often vision shorthand for showing you things about your role in life. "They have to do with what the dreamer is doing, created to do, and his or her current purpose in life."[119]

Periodically I notice that the vehicle appearing in my dreams or visions changes. A couple of years ago my usual gold car disappeared and instead I began to notice a car transporter, taking other cars (ministries) out from the factory (place of equipping and preparation) to get them on to the road. I was driving the car transporter.

On the back of my car transporter was towed a little speedboat. God showed me that it was made to pull a water-skiing team (my outreach team). Jesus drove the speed boat, and my team were doing the water-skiing displays in a pyramid, for the display of His splendour, displaying the love and power of God as they ministered to people in the gifts of the Spirit (the water).

We use this same vision exercise on our courses, asking God to show people a symbolic vehicle representing their lives, so that they can practise interpretation.

When you are interpreting vehicles in dreams and visions, it's useful to ask some questions:

- What sort of vehicle is it:
- What colour is it?
- How big is it?/How many people does it carry?
- Who is driving? If it's you, you are in charge. If you're in the passenger seat, you are helping. If you are in the back, you are part of that ministry.
- Is it made to go over rough ground effectively – a 4x4/tractor?
- Is it a high-performance and powerful vehicle, free and flexible?
- Is the vehicle used locally or internationally?

119      Streams Top 20, Dream Symbols Interpretation Card, Streams Ministry International, 2004 .

- Does it move on the land or the water (in the things of the Spirit), or in the air (the arena of prayer or international travel)?

## Exercise 4.12: Gena and Pete's car vision

### The context

Gena and Pete run a ministry to the homeless.

### The vision

"My husband and I were driving a big, gleaming red car; it was a Mercedes. It stopped at the pavement and lots of people got in the back."

Write down the answers to these questions and use them to come up with an interpretation to give to Gena and Pete:

Answer the questions which unlock the vision:

- Who or what is this vision about?

- What type of vision is it and what is its source?

- What type of protocol do I need to apply to interpret this type of vision?

First look at the sense of the story: what is the headline of the vision story?

These questions will help you think about the vehicle in the vision:

- What vehicle are Gena and Pete driving?

- What do you know about a Mercedes?

- What colour was it? And what does that colour say about their ministry?

- Who was driving?

- How many people got in the back?

- Where did they come from?

- Use the helpful symbolism list below to explore the important parts of the vision. What do they add to the sense of the story?

- What are the important elements in the vision?

- Are these elements literal or symbolic, positive or negative?

- They might be: key statements, items, people, places, colours, names, numbers, feelings, quality of light, or colour.

These symbol meanings are for this vision context. In another context they may mean something quite different.

### Important parts of the vision

**My husband and me** (literal): the seer and her husband

**Gleaming** (positive symbol): well kept

**Mercedes** (positive symbol): quality car, well made

**Red** (positive symbol): anointing, wisdom, power, blood of Jesus, strength

**Pavement** (positive symbol): the street, interacting with the world

**The back** (positive symbol): people who are part of the ministry, being carried

Use the sense of the story, the answers to the questions, and the helpful symbolism list above to write an interpretation of the vision that you would give to the seer.

Compare your interpretation with the interpretation at the end of the chapter. Was there anything you missed?

## Exercise 4.13: Andrew's 4x4 vision

### The context

Andrew is a young, single Church of England curate who is asking questions about his next move. Andrew has been through a lot in his life, through no fault of his own, and he was overcoming some feelings of anxiety which had begun during his childhood.

## The vision

"I had a big black Range Rover with a trailer on it. I was driving the Range Rover and it had a family in it. It was a really rough road; no other car could drive it. The trailer was there for people to get on and off easily without having to get inside. It wasn't fast, but it kept going in the same direction whatever was put in its way. Nothing was too hard for it to cross.

"And when it reached its destination by the coast, all the other vehicles looked battered and bruised. The Range Rover was shiny like nothing had ever happened to it, almost like brand new."

Answer the questions to unlock the vision:

- Who or what is this vision about?

- What type of vision is it and what is its source?

- What type of protocol do I need to apply to interpret this type of vision?

First look at the sense of the story: what is the headline of the vision story?

These questions will help you think about the vehicle in the vision:

- What vehicle is Andrew driving?

- What colour is it?

- Is the colour symbol positive or negative in this vision?

- How and where were the people carried?

- Where were the people carried, in contrast to where the family was?

- What does Andrew's vision point out about the journey?

Use the helpful symbolism list below to explore the important parts of the vision. What do they add to the sense of the story?

- What are the important elements in the vision?

- Are these elements literal or symbolic, positive or negative?

- They might be: key statements, items, people, places, colours, names, numbers, feelings, quality of light, or colour.

These symbol meanings are for this vision context. In another context they may mean something quite different.

### Important parts of the vision

**I** (literal): seer

**Range Rover** (positive symbol): solid, strong vehicle for all terrain

**Black** (positive symbol): authority, security, and power

**Road** (positive symbol): life-journey, direction, truth, what lies ahead for you

**Trailer** (positive symbol): congregation/ministry group/followers/something in tow

**Coast** (positive symbol): where earth and heaven meet, our destination in heaven when we have lived our life fully

Use the sense of the story, the answers to the questions, and the helpful symbolism list above to write an interpretation of the vision that you would give to the seer.

Compare your interpretation with the interpretation at the end of the chapter. Was there anything you missed?

## Exercise 4.14: Holvick's schooner vision

### The context

Holvick is a Lutheran minister. He was coming out of a very busy season where the established church had impacted heavily on his ministry and life.

### The vision

"Today I had a vision of a schooner boat. The trouble is I don't like sailing much at all. I feel a bit like that about ministry recently. When

I was twenty-one I was prophesied over by a visiting team from South Africa. I was told about my heart and ministry. They mentioned a schooner boat. How can I understand this better?"

Answer the questions to unlock the vision:

- Who or what is this vision about?

- What type of vision is it and what is its source?

- What type of protocol do I need to apply to interpret this type of vision?

Your task with this vision is to answer these questions:

- Some frequently noticed interpretations of schooner are: able to influence people/speed on water.

- Is the schooner in the vision positive or negative?

- How is Holvick feeling? What do you need to say about this?

- Is the schooner a life-processing symbol, showing how Holvick is feeling about his ministry right now, or is it a symbol from God to encourage him?

Come up with an interpretation of the Schooner which you could give to Holvick.

Is it relevant that it was a repeating symbol?

You may like to google an image of a Schooner to help you interpret what Holvick is seeing.

Compare your answers to the questions and interpretation against the answers and interpretation at the end of the chapter. Was there anything you missed?

## Developing as an interpreter: Dealing with negative symbols in interpretation

It's easy to give interpretations that contain a happy positive message, but as we develop and hone a gift of interpretation, it's important to understand how to approach negative symbols with wisdom. They need careful handling.

185

The person in front of us is usually very open to everything we have to say. Our words mean so much that we have to measure them carefully. The golden rule of ministry is applicable here: "First, do no harm."

People who have an issue with fear naturally interpret through that lens, and often pull out negative meanings without checking the context or the real interpretation of the revelation. An unhealed part of them is affecting how they view and respond to information. We sometimes see this in our classes.

Black is often interpreted as "an absence of light; darkness or black magic". But it also happens to be the colour of the door of the Prime Minister's headquarters: Number 10 Downing Street. It represents a secure place – a place of rule and authority.

Black cats are often considered by the superstitious to be unlucky. The witch's black cat often seen in fairy stories symbolizes the familiar spirit attached to a witch known as a "cat".

But my daughter has a gentle cat which is a black, fluffy ball of fur. It has been her loving companion throughout her childhood. Black cats and black doors are neutral. It is the context which gives a positive or negative meaning.

When people see a black door or a black cat in a revelation exercise and go into fear, it only means that the unhealed part of their life is being exposed. When people bring us a revelation which has a negative content, or a negative interpretation, we are able to carry light into that part of their life.

There is a particularly high need for care if the picture of a hearse or coffin appears in a dream or vision. This causes fear. Interpret this symbol silently, for your own use in the interpretation encounter. You may be seeing a snapshot of the future, or into a recent bereavement. This is not the province of a casual dream interpretation, but of huge life-and-death issues. It is best not to mention this symbol, even if it becomes apparent during conversation that there has been a death in the family.

You can, of course, pray privately for the person involved, ask them how things have been going lately, or mention it to pastorally responsible people if you are worried. But your job is to bring encouragement, edification, and comfort, to display God's love and compassion.

We have a vision exercise that asks God to show delegates a symbolic vehicle representing their lives. People will see either a positive or a negative symbol.

The two following vehicle visions contain symbols which need careful interpretation. They will help you to identify and interpret negative symbols sensitively and wisely. The colour of the vehicles adds to the symbolic detail of the visions. The colour red often appears in vehicle visions, and it can have both positive and negative meanings depending on the context of the vision story. Common possible meanings are:

| | Possible positive meanings | Possible negative meanings |
|---|---|---|
| Red | Anointing, Wisdom, power, passion, zeal, strength, evangelism, blood of Jesus Christ | Anger, suffering, war |

## Amanda's red delivery truck vision

### The context
Amanda is an evident leader. With two small children at home, she ministers to those around her in both her local community and the church. Amanda had this vision at a training course in her church.

### The vision
"I was driving a red delivery truck with monster truck wheels. The truck had no roof on the cab."

### The interpretation
This vision is about Amanda. It is a life-processing vision with a revelation element from God, showing us the condition of Amanda's heart.

The protocol here is to interpret the dream sensitively in a way which achieves the purpose of the vision: to help Amanda access the support that she needs. The sense of the story is: I have a great truck, but it has no cab.

It was vital to ask Amanda some questions about her vision, to help us discern whether the symbols in her vision are positive or negative.

We asked:

- "Have you perhaps been feeling challenged or vulnerable lately?" Her answer was, "Yes."

- "And maybe a bit cross about that?" Her answer was, "Yes."

This vision carries two symbols which carry negative meanings:
**No cab** to keep her warm and covered: she feels uncovered. (Having no cab equally could have symbolized a love of being free in another context.)
**Red**: in this context shows Amanda's feelings of suffering and anger.

The literal interpretation of Amanda's vision is that she is suffering and angry and no one is covering, protecting, or looking after her.

That interpretation is no help to Amanda. She already knows all this – that's the problem. We aren't called to prophesy the problem, but to encourage her.

Here is a gifted, capable woman with the ability to go into different settings (monster truck wheels) and touch others' lives (delivery truck), but she is vulnerable, uncovered, hurting, and angry. As an interpreter, you are able to bring a level of kindness and clarity to her pain to stand with her, to help her understand what she is going through and the need to have a healthy way ahead.

But you need to do this without trespassing normal social boundaries or telling her what to do. That's a learning curve.

We said something like this: "This vision shows me that you are amazing – you have the ability to go into difficult situations and touch others' lives, bringing things that they need. I have a little question about who does that for you. You will do this at your happiest when you are covered and protected. This vision has shown us how you've been feeling. God's heart is to cover you with love. So there are some things to come into place. I'd love to know what He has planned. A vision like this helps us to see any places where God's order and grace need to come. Improvement needs to be done to your 'truck', so that you're at peace and happily covered. Who might be able to help you do that?"

That conversation will be the beginning of covering and protection. The last question is a good one; it transitions ownership of the situation to Amanda to explore a possible pathway ahead.

Practise interpreting these visions, which include negative symbols:

## Exercise 4.15: Rebecca's tractor dream

### The context

The dreamer is a mature, talented, senior manager coming out of a career break. She is looking for her next step. In her Christian worldview, work is her ministry.

### The dream

"I was in my car, driving along country lanes in summer. The skies were blue and clear. There were four tractors in front of me."

Answer the questions to unlock the dream:

- Who or what is this dream about?

- What type of dream is it and what is its source?

- What type of protocol do I need to apply to interpret this type of dream?

First look at the sense of the story: what is the headline of the dream story?

These questions will help you think about the vehicle in the dream:

- What part do the vehicles in the dream play?

- Why were there four tractors?

- What does the number four represent in the dream context?

Use the helpful symbolism list below to explore the important parts of the dream. What do they add to the sense of the story?

- What are the important parts of the dream?

- Are these elements literal or symbolic, positive or negative?

- They might be: key statements, items, people, places, colours, names, numbers, feelings, quality of light, or colour.

These symbol meanings are for this dream context. In another context they may mean something quite different.

### Important parts of the dream

**I** (literal): the dreamer

**Car** (positive symbol): their role/purpose in life

**Country lanes** (neutral symbol): back roads

**In summer** (positive symbol): a place of light and warmth

**Tractors** (negative symbol): delay

**Four** (positive symbol): change of season

Use the sense of the story, the answers to the questions, and the helpful symbolism list above to write an interpretation of the dream that you would give to the dreamer.

Compare your interpretation with the interpretation at the end of the chapter. Was there anything you missed?

## Exercise 4.16: Indian airport dream

### The context

This dreamer was a young minister who was in transition because a church was about to split. He had no personal understanding of the behind-the-scenes situation, but as a sensitive spiritual man he had been unsettled by the dynamics of the deteriorating situation.

### The dream

"I was in a funny little hotel in India and realized I had to try to find my way to the airport by myself to catch a plane home. I only had twenty (not pounds) left in my wallet and I was worried it was not enough.

"I eventually found someone who gave me a number for a taxi, but they were slow to help me as they were chatting and distracted.

"I called for a taxi and a man appeared with this tiny rounded vehicle like an auto rickshaw – no doors and a round roof – and gave me an elastic rope to hold on to. I then realized I had left my case behind and ran into the hotel and found a woman who told me to go back into the room and get it. She didn't help me. I ran and grabbed the case and the taxi man rammed my case in the back. Then we went on this hair-raising journey in very crazy traffic. I then found myself in the grounds of the airport and I was still trying to hang on to the elastic rope, but there was no driver and I realized I was about to swing out into the traffic. It happened in slow motion. I felt a crunch as a truck hit my right ear. I tried to talk and ask my (female) friend if I had died but it was hard to talk as I couldn't open my mouth properly and she smiled and said no! I looked for my case but it was gone."

The chaotic nature of this detailed dream reflects how the dreamer was feeling and experiencing his situation. Refining the details of this dream down to a list helps to bring order to this chaotic dream story, so that you can interpret it. Your job as an interpreter is to identify the key elements and bring a sense of order and understanding to the situation. Answer the questions to unlock the dream:

- Who or what is this dream about?

- What type of dream is it and what is its source?

- What type of protocol do I need to apply to interpret this type of dream?

First look at the sense of the story: what is the headline of the dream story?

Use the helpful symbolism list below to explore the important parts of the dream. What do they add to the sense of the story?

- What are the important parts of the dream?

- Are these elements literal or symbolic, positive or negative?

- They might be: key statements, items, people, places, colours, names, numbers, feelings, quality of light, or colour.

These symbol meanings are for this dream context. In another context they may mean something quite different.

## *Important parts of the dream*

**Hotel** (positive symbol): transitional location, church

**Plane** (literal): travel; (positive symbol): large ministry

**Home** (positive symbol): where I belong

**Twenty in my wallet** (positive symbol): holy, tested, well tried, found to be faithful, redemption, favour

**"Find my way"** (negative feeling): challenge

**"By myself"** (negative feeling): alone

**"Worried it was not enough"** (negative feeling): concerned about the future

**Woman** (negative symbol): feeling unhelped

**Forgetting my case** (negative symbol): initially unprepared for departure

**Auto rickshaw** (negative symbol): vulnerable chaotic journey with no one in charge to protect the dreamer

**No driver** (negative symbol): no one was leading the transition process

**Truck** (negative symbol): problem, deceit in ministry, opposition, difficulties

**Right ear** (positive symbol): listening, discerning, obedience to God

**Damage to his mouth** (negative symbol): losing your voice

**Female friend** (positive symbol): Holy Spirit

**Case** (positive symbol): identity

Use the sense of the story, the answers to the questions, and the helpful symbolism list above to write an interpretation of the dream that you would give to the dreamer.

Compare your interpretation with the interpretation at the end of the chapter. Was there anything you missed?

## Section 5: God is not a Victorian – personal and sexual imagery in dreams and visions

When I'm doing conferences and schools, teaching about personal imagery in revelation, it's not long before someone will sidle up to me and whisper discreetly, "Please could you interpret my dream? I seem to have kissed the worship leader/pastor/children's worker/schoolteacher…"

Usually such a dream means something harmless: kissing is used in a symbolic way in Scripture to symbolize submission,[120] as a sign of peace and love,[121] or a kiss of homage.[122]

But these dreams can also express the longings of a dreamer for love or affection, or express physical desires which they have projected on to a specific figure. To be frank, it depends upon the type of kiss.

One woman shared her story with me. She had been having romanticized processing dreams about a male friend. In real life, her husband, a lawyer, was busy with work and had asked a colleague to do the legwork for a serious legal situation which the family had encountered. The stand-in supported the wife during this time. Needless to say, the need for support and protection was met by the friend, not by the husband, and the woman's heart began to gravitate toward the source of safety.

The wife recognized her vulnerability and wisely shared her dreams with us. We recognized the dreams as soul dreams, so she took steps to distance herself from the man who had come in to protect her, and renewed her relationship with her husband. The process was followed up by her frank conversation with her husband about the effects of his working hours on the family.

Body imagery is part of life, our reality, and therefore part of our normal conscious and subconscious language. So it's natural that it appears in our dreams and visions. Moreover, God seems to use really intimate and matter-of-fact personal language and symbolism in the Scriptures. He is evidently no prude. Perhaps one of the best examples of a culturally impolite symbol is found in Isaiah 30:22.

I don't find this easily trips off the pen – and I'm not the only one: in looking through the different Western translations of this verse, I notice

---

120     Psalm 2:12.
121     Romans 16:16; 1 Peter 5:14.
122     Job 31:27.

that out of twenty-three versions, fourteen fail to translate the symbol literally, and only nine use the literal translation. Instead the translators use phrases such as "sickening thing", "unclean thing", "impure thing", or "ruined by stains". The nine versions which bite the bullet contain the literal translation: "Then you will desecrate your idols overlaid with silver your images covered with gold; you will throw them away like a menstrual cloth and say to them, 'Away with you!'"[123]

The Bible continues to pull no punches in the Song of Songs. That beautiful little book, tucked between Ecclesiastes and Isaiah, is a personal as well as an allegorical love story. It describes in intimate detail the sensual beauty of the woman who "queens and concubines praised…"[124] Song of Songs spares no blushes and glories in sensuality.

These everyday personal and intimate themes are reflected in our dream life. Especially where sexuality is concerned, the normal weighing process is important, as is asking the questions, "Where does this dream or vision come from?" "Is it life-processing revelation, processing physical desires, or is it a revelation dream or vision, using symbolic language?"

Dreams and visions containing imagery concerning washing and bodily functions are among the ten most common types of revelation. The meaning of the symbolism will always be unique to the context of the dream story. Nevertheless, we see the following universal and cultural symbolism crop up frequently as it reflects part of our everyday lives.

You may find it helpful to use the common meanings below as you look at the following dream and vision exercises:

**Bathroom** (positive symbol): a place of cleansing; (negative symbol): dirty/broken bathroom – there is a need for a clean place to deal with issues. This area seems to have been neglected. The dirty/broken/missing/locked bathroom may not be just a personal issue – there may not be an adequate place of cleansing (inner healing/counselling) available in the real-life context.

**Using a bathroom in full view of people**: there is a cleansing process which will be apparent to others.

---

123     Isaiah 30:22.
124     Song of Songs 6:9.

**Dreaming of being naked in public**: feeling or being vulnerable. It's not necessarily a bad thing to be vulnerable with those you trust, in a safe place.

**Toilet**: natural cleansing and process as we walk through life.

**Shower**: cleansing away the things that have affected us. If undealt with, these will have a consequence.

**Bath** (positive symbol): cleansing, relaxation, soaking, time to yourself. You could ask if there were candles and music, whether the water was pleasant to be in (negative symbol): dirty water indicates a lack of a clean context to bathe in.

## Mobile toilet dream story

### The context

This year, we took a group of women from a discipleship hub group away to an overnight retreat centre. We had teaching sessions, shared delicious food, lit a fire, and got into our PJs to watch a movie. It was a delightful expression of community. There was also a spiritual agenda, with time for God to impact the culture and spirit of each woman. As I was seeking God about His agenda for the twenty-four hours away, he gave me a dream.

### The dream

"In my dream I went into a cloakroom. The toilet stall doors were open and they were gleaming super white. Everything was very light.

"The first stall was a family toilet, with a big toilet and a small toilet next to it. The second and third stalls were normal toilet stalls. The fourth toilet stall was a toilet with an engine and a steering wheel, all beautifully clean and white. It was a mobile toilet.

"Suddenly the scene changed and I was in the men's toilet block, with urinals and some stalls. It was all a dirty yellow. There were yellow stains like a pool on the floor. The toilets and the walls were all dirty and dull yellow."

### The interpretation

The interpretation was interesting and the symbolism somewhat politically incorrect. I knew that the men's toilet block represented the things of "man", symbolizing humanity, the things of the flesh, intellectual pride (yellow), and of some issues to do with literal men. As I looked at the difference between the two cloakrooms, I knew that God was speaking to us about a cleansing from the things of our humanity and other people's humanity and a time of coming into a place of revelation, cleansing, beauty, peace, and light.

I knew the symbolic toilets were for the discipleship group, and they spoke of issues of cleansing for families and individuals. The mobile toilet was to be taken with us for the twenty-four-hour retreat. We were being taken into a time of cleansing.

During the weekend, as we shared together, the women were very clear about where God's cleansing was needed in their lives. We took the dream and journalled to ask God where it applied, asking God the question, "What do you want to do with me during this time of cleansing?"

When they came back with the answer to the question, sharing and prayer followed, as the sweetness of God's voice spoke into each situation. The women each came back with a different answer.

- "I was to be cleansed of the ball of fear that is ruling my life. God wanted to screw it up and kick it so far away that it doesn't bother me again."

   For this dreamer we arranged a time with an experienced inner healing and deliverance minister on our return, so that this discipleship group member could follow up on God's desire for her life.

- "I want to reaffirm your faith in community after your experience with the things of man has dirtied and stained your faith in community and in man's leadership."

- The answers to the question from the other women all concerned literal individual men: they were about husbands, marriages, ex-boyfriends, and work colleagues.

In that safe place the women were able to examine the impact of these relationships on their lives and go through a time of cleansing and prayer.

The next series of exercises contains bathroom symbolism.

## Exercise 4.17: Bizarre dream

### The context

This woman was about to go for counselling.

### The dream

"I was at the zoo and just going off to the toilets. Outside were four large information posters about solid waste. The first was a picture of human dung titled "Normal Dung", the second had a picture of a "floater", the third had a picture of a gorilla and a title of "Gorilla Dung", and the fourth had a picture of a huge steaming pile of mammoth dung. I saw this and thought, 'How extraordinary. Thank goodness I'm in the normal category.' I went to the toilet and saw to my horror that I had a floater. I flushed the toilet again and it went. I woke up."

Answer the questions which unlock the dream:

- Who or what is this dream about?

- What type of dream is it and what is its source?

- What type of protocol do I need to apply to interpret this type of dream?

First look at the sense of the story: what is the headline of the dream story?

Use the helpful symbolism list below to explore the important parts of the dream. What do they add to the sense of the story?

- What are the important parts of the dream?

- Are these elements literal or symbolic, positive or negative?

- They might be: key statements, items, people, places, colours, names, numbers, feelings, quality of light, or colour.

These symbol meanings are for this dream context. In another context they may mean something quite different.

### Important parts of the dream

**Zoo** (positive symbol): a place of learning and revelation

**Dung** (negative symbol): something left over that needs to be processed and cleared away

**Toilet** (positive symbol): going through a cleansing and purifying process

**Floater** (negative symbol): persistent issue that you've been processing, but it isn't complete

**Flushing the toilet** (positive symbol): 1) you can do it; 2) it will go

**Information posters** (positive symbol): useful information for you to use

**Number four** (positive symbol): there's a change of season coming

Use the sense of the story, the answers to the questions, and the helpful symbolism list above to write an interpretation of the dream that you would give to the dreamer.

Compare your interpretation with the interpretation at the end of the chapter. Was there anything you missed?

## Exercise 4.18: Washing vision

### The context

This seer was attending a church worship meeting when she saw this vision about the church.

### The vision

"Everyone in the building was submerged in water, except for a few heads that could be seen bobbing above the water. Those heads were very gently pushed downward.

"The church leader was lying face down, facing the door, in front of the congregation. At some point as he talked about repentance.

Some froth-producing material (a soap bar?) was being used to wash everyone's hair, with heads kept just above the water. There were many soapy heads, as everyone seemed to happily cooperate with the process, and appeared to be enjoying it. In addition, one person had a change of clothing, into a silvery suit, as the old clothes were taken away and they were moved forward. The church leader also had a change of clothing into a sort of silvery-grey suit. Initially he was made to sit facing forward, and then he walked slowly down the middle aisle, talking, all the way to the front door, where he stood looking out.

"The same stuff that had been used to wash heads was placed on the youth worker's head as she stood by the door. She was amused! Soapy water then flowed from the church through the front of the entrance into the street."

Answer the questions which unlock the vision:

- Who or what is this vision about?

- What type of vision is it and what is its source?

- What type of protocol do I need to apply to interpret this type of vision?

First look at the sense of the story: what is the headline of the vision story?

Use the helpful symbolism list below to explore the important parts of the vision. What do they add to the sense of the story?

- What are the important elements in the vision?

- Are these elements literal or symbolic, positive or negative?

- They might be: key statements, items, people, places, colours, names, numbers, feelings, quality of light, or colour.

These symbol meanings are for this vision context. In another context they may mean something quite different.

### *Important parts of the vision*

**Water** (symbol): things of the Spirit

**Church leader** (literal): church leader

**Congregation** (literal): congregation

**Talked about repentance** (literal): repentance

**Soap bar** (positive symbol): cleansing, conviction, repentance, and forgiveness

**Washing hair** (positive symbol): cleansing minds and thinking

**Happily joining in** (positive symbol): the process brings joy[125]

**Change of clothing** (positive symbol): look at Zechariah 3:4

**Silver suit** (positive symbol): purified, redeemed, and reclothed in strength through grace (the negative is slavery, domination, and legalism)

**Aisle** (positive symbol): transition

**Front door** (positive symbol): place of interacting with the outside world

**Youth worker** (literal): she was amused, bringing joy

**Soapy water from the church** (positive symbol): cleansing – repentance in the church is affecting the world

**Street** (positive symbol): outside world

Use the sense of the story, the answers to the questions, and the helpful symbolism list above to write an interpretation of the vision that you would give to the seer.

Compare your interpretation with the interpretation at the end of the chapter. Was there anything you missed?

## Developing as an interpreter: Dealing respectfully and competently with sensitive dream and vision content

Health warning: this development section looks at sexual imagery in dreams and visions. If it is likely to be sensitive for you, I would ask you to consider giving yourself full permission to leave this section and move on to the next chapter where we begin to deal with less emotive issues.

---

125    Hebrews 1:9.

When preaching about sexuality, one preacher dispelled embarrassment by telling a joke about a minister who took up sailing. After just two lessons the minister is said to have told his wife he was going to preach a sermon based on sailing as his new hobby. At the last minute he changed his mind and preached on sex. Unfortunately, his wife didn't make it to worship that Sunday and did not realize he had made the change. On Monday she ran into a church member in the grocery store who commented how much she had appreciated the sermon. The unwitting preacher's wife replied, "Well, I don't know why he tried to preach on that. He only tried it twice – the first time he got seasick and the second time he lost his hat."

Recognizing body and sexual symbolism and knowing how to interpret it accurately in dreams and visions is just the beginning of interpreting these extremely private pieces of revelation. For anyone to let you into their world in this way expresses real vulnerability. Our job is to respond with respect and sensitivity, as well as skill surrounded by great protocol.

There's still a hint of embarrassment around this area. A matter-of-fact approach and some wise protocol can bring a place of safety and respect.

One of the comments we most frequently receive about our ministry is that we are "a safe place". We achieve that in two ways: by genuinely honouring and caring about each person who comes to us, and by treating them with wise protocol and consideration.

There are five options which we have come across for this type of dream or vision.

The first is that they are symbolic, using cultural norms or biblical symbols to represent other things. Sometimes intimate imagery can be used to tell a story. The key to this category of dreams is the feel of the dream – it's so extremely non-sensual and unsexy that it's amusing.

The best way to illustrate this is by telling you one of my dreams.

## Brothel dream story

### The context

I had been asked to go and work with a prophetic teaching and training ministry which worked worldwide. The people were lovely, the ethics and culture were excellent, and the opportunity would have been exciting. It came at a time when we been praying through the way forward. From the family point of view, it would be beneficial because I could choose how much travelling I would do, and it would be a blessing financially. Dave saw these advantages, and asked me to consider taking the job.

That night I had a dream.

### The dream

"I dreamt I was working in a brothel. I was wearing a very baggy pair of thick jeans, flat lace-up shoes, and a big polo-neck, cream, chunky-knit sweater. It was bright daylight and I was dusting the empty room, which looked like a normal, empty coffee shop. The whole dream was entirely unsexy and non-threatening; there were no other people in it. But I knew my husband owned the brothel!"

### The interpretation

This dream was about us a couple – it was a revelation dream from God. The protocol for us was to listen to the message of the dream and act upon it.

The sense of the story is that I was shown a place that merchandized something precious and holy.

The dream implicitly refers to a well-known phrase used in prophetic circles to talk about doing things for practical benefits rather than being called by God: "prostituting the gift". The dream was very matter of fact and hygienically pure in attitude and action – it was the opposite of a sensual dream. But the message was clear: "You would be taking a job for the wrong reasons." We turned the opportunity down without another thought and continued on our way. And God has been faithful to us financially each time we've made a decision to follow His will.

The second option is that dreams can sometimes have sexual content which processes normal biological feelings

From time to time, when the team and I are out on outreach, we will meet a man who wants to tell us one of "those" dreams. This never seems to happen, thankfully, in the café, where our kingdom culture is the predominant culture. But for pop-up outreach, we have briefed the men on team that they need keep an eye out for a certain sign from our girls so that we can replace them immediately.

It is generally best not to be too intense about the interpretation of biological dreams. The best thing to say is, "They are just processing dreams. They happen." And that's the extent of the interpretation.

Within a pastoral relationship, these dreams may be part of a wider conversation. Disturbing sexual content can sometimes be part of a wider life story, reflecting problems people are experiencing. They may come to a familiar interpreter asking genuine questions. The stories they tell are of dreams that they have enjoyed sensually. I point this out because this category of dreams (or less usually, visions) is defined by that fact.

## Casual sex dream

### The context

The dreamer was asking sincere questions about her recurring graphic dreams. She had been faithful in her marriage and was concerned about the implication of the dreams, asking, "Am I going to be unfaithful?"

### The dream

"I am having repeating dreams about sleeping with different men: including the doctor, the children's headmaster, and my husband's boss's boss."

### The interpretation

This dream is a life-processing dream about the dreamer. The protocol is to interpret it sensitively and considerately, removing her fears and explaining the content. It's necessary to be totally non-judgmental.

The sense of the story is, "Help, I'm having sex with different men."

The dream suggests that the dreamer's normal desires were being channelled toward "safe figures" who were out of reach. It became apparent as she talked that her marriage needed a little attention, so that there was a natural outlet for her sexuality.

The whole conversation was accomplished without embarrassment in a very matter-of-fact way. We explained to the dreamer what was happening in her dreams, so that she could understand herself and work gently toward building her relationship with her husband, whom she dearly loved.

The wisdom and care we need to show with the next two types of dreams and visions with sexual content is immense. This type of sexual revelation differs drastically from the previous two types, which deal with symbolic or sexually enjoyable dreams. By contrast, these dreams and visions are unpleasant and bring distress.

This material is so sensitive that we have chosen not to use a teaching example here. We will briefly describe those dreams in general instead.

The third category of trauma dreams and visions with sexual content can contain a literal component, reflecting traumatic events of the past which a person may have experienced. This means that you need to be wise, gentle, and careful to avoid retraumatizing someone if they bring you a dream in this category. If a seer is sharing a genuine dream or vision with you that they clearly find unpleasant, upsetting, or fearful, or which has graphic unpleasant sexual or violent content, as an interpreter you need to have an automatic cut-out which stops the interpretation process but allow the person to fully recount their dream. This may be the first time they have told someone and it's important not to shut them down. Listen compassionately.

We would like to offer you some safe questions to use in guiding the encounter.

- First, compassionately, casually, and gently ask a question to see if you are encountering a trauma dream or vision.
- Check your facts: "I wonder if this is a recurring dream or vision?" "And it is a difficult dream or vision?"
- Gently emphasize without making a big thing of it, "You are very brave to ask about this type of dream because this may be hard for you."
- Explain your protocol: "These recurring dreams or visions can be very sensitive." (Using the term "recurring dream" rather than "traumatic dream" again covers the person with dignity and continues the gentle, non-invasive approach.)

In expressing this compassionately, you are not turning the person away or dismissing their dream or vision. On the contrary, you are receiving them, hearing them, and being hospitable to them at this point in their life. Do not comment on the dream content or ask questions. Don't hurry on to the next person, if they chose to continue the conversation. When they have finished, gently build a bridge to more normal conversation. Dealing with trauma is a specialist counselling area, which as interpreters it's not appropriate for us to engage in. Our job is simply to refer people to the type of kind, capable expertise that can bring the necessary healing. If by following these guidelines you suspect the dream reveals past abuse, it is important to signpost people to the GP or specialized counselling; our responsibility lies in keeping a confidential record of the conversation with basic facts: name, date, bullet points of the conversation, including none of our own opinions, just reporting the simple facts.

It's unlikely that the telling of a dream would count as legal, "first disclosure" of a past incident, but a record may be of worth in the future if the police do investigate any specific case. At that point, it would corroborate a story if the person chose to later report an incident or cycle of past abuse. There is no legal responsibility to report historical abuse if the subject is now an adult.

However, if a child reveals potential abuse, the advice in addition to that above is:

- Never promise to keep a secret.
- Never ask a child leading questions.
- Never attempt to investigate the allegations yourself.
- On our team we have a nominated, qualified safeguarding officer who is our "go to" person.
- Official avenues of reporting are the NSPCC, the police, or the local council's social work department.

The fourth category is another type of dream which isn't very pleasant at all. But because I've been asked this question several times, I'm going to include it here, so that if you are asked the same question you have some input and experience with which to meet it. I have never been told a vision in the category of dreams about God which represented a pagan or unhealed sexuality, but that doesn't mean that they don't exist.

Before I talk about this category of dreams, let's be very clear that we're not talking about an echo of the Song of Songs symbolism. Song of Songs is a piece of biblical symbolism on two levels: first, the literal celebration of the artistry and sensuality of the love between Solomon, a literal man, and the Shulamite, a literal woman; secondly, many commentators point out that Song of Songs is symbolic, representing the forthcoming marriage between Christ and the universal corporate church.[126]

Both these concepts are scriptural, but there is a distortion which sometimes appears in dreams. And there's no nice or good way to say this, other than just to say it: occasionally a woman will come with a dream of God and herself in a sexual encounter. The message and value of the dream and the symbolism – of God loving the woman with that kind of sexual expression – are unscriptural. It reflects a pagan value set where deities and humans interact sexually. So what is going on here?

There are two options:

- A background of unhealthy sexuality and spirituality is being expressed in a soul dream. The issue is not the dream, but the theology of sexuality and spirituality, which needs to be redeemed.

- Past hurts and unmet needs, romantically or sexually, are being projected on to God. Again, the issue isn't the dream; the issue is the wounded heart of the dreamer, who will usually quote Song of Songs as a reference point.

The first is a discipleship issue and the second is a pastoral healing issue, both of which are hard to deal with within a dream interpretation context. These dreams express broken or unhealthy relationships or marriages, broken histories, or pagan spirituality. The very last thing these people need is shock or judgment. It's simply an issue of healing and discipleship.

Our dreams and visions are uncensored. I find it moving that people are willing to trust us and invite us into their personal world. And our response needs to be to cover their dignity: love covers.

---

126     Revelation 19:7–9; 21:9; Ephesians 5:25; John 3:29.

> *If I have the gift of prophecy and can fathom all*
> *mysteries… but do not have love, I am nothing.[127]*

So in an interpretation situation, limit yourself to general statements about sexuality and pick up on the underlying issues in the revelation: "That's an unusual and unorthodox dream. Such dreams can suggest a need to feel safe and loved, unhealed areas around sexuality, or unorthodox theology about sex.

In a pastoral context, the interpretation is the beginning of a conversation.

The fifth option is transference. Dreams and visions with an out-of-the-blue, unusual, graphic sexual content can occur after interactions with someone who has been carrying a certain type of demonic spirit. If a minister has been pastoring or working with someone who has a problem with sex addiction or perversion, it's not uncommon for them to have a dream or vision which displays that particular type of sexual problem.

It's important to have a complete lack of shame about our dreams. Just this week we have been working with a young minister who has been counselling a young man with a profound sexual problem. The minister's dream life has been affected, and it has taken prayer and support to bring him to a place of freedom and peace. This type of revelation can only usually be recognized by knowing the context or character of the seer. It's unusual, although not impossible, to recognize this category of dream or vision in an interpretation encounter.

## A Protocol for interpreting personal and sexual dreams and visions

In an interpretation situation, don't initiate the conversation about sexual dreams and visions. If, however, the subject comes up naturally, deal with it after assessing which type of dream or vision it is.

- Symbolic dreams and visions use sexual and personal universal symbolism to represent other things. They are non-sensual in content.

---

127    1 Corinthians 13:2.

- Graphic dreams process biological feelings or emotional needs.

- Trauma dreams and visions are not to be interpreted, but the seer is to be dealt with gently and listened to, to the extent that they want to talk before being pointed to access any help.

- Dreams about God which represent a pagan spirituality or unhealed sexuality.

- Transference dreams. If the seer has a Christian worldview, a prayer for cleansing, perhaps choosing to break bread during prayer, is very effective.

Develop an unembarrassed, matter-of-fact approach to the dream or vision. These areas of our lives are simply part of the universal symbolism on which our subconscious draws.

Create a zone of safety and respect. Be sensitive about the volume of the conversation in a public place.

Have a thought-through exit strategy when people are sharing inappropriate material with the opposite-sex members of your team. For example, "Let me stop you there – we have a same-sex policy on this category of dreams and visions. I'll just get someone to complete your session."

Have a thought-through procedure of referral for those you may encounter who are processing real past needs and of reporting past or current abuse which comes to light.

Have responsible people to whom you can offload after interpreting this type of dream or vision. This covers you as an interpreter. Unless there is abuse or a pastoral need to follow up, names and identities can be left out of this discussion to protect people's privacy.

## Exercise 4.19: Kissing dream

### The context

The two couples represented below belong to the same church. As part of a larger group of families, they go on holiday together. They all hold various positions in ministerial areas of that church.

The dreamer was a woman. Both she and the man of the other couple involved in the dream were godly people.

## The dream

"I was with Chris, my husband, at the ticket office. Alan and Ruth, another couple from the church, were there. Alan and I had apparently just got engaged. We shook hands formally and kissed on the lips in a mother-to-child type kiss. Our spouses were there and it seemed totally appropriate.

"The couples remained couples and went off in different directions. My husband and I went swimming in a deep-blue, clear swimming pool with our children. Alan and Ruth said that was much too expensive for them and they left."

Answer the questions to unlock the dream:

- Who or what is this dream about?

- What type of dream is it and what is its source?

- What type of protocol do I need to apply to interpret this type of dream?

First look at the sense of the story: what is the headline of the dream story?

Use the helpful symbolism list below to explore the important parts of the dream. What do they add to the sense of the story?

- What are the important parts of the dream?

- Are these elements literal or symbolic, positive or negative?

- They might be: key statements, items, people, places, colours, names, numbers, feelings, quality of light, or colour.

These symbol meanings are for this dream context. In another context they may mean something quite different.

## Important parts of the dream

**Ticket office** (positive symbol): booking a journey, a transitional place

**Engaged** (positive symbol): joined to do something together in the future

**Handshake** (positive symbol): formal, not personal sign of agreement

**Kiss** (positive symbol): to seal the bargain – a sign of peace and charity;[128] kiss of allegiance[129]

**Swimming pool** (positive symbol): place of learning, gifts of the Spirit, place of anointing in the Spirit

Use the sense of the story, the answers to the questions, and the helpful symbolism list above to write an interpretation of the dream that you would give to the dreamer.

Compare your interpretation with the interpretation at the end of the chapter. Was there anything you missed?

## Exercise 4.20: Embarrassing dream

### The context
This gentle woman was being brought into leadership in her church.

### The dream
"I came out of a public toilet and was washing my hands when I noticed I had male genitals protruding from boxer shorts that I was wearing (I am a woman). I felt embarrassed and tried to hide them but the boxer shorts were too small and I couldn't. I was going to join a meal/banquet and was relieved to be able to sit at the table and hide the lower part of my body."

Answer the questions to unlock the dream:

- Who or what is this dream about?

- What type of dream is it and what is its source?

- What type of protocol do I need to apply to interpret this type of dream?

128    Romans 16:16.
129    1 Samuel 10:1.

First look at the sense of the story: what is the headline of the dream story?

Use the helpful symbolism list below to explore the important parts of the dream. What do they add to the sense of the story?

- What are the important parts of the dream?

- Are these elements literal or symbolic, positive or negative?

- They might be: key statements, items, people, places, colours, names, numbers, feelings, quality of light, or colour.

These symbol meanings are for this dream context. In another context they may mean something quite different.

### Important parts of the dream

**Male genitals** (positive symbol): authority and strength (cultural symbol); (negative symbol): shame

**Meal/banquet** (positive symbol): place of fellowship and provision and welcome among others

**Boxer shorts** (positive symbol): inadequate covering, feeling exposed, inadequate preparation

Use the sense of the story, the answers to the questions, and the helpful symbolism list above to write an interpretation of the dream that you would give to the dreamer.

Compare your interpretation with the interpretation at the end of the chapter. Was there anything you missed?

The next two dreams deal with pregnancy and baby imagery in dreams and visions.

If you see that somebody is pregnant in a dream or vision, it's definitely best to ask a question and not to tell them that you think they may be pregnant. If you are wrong, you can cause huge hurt.

In dreams and visions, we've noticed that "I was pregnant" can occur in both men and women, emphasizing that it can be used in a symbolic way, that they are carrying something that can be birthed, shortly to be brought into being.

Particular sensitivity is needed when it comes to bleeding dreams, which represent the loss of something precious, premature ending, miscarriage of justice. But there is always the possibility that the dreamer is processing a life event. The loss of any pregnancy is hugely sad. Because these dreams may refer to a literal loss, ask the question, "How do you feel about this dream or vision?" If the answer to your question shows that a literal event is being processed within the dream, simply say how very sorry you are, and sit with the person in their grief.

## Exercise 4.21: Homeless man's dream

### The context

Gareth came into our outreach café and told us that he was living rough. He had been an IT engineer until the break-up of his marriage coincided with problems with his boss, leading to the end of his employment. He has lost contact with his family, who are fit and well, and he doesn't have a current relationship.

### The dream

"I dreamt that I had a girlfriend and then got married. We had a baby, then my wife died."

Answer the questions which unlock the dream:

- Who or what is this dream about?

- What type of dream is it and what is its source?

- What type of protocol do I need to apply to interpret this type of dream?

First look at the sense of the story, what is the headline of the dream story?

Use the helpful symbolism list below to explore the important parts of the dream. What do they add to the sense of the story?

- What are the important parts of the dream?

- Are these elements literal or symbolic, positive or negative?

- They might be: key statements, items, people, places, colours, names, numbers, feelings, quality of light, or colour.

These symbol meanings are for this dream context. In another context they may mean something quite different.

### Important parts of the dream

**Gareth** (literal): the dreamer

**Girlfriend** (positive symbol): temporary relationship

**Wife** (positive symbol): formal contractual relationship

**Died** (negative symbol): the loss of something

**Baby** (positive symbol): a surviving dream

Use the sense of the story, the answers to the questions, and the helpful symbolism list above to write an interpretation of the dream.

Compare your interpretation with the interpretation at the end of the chapter. Was there anything you missed?

## Exercise 4.22: Bleeding dream

### The context

Both women were leading the same ministry, working together in the prayer area of a small church. Both are lovely godly women.

### The dream

"I was with my leader in the toilet block. She was haemorrhaging extensively; it was beyond anything you'd expect. Then I noticed that I was bleeding too."

Answer the questions which unlock the dream:

- Who or what is this dream about?

- What type of dream is it and what is its source?

- What type of protocol do I need to apply to interpret this type of dream?

First look at the sense of the story: what is the headline of the dream story?

Use the helpful symbolism list below to explore the important parts of the dream. What do they add to the sense of the story?

- What are the important parts of the dream?

- Are these elements literal or symbolic, positive or negative?

- They might be: key statements, items, people, places, colours, names, numbers, feelings, quality of light, or colour.

These symbol meanings are for this dream context. In another context they may mean something quite different.

### Important parts of the dream

**Dreamer** (literal): the dreamer

**Leader** (literal): the leader

**Bleeding** (negative symbol): something precious that they're involved in is finishing prematurely (it can also mean a miscarriage of justice)

**Toilet block** (positive symbol): a safe place to deal with this

Use the sense of the story, the answers to the questions, and the helpful symbolism list above to write an interpretation of the dream that you would give to the dreamer.

Compare your interpretation with the interpretation at the end of the chapter. Was there anything you missed?

## Teaching points from chapter 3

There are two points of view about dreams and visions and their symbols. These largely reflect:

- therapeutic interpretation: recognizing dreams and visions that come from the individual processing their own lives, using highly individual symbolism

- spiritual interpretation: recognizing dreams and visions that come from God using a variety of symbols from Him, from the Bible, or from the different cultures and subcultures in which we live. (Nightmares also use language from our culture and subcultures in the form of dark revelation.)

In reality, these two types of revelation are often overlapping. A balanced, mature approach will draw on both understandings and remain open-minded when approaching each individual dream or vision.

The ability to hold two truths in tension is a mark of maturity. Symbolism in dreams and visions can come from:

- biblical symbolism;

- cultural symbols on which we sub-consciously draw, as part of our everyday world;

- universal symbols as part of our common human experience;

- personal symbols meaningful only to the individual seer.

These types of symbols are the language of our thought life.

A few things to consider when interpreting symbols:

- Consider all the options when interpreting symbols. Don't be seduced by simple rote meanings. Wait on the Holy Spirit to guide you. Be determined to develop a mature understanding of the breadth and depth of symbolism.

- Looking at symbols and understanding what they represent in the dream will add to the sense of the dream or vision story, giving clarity and greater depth to the interpretation.

- The symbols are not the main part of the interpretation; the dream/vision story is the basis of the interpretation.

- The important parts of the revelation may be: key phrases or statements, people, places, items, feelings, colours, numbers, light, or weather.

When interpreting consider:

- Anointed interpreters will release God's peace and power into the interpretation of revelation dreams.

- Relax as you learn – even Jesus had a learning curve.[130]

- Accurate and anointed interpretation will bring about God's purpose for which the dream or vision was sent.

- Discerning the source of revelation allows us to compassionately listen to the voice of our own soul and to trump dark revelation with light and truth.

- We interpret what we see with mercy and grace, truth, and accuracy to help each person fulfil their potential.

- Giving the interpretation of the revelation into a real-life context:

    – In each interpretation encounter, we will have a level of favour and credibility with the seer, which limits how much we can say.

    – In each interpretation we will have a different level of positional authority. What level of formal responsibility do I have in this situation (parent/counsellor/mentor/teacher)?

    – In each interpretation encounter we have different relational authority – how good a relationship do I have with the person to whom I'm giving the interpretation? What is it ordinarily ok for me to talk with you about?

    – "Behind-the-counter" medicines should be confirmed by other outside information and independent revelation from separate sources and dealt with in a pastoral context.

---

130    Isaiah 7:14–15.

– These interpretations should be weighed in team, not by an isolated interpreter.

– Practise putting interpretation tactfully and well. Calibrate your interpretations with the real-life examples in the answers.

- Some children see revelation easily. They benefit from an atmosphere of peace and love. As parents, we can first cover them and then train them as they grow to feel secure and gradually settle their own spiritual atmosphere. They learn this by seeing us bring peace and order into real-life situations.

- We have a learning curve as revelatory people to walk in more peace, joy, and victory.

- Figures in dreams and visions:

    – Do I know this person?

    – Are they literal, themselves, in the story? Do they represent someone/thing else?

    – Does their name carry meaning?

    – What is their part in the story?

    – Are they a positive or negative figure in the story?

    – If the figures, and the feelings about them, are the focus of the dream/vision story, they are crucial to the meaning of the revelation.

- The Trinity:

    – Predictably, God the Father often appears as one having authority or as a father.

    – Jesus often appears as a young man of love and authority or is often represented by a version of His name, even if that name appears feminine. For example, Carol, meaning champion, manly, strong, and freeman.

    – The Holy Spirit is shown far more symbolically, for example, as a strong wind, a cleansing fire, or a gentle dove.

– Where the Holy Spirit is personified, we have found to our surprise that this tends to reflect the symbolic feminine grammar used in the Old Testament (Hebrew – *Ruach* and *El Shaddai*) and the New Testament (Greek – *Peristeran*), presenting a symbol of gentleness, nurture, and nourishment. Those who don't fully appreciate the use of symbols may find this hard to understand. The Holy Spirit is not a woman any more than He is a dove. It's not literal; it's symbolic.

– But put this information to one side and see what patterns you recognize as you begin to interpret dreams and visions.

- Symbols can be weird and wonderful, but the values and interpretation of a revelatory dream or vision must line up with scriptural values and its message, if it is said to be from God.

- Biblical literacy precedes prophetic literacy, and discernment is key.

- Figures without faces, or hidden faces, sometimes represent angels or demons. The interpretations we give in these cases need to be general, and the language describing "negative spiritual influences" must use soft words to avoid raising fear (for example, "unsettled spiritual atmosphere").

- Don't focus on the negative; focus on what God can do.

- Numbers in dreams can be interpreted mathematically, biblically, culturally, or in relation to how they sound.

  – Think outside the box.

  – There is also an interesting pattern of frequently noticed number meanings as well as the highly creative use of personal number symbolism that appears in our dreams.

  – Frequently noticed number interpretations are not a list of definitive meanings.

  – Different schools of interpretation translate numbers, colours, and symbols differently. Don't worry about trying to calibrate the whole world of interpretation.

– There is no dogmatic rote meaning system, but rather an overlapping symbolic language which can sometimes help you.

– Your own soul will naturally use the language that you know.

– God will choose what dream or vision story to tell you using symbols from your own mental library and from the world around you. His Holy Spirit will then lead you to the interpretation in a relational treasure hunt.

- Seeing visions isn't hard; it's impossible. God is the one who is in charge. Relax – you are learning about how you see, as well as about what He shows you.

- Vehicles in revelation are one of the most commonly occurring symbols we see.

– These often speak into what the seer is doing currently, what they are created to do, or their purpose in life.

– Ask, "Are you in the driving seat (in charge), in the passenger seat (helping), in the back (part of the ministry)?" "How large is the vehicle (an individual role/an organization)?"

– Negative symbols: it's important to interpret negative symbols carefully or not at all.

– Interpret negative revelation redemptively, using the truth of God's word: what does God say into the situation?

– Hold back from interpreting symbols to do with death, pregnancy, or marriage. They create tremendous hope or fear. Bring words of comfort and life in place of these pictures.

– If someone has been "stung" by a negative dream, your interpretation brings the antidote.

- Personal and sexual symbolism is part of our language because dreams and visions reflect life.

– Be prepared for it to come up in revelation.

– It's often highly symbolic.

– Sometimes it is simply a manifestation of biological processes.

– Repeating trauma dreams reflecting past abuse need to be left well alone in the context of a calm, relaxed, and caring verbal exchange at the presentation of a person's dream.

– You can gently suggest that the person talks to someone they trust and perhaps find someone who can help them process their dream in a safe therapeutic environment.

– If any historical or current sexual abuse is disclosed, there is a recognized process of reporting and handling such abuse.

# CHAPTER 3: ANSWERS AND INTERPRETATIONS

## Exercise 4.1: Adam's "Noah's Ark" dream

### The dream

"I am stood on the deck of the ark with a man with a white beard and who was wearing an oatmeal-coloured floor-length gown. I thought this was Noah. We are looking out over a desert setting. I then said to him, 'So you have to get all the animals in here then?'"

"He then replied, 'Yes,' and smiled."

"I then said jokingly, 'Spiders as well?'"

"He grinned broadly and said, 'Yes, spiders too.'"

"I then said, 'But no people as they're not worth it?'"

"His expression suddenly changed to a slight frown and he looked at me with disappointment."

- Who or what is this revelation about?

The dreamer.

- What type of revelation is it and what is its source?

Revelation/correction dream from God.

- What type of protocol do I need to apply to interpret the revelation?

Simply interpret the dream. Don't correct the person unless you have the specific responsibility to disciple them.

Record your interpretation for future reference.

Work in team.

Ensure the seer knows the weighing procedure for weighing your interpretation.

Be general, not directive.

- What is the sense of the story?

God really enjoys this person and is sad if they feel judgmental.

### The interpretation

This dream suggests that the dreamer has a great sense of humour and an awareness of God, but that they have been through things in life that have caused them to become hurt and disillusioned by people. There is also an underlying judgmental attitude. The Old Testament story brings together the themes of judgment and grace; the ark is a vessel for salvation. The interpretation needs to be put very well, to allow the dreamer to understand the two aspects of the dream, perhaps by asking a question: "I love that you were safe and in conversation with God. Why do you think He was disappointed?" The interpretation needs to have and model grace toward the dreamer so that they don't go into condemnation. This dream is about cleansing and freedom from old attitudes.

## Exercise 4.2: Teddy bear dream

### The dream

"I was watching a young woman in her twenties whom I knew. She was walking through a bright hallway, dividing two rooms. As she did, I noticed she was carrying a teddy bear. The teddy bear suddenly changed and became covered in attached colourful little bears of different sizes, about six or seven of them. The bears were each part of the fabric of the teddy bear."

- Who or what is this revelation about?

The young woman.

- What type of revelation is it and what is its source?

A revelation dream from God (the story was significantly in bright light).

- What type of protocol do I need to apply to interpret the revelation?

Interpret the dream for the dreamer clearly, so that they can apply the message, in accordance with the level of authority, influence, and expertise that they have with the young woman.

Record your interpretation for future reference.

Work in team.

Ensure the seer knows the weighing procedure for weighing your interpretation.

Be general, not directive.

- What is the sense of the story?

Someone is going through a hallway (transition), and they are carrying something quite complex.

- What question would you like to ask the dreamer?

"Do the teddy bears mean anything to you, and what do they have to do with the dreamer?"

Answer: "That speaks to me of a fractured personality."

### The interpretation

The young woman is carrying pain and hurt from her past, which was deep enough to bury her pain at different points in her history. There is a need for healing as she comes into transition in a place where God is revealing this, so she can move on with her life, in a healthy and settled way.

## Exercise 4.3: Tick dream

### The dream

"I dreamt I was in a hospital setting – I was visiting the hospital. I found a tick in my right ear. I got it out and I made sure I had the head of the tick.

"I was really annoyed in the dream that the tick had dared to be there. My response to it was, 'How dare you!' My right ear was really important in the dream. Strangely the dream felt good, and once I'd got rid of the tick I felt happier.

"The tick's body was green with red legs, to try and attach itself."

- Who or what is this revelation about?

The dreamer.

- What type of revelation is it and what is the source?

Revelation/prayer ministry dream from God.

- What type of protocol do I need to apply to interpret the revelation?

Interpret the dream gently and encouragingly.

- What is the sense of the story?

Something yucky has been affecting me. It needs to be dealt with in a place of healing.

223

### Interpretation

This dream suggests that someone has got under the dreamer's skin, who has been operating out of jealousy and anger against the dreamer. This may have affected the dreamer's ability to hear God and to operate in peace. It may even have affected their ability to follow His teachings in some parts of their life. But the dreamer seems to have a healthy, proactive attitude to protect their boundaries; and is in a time and a place of healing to deal with these issues.

It's interesting that the head of the tick was completely removed, which is encouraging, because that would mean that its authority, and any spiritual authority working through it, is completely broken.

## Exercise 4.4: Isaac's spider dream

### The dream

"I went to Australia with school and my class. It was a trip. I was excited. I was there for ten days. God was there. The whole reason for the trip was to look for spiders. On the last day before we went home, I was looking for redback spiders. But instead I found a spider under my bed. I was not frightened; it was not scary. The spider I found was green and big. It had gold legs and the spider had a crown on his head. We left it under the bed."

- Who or what is this revelation about?

The dreamer.

- What type of revelation is it and what is its source?

Revelation dream from God, bringing encouragement and comfort.

- What type of protocol do I need to apply to interpret this revelation?

Interpret the dream, highlighting the reassuring message for the mother.

- What is the sense of the story?

Isaac is going on a school trip covered by the safety of his teachers. He was excited, not scared. God was there. And he didn't find any redback spiders.

- Are the spiders in Isaac's dream positive or negative?

Literally, redback spiders are highly venomous and aggressive, and some people have a life-threatening reaction to their venom. They cause intense pain, red swelling, and sweating. Anti-venom is available at hospitals. These literal facts back up the common symbolic interpretation of the colour red in dreams: suffering, anger, and aggression. The redback spiders in Isaac's dream are negative.

The spider under the bed has a gold crown – it is welcomed, not killed or removed in the context of the story. The gold crown is a cultural sign of authority and rule. The spider under the bed is a positive symbol and represents God's authority, kingship, and protection for Isaac in his place of rest (his bed).

### The interpretation

Isaac is in a stage of learning. He's aware of both positive and negative spiritual things but he is in a safe place.

The Good Shepherd is nearby to bring protection and the authority and rule of King Jesus into the place of Isaac's peace and rest. This dream is sent to reassure the mother that Isaac is safe and protected. It also raises up the need for his present learning to be led and guided in this stage of his life.

## Exercise 4.5: Jesus and the wagon dream

### The dream

"Jesus and Emma are sat on a wagon, like the ones you see in Westerns. There are two white horses pulling this wagon and they're walking calmly along a long road. All around is just desert.

"Jesus has hold of the reins for the horses. He looks at Emma and says, 'I have the reins, don't I, Emma?' Emma nods in agreement.

"Jesus then asks, 'Have I ever let you have these reins, Emma?'

"Emma replies, 'No.'

"Jesus then says, 'Nor will I ever let you hold these reins, Emma, because I am in control.'

"Suddenly, a rumbling comes from the distance, and it's cowboys on horseback. There are many of them, and they all gallop round the wagon, shooting their guns off and shouting, 'Yee ha!'

"Jesus then calmly looks at Emma and says, 'Pay no attention to them; it's just a distraction.' The wagon is still moving through this.

"Jesus and Emma end up in a town. They are both near a saloon. The wind is blowing, and little bits of paper are being tossed around.

"Jesus points to a poster pinned to a post. They both look at it: it is a 'Wanted' poster and it has Emma's face on it. Jesus says, 'Read it.'

"It said, 'Wanted everywhere I am.'"

- Who or what is this revelation about?

Emma.

- What type of revelation is it and what is the source?

Edification, encouragement from God.

- What type of protocol do I need to apply to interpret the revelation?

Build up and encourage Emma.

What is the sense of the story?

The dream suggests that she needs to know how precious she is.

### The interpretation

This dream speaks of the landscape of the dreamer's life feeling quite barren at the moment in some respects. They may have felt that they've been on a long journey. They seem to be a strong person on the one hand, but also to feel the weight of responsibility on the other. But this dream carries a lovely sense of Jesus being in charge, that they can rest in His control. The dreamer may have been in total control of everything at some stage, but the message here is shifting, with a firm statement that Jesus is now in charge. But the key message of this dream is that the dreamer is wanted and loved. It's a message of affirmation and acceptance.

## Exercise 4.6: The palace awards ceremony

### The dream

"I was arriving at an awards ceremony in the king's castle. I was wearing a long, gold, beautiful dress. I expected as I was arriving that the prince would be invited as well, though I didn't see him in the room.

"We sat in a large studio with blue seats, almost like a lecture hall. I was sitting towards the left side, halfway back. There were about fifty people in the room.

"As people's names were called, they came forward to collect their awards. On the awards were written their names and what they were being awarded for doing. I didn't see or know any of the people in the ceremony or in the audience. I was called forward and received my award, but my name was wrong and it wasn't for what I had done. In the dream I was upset. On my way to the awards dinner, I stopped off at a beautiful palace sitting room. It had a high marble mantelpiece, and on the mantelpiece was a package wrapped like a gift in blue and silver paper. The duchess was there and she was crying. She was grieved that I had been wrongly named. Then she reached up and undid the package ,which was a beautiful, airy, light shawl in silver and blue, which she gave to me to put on."

- Who or what is this revelation about?

The dreamer.

- What type of revelation is it and what is its source?

Revelation/edification and encouragement from God, with some life-processing elements.

- What type of protocol do I need to apply to interpret the revelation?

Encourage and comfort the dreamer – she needs strength and affirmation.

- What is the sense of the story?

The dreamer was upset but God has something beautiful for her.

### The interpretation

This dream suggests that the dreamer has been through a time of being misunderstood in her context.

The dream speaks of the Holy Spirit being grieved by what has happened to her in the church situation where she was present by His specific invitation. There seems to be an area of lack of understanding and affirmation. But in this very place He has a gift to give her: a gift of an anointing of purity, revelation, and power in the Holy Spirit in which to go forward. Silver often speaks in dream contexts of redemption: redeeming the situation. The fact that the shawl is light and airy indicates the lifting off of any heaviness that the dreamer has been carrying.

## Exercise 4.7: Mel's dream

### The dream

"I was sitting at the table with my family. My father was at the head of the table. He was shouting at me, as usual, criticizing me again and again, about something I had done. My mother sat silently. But my grandmother, who doesn't usually eat with us, was sitting at the foot of the table and she was crying and crying because my father was berating me."

- Who or what is this revelation about?

Mel.

- What type of revelation is it and what is its source?

Revelation from God. This isn't a self-condition dream, because it doesn't talk about Mel's feelings, even though this was how her father was when she was growing up. It talks about God's care for Mel.

- What type of protocol do I need to apply to interpret the revelation?

Be edifying, encouraging, and comforting. Interpret according to Mel's worldview, using neutral language.

- What is the sense of the story?

The father is criticizing the daughter and the mother is doing nothing to protect her, but the grandmother cared deeply. The grandmother is symbolic, representing the Holy Spirit.

> **"Do not let any unwholesome talk come out of your mouths**, *but only what is helpful for building others up according to their needs, that it may benefit those who listen. And* **do not grieve the Holy Spirit of God**, *with whom you were sealed for the day of redemption."*[131]

---

131    Ephesians 4:29–30 (author's emphasis).

### The interpretation

This dream tells us a little about how it was for the dreamer and her family. It suggests it wasn't easy for the dreamer and that her father was sometimes harsh toward her. The dream shows that the Holy Spirit is really sad about the way the dreamer's father behaved and how she was treated. The message of the dream is that God cares deeply about Mel and the way she was treated.

### Real-life story

Following the interpretation of this dream, Mel was able to recognize the Holy Spirit when He figured in her dreams. She would come to us saying that she had seen the Holy Spirit in her dream the night before. Interestingly, Mel never recognized Jesus in her dreams, which fitted with the stage of her real-life spiritual journey so far. She also never recognized God the Father, which also fitted with her broken history of being "fathered" harshly in her childhood.

## Exercise 4.8: Hannah's dream

### The dream

"I'm walking along a road with Alan and suddenly a car pulls up to offer us a lift. As I get into the back I see that the driver is Josh and I'm amazed to see him. Josh has blond hair.

"Then we (myself and Josh) are on a bus. Josh is sat on the right side, and I'm sat on the left but a seat down from him. He then gets up and comes over to the left side and stands two seats in front of me, but he's not looking at me. All this time I cannot take my eyes off him and I think to myself, how gorgeous he is! I then hear him mentally say, I have to go back Thursday.'"

- Who or what is this revelation about?

Hannah.

- What type of revelation is it and what is its source?

Life-processing dream. Source: Hannah, with elements of revelation from God.

- What type of protocol do I need to apply to interpret the revelation?

Be gentle and balance sympathy with encouragement

- What is the sense of the story?

Hannah misses Josh, because he loved and cared for her.

### The interpretation

The interpreter might say, "This is an interesting dream. I imagine that it tells me a little bit about your history.

"It also tells me that you might have been feeling a need to feel safe and loved. Your dream uses an old symbol for someone strong and kind being in charge. Those are feelings you may want to talk to somebody about because the dream emphasizes a need to process and address how you are feeling."

### Teaching point

Some interpreters have assumed that Josh is Jesus, coming to offer love and protection. If this was so, then He would not be leaving. He would stay to protect and care for Hannah. It is, however, interesting that she is on the bus – a bus can be a symbol for a church or ministry. If you had a place of influence and friendship with Hannah, it may be helpful to talk through with her whether the context of her "bus" can provide some of the friendship and care that she seeks. The bus is a vital point of encouragement for her in this dream, because she seems unaware that she's actually en route to her destiny.

## Exercise 4.9: Penelope's "28" dreams

### Dream 1

"I had a dream about the letters W-A-I-T in big black letters, bigger than me; they were on the left side of the path I was walking down."

### Dream 2 (two weeks later)

"I was walking down the same path again and the number '28' was in big black digits on the other side of the same path."

- Who or what is this revelation about?

Penelope.

- What type of revelation is it and what is its source?

Some life-processing elements and revelation from God.

- What type of protocol do I need to apply to interpret the revelation?

This dream is an encouraging dream, so you can interpret it freely, bringing that sense of encouragement.

- What is the sense of the story?

I'm in a transition and I am unsure of what is happening next.

### The interpretation

The interpreter might say, "This dream suggests you may be going through some sort of transition. It's a reassuring dream. I wonder if these dreams may be using a word play to repeat a positive message. '2-8' sounds like to wait, as if God is giving you the same message in a different way. He may be encouraging you to rest and wait for the future to take shape, rather than to be stressed and hurry things. It suggests that you relax into the timings of God, not only to wait, but also to be able to wait confidently and allow things to unfold."

## Exercise 4.10: Stuck in Leicester dream

Did you identify the correlation between the numbers used in this dream and the frequently noticed number meanings for that number?

## Exercise 4.11: Vision exercise using a list of frequently occurring number options in seer revelation

Interpret your own number vision

## Exercise 4.12 – Gena and Pete's car vision

### The vision

"My husband and I were driving a big, gleaming red car; it was a Mercedes. It stopped at the pavement and lots of people got in the back."

- Who or what is this revelation about?

Gena and Pete.

- What type of revelation is it and what is the source?

Edification, encouragement, and comfort from God.

- What type of protocol do I need to apply to interpret the revelation?

Edification, encouragement, and comfort.

- What is the sense of the story?

Cool car, used for others.

### The interpretation

The interpreter might say, "Your vision carries an inherent commendation and speaks about the exceptional quality, condition, and effectiveness of your ministry to the poor. It will care for and carry lots of people from the streets. It suggests how well you work as a team to care for people. You've done incredibly well and you have the wisdom, anointing, power, and strength in your ministry to get the job done."

## Exercise 4.13: Andrew's 4x4 vision

### The vision

"I had a big black Range Rover with a trailer on it. I was driving the Range Rover and it had a family in it. It was a really rough road; no other car could drive it. The trailer was there for people to get on and off easily without having to get inside. It wasn't fast, but it kept on going in the same direction whatever was put in its way. Nothing was too hard for it to cross.

"And when it reached its destination by the coast, all the other vehicles looked battered and bruised. The Range Rover was shiny like nothing had ever happened to it, almost like brand new."

- Who or what is this revelation about?

Andrew.

- What type of revelation is it and what is the source?

Edification, encouragement, and comfort vision from God, with one element of directional encouragement.

- What type of protocol do I need to apply to interpret the revelation?

Interpret freely, but don't comment on the family piece of the puzzle – God has already done that. It's not up to an interpreter to foretell the future.

- What is the sense of the story?

It might be rough terrain, but the vehicle copes with everything life throws at it. The family are insulated in a comfortable, secure place.

### The interpretation

The interpreter might say, "This vision speaks about your life. It suggests that you are super-equipped. You are a quality person. There's an encouragement just to steadily keep going, because you're well able to do that and you will reach your destination. You will reach it with style, even though the terrain might not always be easy. You will have two parts to your ministry, and they are to be two distinct parts. A public role – effectively touching many – and a private, comfortable space, which is away from public access."

## Exercise 4.14: Holvick's schooner vision

### The vision

"Today I had a vision of a schooner boat. The trouble is I don't like sailing much at all. I feel a bit like that about ministry recently. When I was twenty-one I was prophesied over by a visiting team from South Africa. I was told about my heart and ministry. They mentioned a schooner boat. How can I understand this better?"

- Who or what is this revelation about?

Holvick.

- What type of revelation is it and what is the source?

Revelation dream from God to encourage Holvick.

- What type of protocol do I need to apply to interpret the revelation?

Be encouraging and sensitively general about the issues involved.

- What is the sense of the story?

Holvick is being given a schooner.

### The interpretation

The interpreter might say, "This is a great vision. Because it repeats a symbol from the previous prophecy, it shows God drawing your attention to an important message for you at this time, especially because you seem to be a little tired and even discouraged.

"The schooner symbol is a glorious picture of your church, in full sail, catching the winds of the Spirit. It has speed and agility but it's also a "dangerous" vessel – able to hold canons and be fierce in an attack, able to out-manoeuvre the enemy. It is both an encouragement and a help for the journey ahead. Let's talk about letting those sails catch the wind of God."

## Exercise 4:15: Rebecca's tractor dream

### The dream

"I was in my car driving along country lanes in summer. The skies were blue and clear. There were four tractors in front of me."

- Who or what is this revelation about?

Rebecca.

- What type of revelation is it and what is its source?

Rebecca is processing her life and God is speaking to her about it in revelation.

- What type of protocol do I need to apply to interpret the revelation?

Encourage Rebecca.

Record your interpretation for future reference.

Work in team.

Ensure the seer knows the weighing procedure for weighing your interpretation.

Be general, not directive.

- What is the sense of the story?

There's a frustration here.

### Teaching point

The sunny skies indicate a positive revelation dream.

### The interpretation

The interpreter might say, "You are in a good place in your life's journey – the skies are sunny and clear and you are functioning well. But there seems to be some delay in getting to your destination. You may be expressing some frustration through your dream. But you are in the process of a journey, and a change of season may well be coming very soon."

### Dream story

After some delay (a year – four seasons), this lady was offered and accepted a very high-profile, high-powered job managing a secular care agency. All her skills were drawn on to change a culture as well as to transform an agency to affect the lives of many staff and clients.

## Exercise 4.16: Indian airport dream

### The dream

"I was in a funny little hotel in India and realized I had to try to find my way to the airport by myself to catch a plane home. I only had twenty (not pounds) left in my wallet and I was worried it was not enough.

"I eventually found someone who gave me a number for a taxi, but they were slow to help me as they were chatting and distracted.

"I called for a taxi and a man appeared with this tiny rounded vehicle like an auto rickshaw – no doors and a round roof – and gave me an elastic rope to hold on to. I then realized I had left my case behind and ran into the hotel and found a woman who told me to go back into the room and get it. She didn't help me. I ran and grabbed the case and the taxi man rammed my case in the back. Then we went on this hair-raising journey in very crazy traffic. I then found myself in the grounds of the airport and I was still trying to hang on to the elastic rope, but there was no driver and I realized I was about to swing out into the traffic. It happened in slow motion. I felt a crunch as a truck hit my right ear. I tried to talk and ask my (female) friend if I had died but it was hard to talk as I couldn't open my mouth properly and she smiled and said no! I looked for my case but it was gone."

- Who or what is this revelation about?

The dreamer.

- What type of revelation is it and what is its source?

Life-processing dream with an element of revelation from God to encourage the dreamer.

- What type of protocol do I need to apply to interpret the revelation?

Comfort and encourage the dreamer.

- What is the sense of the story?

I feel totally alone with no help, on a journey that I don't understand. I'm worried about missing my plane home.

Refining the details of the dream down to a list helps to bring order to this chaotic and complex dream story so that we can interpret it.

### The interpretation

The interpreter might say, "This dream has lots going on and suggests you may have been feeling unsettled in a situation in which you are involved. There are a lot of feelings expressed in the dream that are quite demanding – feeling alone, without the help you need, no one in charge, and you may be feeling that you have lost favour and identity in this journey. On a deeper level, its chaos may have affected your ability to hear God clearly, and that may have affected your sense of having a voice to influence the situation. But throughout this dream, there is real reassurance for you. The twenty in your wallet is not only enough, but you also have the favour you need to get through this situation. It speaks of how you have been tested and well tried through this situation and found to be faithful. You've stood in a holy place. This speaks well of you. But I feel God is telling you that you that although you have sustained some losses and it has affected your sense of identity, you are on a journey home."

## Exercise 4:17: Bizarre dream

### The dream

"I was at the zoo and just going off to the toilets. Outside were four large information posters about solid waste. The first was a picture of human dung titled "Normal Dung", the second had a picture of a '"floater", the third had a picture of a gorilla, and a title of "Gorilla Dung", and the fourth had a picture of a huge steaming pile of mammoth dung. I saw this and thought, 'How extraordinary. Thank goodness I'm in the normal category.' I went to the toilet and saw to my horror that I had a floater. I flushed the toilet again and it went. I woke up."

- Who or what is this revelation about?

The dreamer.

- What type of revelation is it and what is the source?

Revelation, encouragement, and comfort from God.

- What type of protocol do I need to apply to interpret the revelation?

Encourage and comfort the dreamer.

- What is the sense of the story?

This person seems very focused on dung!

### The interpretation

The interpreter might say, "What a great dream. It's such great symbolism – really clear. It suggests that there's some information that will help you in the things you're trying to process. You may be going through a time of cleansing away some stuff from the past. That's totally normal and you are well in process. This is an encouraging dream to tell you that it can be processed and it will go. The message is really reassuring. It suggests you face it, but keep things in perspective – you're doing really great."

## Exercise 4.18: Washing vision

### The vision

"Everyone in the building was submerged in water, except for a few heads that could be seen bobbing above the water. Those heads were very gently pushed downward.

"The church leader was lying face down, facing the door, in front of the congregation. At some point as he talked about repentance. Some froth-producing material (? a soap bar) was being used to wash everyone's hair, with heads kept just above the water. There were many soapy heads, as everyone seemed to happily cooperate with the process, and appeared to be enjoying it. In addition, one person had a change of clothing, into a silvery suit, as the old clothes were taken away and they were moved forward. The church leader also had a change of clothing into a sort of silvery-grey suit. Initially he was made to sit facing forward, and then he walked slowly down the middle aisle, talking, and all the way to the front door, where he stood looking out.

"The same stuff that had been used to wash heads was placed on the youth worker's head as she stood by the door. She was amused! Soapy water then flowed from the church through the front of the entrance into the street."

- Who or what is this revelation about?

The church.

- What type of revelation is it and what is the source?

Revelation cleansing vision from God.

- What type of protocol do I need to apply to interpret the revelation?

Record your interpretation for future reference.

Work in team.

Ensure the seer knows the weighing procedure for weighing your interpretation.

Be general, not directive.

- What is the sense of the story?

Everyone is being washed clean.

### The interpretation

The interpreter might say, "Your church is being invited to a place of cleansing. Some people will need gentle encouragement to engage with that process. It will have several effects: happiness and peace in the congregation, the church leader will be redeemed from slavery to sin, the youth leader will find a place of happiness, and the world around the church will be impacted."

## Exercise 4.19: Kissing dream

### The dream

"I was with Chris, my husband, at the ticket office. Alan and Ruth, another couple from the church, were there. Alan and I had apparently just got engaged. We shook hands formally and kissed on the lips in a mother-to-child type kiss. Our spouses were there and it seemed totally appropriate.

"The couples remained couples and went off in different directions. My husband and I went swimming in a deep-blue, clear swimming pool with our children. Alan and Ruth said that was much too expensive for them and they left."

• Who or what is this revelation about?

The dreamer and Alan.

• What type of revelation is it and what is the source?

Revelation/foretelling from God.

• What type of protocol do I need to apply to interpret the revelation?

Make it very clear that it's symbolic! It's not about a personal relationship. Be very clear. Very.

Record your interpretation for future reference.

Work in team.

Ensure the seer knows the weighing procedure for weighing your interpretation.

Be general, not directive.

• What is the sense of the story?

Alan and the dreamer are engaging in something together, but then they go their separate ways.

### The interpretation

The interpreter might say, "You seem to be in a place of transition and may be partnering with Alan in a professional role which will be short lived as you are about to go on separate journeys. In the meantime the dream suggests that you will be working together before your journeys separate, because you are willing to pay a high cost to get where you want to go, where the whole family will learn and enjoy new things and experience life in the Spirit in the place of deep revelation. Alan and his wife don't want to pay that high cost."

## Exercise 4.20: Embarrassing dream

### The dream

"I came out of a public toilet and was washing my hands when I noticed I had male genitals protruding from boxer shorts that I was wearing (I am a woman). I felt embarrassed and tried to hide them but the boxer shorts were too small and I couldn't. I was going to join a meal/banquet and was relieved to be able to sit at the table and hide the lower part of my body."

- Who or what is this revelation about?

The dreamer.

- What type of revelation is it and what is the source?

The dreamer is processing some feelings, and God is encouraging and comforting her.

- What type of protocol do I need to apply to interpret the revelation?

Be very laid back, positive and matter of fact. Reassure and recognize how she feels. Dwell on the place of covering and welcome at the banquet.

- What is the sense of the story?

This lady is feeling uncomfortable and exposed.

### The interpretation

The interpreter might say, "I would imagine you feel a bit vulnerable at the moment. You've been through a stage of cleansing and growth and are growing in authority and leadership. But you may feel not at ease with that yet. You may even feel a need to hide away because of the things you've been through before. But this dream speaks about a place of love and fellowship where you are welcomed and feel covered."

## Exercise 4.21: Homeless man's dream

### The dream

"I dreamt that I had a girlfriend and then got married. We had a baby, then my wife died."

• Who or what is this revelation about?

Gareth.

• What type of revelation is it and what is the source?

Encouraging, calling dream from God.

• What type of protocol do I need to apply to interpret the revelation?

Be encouraging and, when interpreting the calling element of the dream, be general.

• What is the sense of the story?

Be general not directive. "You may find you are good at…"/"You may find opportunities in the area of…"

### The interpretation

The interpreter might say, "This dream shows me that you have known a loss in your professional life and you thought your dream job had ended, and your working relationship ended with a loss of hope and support. But the dream contains the information that you carry the gift and the ability to operate in an area of your gifting. You might to talk to somebody about that."

### Real-life story

Gareth was put in touch with a local organization that works with the homeless to get their lives back on track. But what struck us as the wonderful outcome of the encounter was that Gareth totally changed during the interpretation. He became hopeful and animated, telling us that he had always wanted to set up his own software consultancy. The interpretation of the dream reignited hope.

## Exercise 4.22: Bleeding dream

### The dream

"I was with my leader in the toilet block. She was haemorrhaging extensively; it was beyond anything you'd expect. Then I noticed that I was bleeding too."

• Who or what is this revelation about?

Both of the women.

• What type of revelation is it and what is the source?

This is a revelation dream from God for prayer.

• What type of protocol do I need to apply to interpret the revelation?

Be very sensitive. Do not make any assumptions. Ask, "How far have you got with this dream?" If the dreamer doesn't mention the word "symbolic", I would only discuss what it means to them.

• What is the sense of the story?

Something is going very wrong here.

### The interpretation

The interpreter might say, "How far have you got with this dream? What does it mean to you?" Then (if it's not literal), "I think it's a symbolic dream, and often these types of dream mean that things are finishing early. So we might like to pray for you and your leader, and all that she's carrying, and then for any possible effect that could have on what you do together. And that if anything is ending early, that each woman moves on healthily at the right time to new areas of fruitfulness."

*Chapter 4*

# USING DREAMS AND VISIONS IN OUTREACH

*God does not ask us to leave the immediate,
compromised and uncomfortable world and enter some
sort of "spiritual" alternative. The movement of God is
precisely in the opposite direction.*[132]

Jesus had a simple way of dealing with people: He simply looked to see what His Father was doing and joined in.[133] The beauty and simplicity of working with dreams and visions is that it follows that same simple pattern. It sees what God is doing, and articulates and works precisely with that.

Sharing a vision or dream sensitively with an acquaintance or stranger is sometimes very natural. At other times, the skill of the delivery is to build a simple and natural bridge from a very normal and easy conversation to giving something that is out of the normal range of most people's experiences.

I once had a vision for a rather angry, cynical, and intellectual journalist who had been talking to me about her stress levels and how she needed help through some kind of meditation. On my way home, I started to pray for her and saw a vision. This lady was no pushover in terms of giving her something from God. It was time for a matter-of-fact approach, using the "three Bs": "Be Bold; Be Brief; Be Gone". I went

132     The Most Revd Dr John Sentamu, *Daily Telegraph*, 22 December 2007.
133     John 5:19.

and bought a local speciality – a soft, crispy Bath Bakery doughnut – and put it into an American-style paper lunch bag, along with a napkin and the written vision, including an explanation that I had received a very distinct picture of her in my mind's eye after we'd talked. I handed it to her later with the words, "I was thinking about you today – this is 'soul food.'" I smiled, turned round, and walked away.

Later I discovered what happened after that. Rachel went home, went to her bedroom, wrapped herself in her duvet, and meditated on the words of the vision, in which God her Father arrived at a very busy, noisy children's party and searched for a very young Rachel. He found her and held her closely with her head cupped in His hand against His shoulder. She found rest in his arms.

I had found a way to respect Rachel's boundaries, but still to reach out to her with God's love.

At first this can seem a challenge. But as we gain experience and develop language to communicate to people with different worldviews, it becomes great fun.

I am always amused when I send people out on to the streets to interact with the public – from a nice, warm, comfortable training room during a dreams and visions interpretation day. Delegates need to get used to interpreting dreams from people of all worldviews. So they leave with a clipboard, lanyards, and a collection sheet, resignedly buttoning their coats. Typically, thirty minutes later, they burst in through the door, their faces animated by the discussions and encounters they have had about people's dreams.

The next hour in the class is spent interpreting those same dreams. Inevitably, for some of those delegates, the exercise has moved beyond theory and they are texting, emailing, and leaving the room to get the interpretations to interested members of the public.

At our outreach evenings, we find this same enthusiasm ignites as we interpret dreams and give vision readings. Recently I drove a group of musicians and interpreters to one of our new outreach café venues. It was a Friday evening. Some of the team had had a busy week and they were fairly quiet. But on the drive home, they were bubbling over with fun and laughter, with stories and enthusiasm for what God had done as they saw Him touching people in incredible ways through dreams and visions.

In this chapter we will interpret dreams and visions that have come up in an outreach context. Part of our development as an interpreter is to learn to use dreams and visions effectively with people of different beliefs and lifestyles. To do that, we need to understand the spiritual landscape of the people around us, and to be able to articulate that to the people we meet.

Through dreams and visions God speaks to people about their lives and concerns, and we make a space where people can hear God's voice and experience God's love in an intimate, easy-going, and specific way.

In our culture, we have historically left the seat of supernatural revelation, comfort, and counsel, where many people turn in times of need or curiosity, to psychics and mediums. As the people of God, we have vacated that influential role. As a ministry, we are raising a team of people to reverse the trend.

People wander into outreach cafés, which are held monthly at a growing number of secular venues, and they drink coffee and listen to live music. They are met by one of the welcomers with a menu explaining the opportunity for a free trial session of "Your Dream Explained" or "Vision Readings" and "Insight Readings" (we needed to come up with a more descriptive term for "prophecy", otherwise people expect us to tell their future).

People can book in for a free professional massage to unwind while our physios or massage therapists pray a silent blessing over them. One recent visitor received a massage and prayer for a sore back. She returned to her table completely well, much to her amazement: she had come to us after seeking help from the doctor, a chiropractor, and an osteopath.

It's a fun, relaxed evening which becomes a life-changing event for some people.

Our vision readings use a vision-based exercise called, "When I look at you I see..." which begins using a word of knowledge. If friends come together, they often nudge each other at this point and exchange surprised glances or begin to laugh as the subject's life and character are accurately described. Then we switch into visions and look to see what God is doing with the person in their life. As we do, an encounter between that person and the Lord takes place as He touches them.

For a moment in time, they sit in His presence, hear His voice, and experience the depth of His love.

We are simply serving what God is doing in the vision; we are not trying to make anything happen. We aren't selling anything. We are giving it away and, just like in the parable of the sower, seed flies everywhere, irrespective of the fruit it yields. "Freely you have received; freely give."[134] This "serve, don't sell" principle means that it's a very easy-going environment for the team and for the people who come in.

One of the symptoms of peace is the increasing ability to let things unfold, rather than trying to shape any particular encounter. This is a beautiful process in outreach, because we journey with people in a relaxed way while God touches them and meets them in the way He chooses. People feel comfortable around this genuine approach – it's a safe place.

# DREAMS AND VISIONS EXERCISES
# EXERCISE SET 5: QUESTIONS TO UNLOCK AN INTERPRETATION

This next dream exercise illustrates the importance of that relaxed and real dynamic.

## Exercise 5.1: Patrice's supermarket dream

### The context

This dream was brought to a café by an ardent evangelist who was working with foreign language students. Patrice was a French student who had told him this dream she had had the previous week.

### The dream

"I was shopping in a supermarket, choosing things from the shelves, when a guy came along who I liked, but wasn't in love with. He was really into me, and grabbed me and kissed me. But I wasn't that into him."

How would you interpret this dream, and handle this encounter? What does this dream mean? Answer the questions to unlock the dream:

---

134     Matthew 10:8.

- Who or what is this dream about?

- What type of dream is this and what is its source?

- What type of protocol do I need to apply to interpret this type of dream?

First look at the sense of the story: what is the headline interpretation? Use the helpful symbolism list to explore the important parts of the dream. What do they add to the sense of the story? Please remember that these symbols and those listed in the rest of the chapter in a different context would mean something quite different.

## Helpful symbolism

**Supermarket** (positive symbol): evangelistic outreach ministry
**Choosing** (neutral symbol): making selections
**Kiss** (neutral symbol): over-eager close contact (The key to this symbol meaning was to ask Patrice how she felt about being kissed and what type of kiss it was. The answer in this case was that it was non-threatening and non-sexual, but very enthusiastic.)

Compare your interpretation with the interpretation at the end of the chapter.

When we are on outreach we are very clear about our own Christian worldview, but we also have a genuine interest in and respect for other people's worldviews. In a very relaxed introduction to the vision reading we explain that there are two ways to do insight readings, and say something like, "The first group of people seek guidance from the spirit world. Because of our worldview (it doesn't have to be your worldview), we ask God to show us about you because He made you. And you get to see how accurate that is."

And at the end of their session, if they have had a personal spiritual encounter, we ask permission to bless them in the name of Jesus. In all the years we've been doing this, only one man has ever said "No", and we happily blessed him in the name of God.

There is a follow up mini postcard that we can give to people on leaving called, "Tips for Spiritual Readings". It explains the principles of the different sources of spirituality that we talk about in this chapter, so that people can make informed and healthy decisions going forward.

Dreams and visions touch hearts deeply.

> *If this is not a place where tears are understood, then where can I go to cry?*[135]

When people experience God speaking into their needs and hurts, tears flow. Listening is hospitality at heart level, an expression of healing community in action. We take time to sit with people, bringing God's love into a dark place or a challenging time in their lives.

Years ago I hadn't understood this profound dynamic. Early in my ministry I was called in to a church team in crisis. Two elders asked to talk to me. My immaturity was clear, as I began to feel after two hours of simply listening to these weary and stressed leaders, contributing little to the situation, that I was wasting my time. I didn't initially realize that God cared first about these hurting people, and that the healthy resolution of the situation depended on their own health. As I got up to leave, the penny dropped: "Liz, thank you for coming. No one has listened to us; we've been so alone." God met them as they processed their grief and confusion. Sometimes listening is enough.

Other visitors to the outreach café discover a fresh perspective on what is happening in their lives through visions, prophecy, and interpretation of their dreams They receive clarity, revelation, and help from God for their lives. That clarity astounds them, and they sometimes stay at the table at the end of their session and ring their friends to come down: "You have to get down here now!" They return to their table, and we overhear their enthusiastic, if exaggerated, commentary which echoes the woman at the well of Samaria: "Come, see a man who told me everything I've ever done."[136]

There will be those, though, who are searching. In an encounter with God, their heart recognizes in Him a place where they are known, fully accepted, and understood. These people tend to stay with us, and we accompany them on their journey. They become friends, and sometimes they become part of one of our vibrant and colourful visionary communities.

---

135    Ken Medina, *Celtic Daily Prayer*, Harpercollins, 1994, pp. 4–6.
136    John 4:29.

*"I have other sheep that are not of this sheepfold. I must bring them also. They too will listen to my voice."*[137]

## Raj's vision story

Raj dropped into one of our outreach cafés and had a vivid encounter with God. He joined our community and defined for me one of the values of our ministry. One of my tests for our "serve, don't sell" culture of unconditional acceptance is whether those who aren't leading the ministry can naturally express our values. Raj did this beautifully when he came and said to me, "Before I came to community, I used to ask this question: What do people think of me? But now I come to community, I know that I am loved. Now instead of asking what people think about me, my question has changed. I ask a different question: Why should I care?"!

Raj joined us for nearly a year, hanging out and joining in our evenings where we interpret dreams and encounter God through simple vision workshop exercises. And as he did, he became familiar with the presence and peace of the Holy Spirit.

And then it came time for this lovely Indian businessman to return to Delhi. So on our last community evening we had an evaluation session. I talked with Raj about how he had encountered God and experienced the Holy Spirit, and I asked him if he had met Jesus. Raj told me that he had been on a search for God ever since his grandfather's funeral. Having grown up without a father, his grandfather had meant everything. He had been his mentor, his protector, and his role model. As Raj sat alone with his grandfather's body, a light shone down upon them. Raj knew it was from God, and the light comforted him.

He never forgot that light.

We sat and talked about Jesus, the Light of the World, and Raj said that there was a problem: he was a Hindu and he lived within a radical culture; it could be dangerous for him to believe in Jesus. We continued to talk until it became so clear that Raj was on a deliberate search for that light, that reality, and whatever it was, he wanted to find it. But he repeated that there was a problem: "I am a Hindu; it could be dangerous for me to believe in Jesus."

---

137     John 10:16.

Instead of talking any more, I asked his permission to gently put my hand on his eyes and ask God to give Raj a revelation of the light. I prayed in tongues for perhaps three minutes and then removed my hand.

Raj sat as if I had struck him with a plank of two by four. He reeled in his seat. He had obviously seen something profound. I, on the other hand, had seen and felt nothing. Raj opened his eyes and said to me, "What do I have to do?"

I, caring about this young man, said, "But Raj, there's a problem: it could be dangerous for you to believe in Jesus."

With boldness and confidence, he replied, "It doesn't matter."

He had just found what he had been looking for: he had seen the Light of the World, Jesus, in a vision. Jesus is the highest revelation to be revealed through dreams and visions.

"What do I have to do?" is a phrase I hear again and again. Wait for it: it delineates the seeker from the found. When someone asks this question, "What do I need to do?" there is a window of time. Power hangs in the air, and with it the promise of a new day. Time and eternity meet. This window doesn't last. Drop everything: it's a *Kairos* moment. God is at work above and beyond anything you are personally doing in that encounter. This is the ultimate moment of timing in response to revelation.

This question, "What do I need to do?" takes the stress out of the journey for everyone. People know what they want – they aren't stupid. Trust them. Serve, don't sell.

This question was first asked on the day of Pentecost when there was a powerful outpouring of the Holy Spirit. "'Be assured of this: God has made this Jesus, both Lord and Messiah...' When the people heard this, they were cut to the heart and said... 'Brothers, what shall we do?'"[138] The answer, of course, was to receive a radical, empowering freedom to live a new life. Free from destructive patterns. Free to be fully who they were made to be and to do all they were destined for in the power of God.

Working with people in these moments is an immense privilege as we watch God at work. As we develop as dream interpreters and

---

138    Acts 2:36–37.

those who use visions in outreach, we have found ways to demystify spirituality by using everyday language to explain spiritual truths.

One enterprising Christian YouTuber illustrates the bewildering world of Christian jargon by filming his secular friends when he asked them to guess what Christians mean by certain phrases. After they attempted to translate the in-house Christian jargon, he explained to them the real meaning of the phrases in simple everyday language.

The friends were first asked to translate "Love offering". Their ideas were enlightening:

- Open your arms to someone?

- Give them a sign of the peace, like a handshake?

- Sex!

None of their comments were more interesting than when they were told that a "Love offering" is the phrase used to explain the practice of passing round the offering plate to take up a collection to pay a preacher. They responded, "Interesting. So money equals love."

The gap between the cultures widens when the friends were asked to translate the phrase, "Washed in the blood":

- "That's horrifying! Does the water represent blood in baptism?"

- "That's totally contradictory – you can't wash something in blood."[139]

All groups use exclusive language; it's one of the defining markers. But exclusive language can promote exclusive rather than inclusive culture. The subliminal message given is, "I'm in, but you are not." The more overt message is, "We are weird and out of touch."

The YouTuber was astute enough to realize that he stood between two cultures, neither of which understood the other. Our job as interpreters is to begin to notice and use language common to people of all worldviews.

As an illustration, some useful examples of more accessible ways to put some of our Christian buzz words are:

---

139    "People Guess what Christian Phrases Mean", 30 January 2016, available at https://youtu.be/T8gmtrOBcgQ (last accessed 15 August 2017).

- Authority: you are able to influence others; you are about to gain greater control over some situations in your life.

- Bondage: trapped or restrained.

- Deliverance: removing any obstacles from you coming into your full destiny.

- Pastor: you are a leader. You are compassionate and concerned about others.

- Purity: staying away from the things that are bad for you.[140]

## Dreams and visions exercises: Using neutral language to interpret dreams and visions

During the exercises in this chapter, the list of helpful symbol meanings still appears with each dream or vision. But in order to move toward a more natural interpretation situation, you may like to photocopy the summary of questions below, to use when you interpret the dreams and visions in this chapter. We give this summary to our interpreters when they are on outreach.

### Summary questions for interpretation

- Record the dream or vision.

- Who or what is the dream or vision about?

- What type of revelation is it and what is its source?

- What is the sense of the story?

- Which are the important parts of the revelation? They might be: key statements, items, people, places, colours, names, numbers, feelings, quality of light, or colour.

- Are they literal or symbolic, positive or negative?

### Types of revelation

- Revelation dreams and visions from God: edifying, comforting, and encouraging; calling: prayer/prayer

---

140    Doug Addison, *No More Christianese*, Fruit-Bearer Publishing, 2004.

ministry; direction; correction (cleansing); foretelling; warning.

- Healthy life-processing dreams and visions.

- Trauma dreams.

- Hallucinations caused by an imbalance in levels of brain chemicals, drugs, or alcohol abuse.

- Nightmares.

### Protocol

- Is the revelation you are interpreting an "over-the-counter" revelation or a "behind-the-counter" revelation?

- Adjust the amount of information you give, and where you will be very general, accordingly.

- By adjusting that to suit the situation and type of revelation, you will express an increasing maturity as an interpreter.

- Serve, don't sell. Simply see what God is doing or saying in the dream or vision and facilitate it.

- Never try to manipulate a conversation about faith.

- Sometimes listening is enough.

- Use neutral-space language.

## Exercise 5.2: Completely full lavatory dream

### The context

This dreamer was working in a care home which was shortly to be shut down because of its abusive culture, although the dreamer didn't know that at that time. The attitude among the staff was one of coldness and bullying.

The dreamer had appealed to the management for help on several occasions because the strain and stress was affecting her. The management kept assuring her that they would help, but in actual fact they did nothing.

### The dream

"It was night-time and I was in a camp, looking for somewhere to go to the toilet. I found a toilet in a shed, but it was full of solids, right up to the brim, so I couldn't use it. I searched round the camp again and found another toilet in a small hut. It was scruffy and ill-kept. I opened the lid but again it was full to the brim and I couldn't use it."

How would you interpret this vision and handle this encounter?

### Helpful symbolism

**Dreamer** (literal): the dreamer

**Camp** (negative symbol): temporary place without strong protective structures

**Lavatory** (positive symbol): time/place of cleansing

**Full to the brim with solids** (negative symbol): a reference to an impolite colloquial cultural phrase! (This cultural phrase refers to false promises in a place which itself isn't clean.)

Compare your interpretation with the interpretation at the end of the chapter.

## Exercise 5.3: Singing a love song dream

### The context

This woman came into the café for a dream interpretation. After we had interpreted her dream, she told us that she was spiritually aware and interested in the New Age scene. Her partner, with whom she was on "the same wavelength spiritually", was a verbally abusive, critical man.

### The dream

"My partner started to sing a song. It was a love song, but he couldn't remember the words. So he stopped halfway through. I was disappointed. Then a young man in his thirties came in. I knew he was a family member, although I didn't have anyone like that in my family. He began to sing the love song to me. He looked directly into my eyes and sang this amazing song – it was beautiful."

How would you interpret this vision, and handle this encounter?

### Teaching point

Jesus appears symbolically in this dream. The fact that He didn't appear directly in the dream suggests that he is not a person with whom she is familiar, relates to, or understands in her cultural view. Your interpretation should mirror that level of awareness and speak into it in neutral spiritual language.

### Helpful symbolism

**Dreamer** (literal): the dreamer
**Her partner** (literal): her partner
**Love song** (positive symbol): a expression of love through words
**Disappointed** (literal): feeling
**Man in his thirties** (positive symbol): Jesus
**Singing** (positive symbol): expressing His love

Compare your interpretation with the interpretation at the end of the chapter.

## Exercises 4 and 5

The following two exercises are visions for people who signed up in the café for a vision reading session.

### Teaching point

We see how comfortable the individuals are with the concept of God, Jesus, or the Holy Spirit by the way the dream or vision story plays out: you will see whether the Trinity figures in the vision literally, symbolically, or not at all.

Broadly, in our experience, if Jesus figures in the vision story, the person tends to have had some Christian education, either through Catholic school or perhaps in their family home or Sunday school. This background has given them a worldview which accepts, or at least understands, the concept of Jesus as a historical figure. It is much more common for visions to include symbolic representations of God as a kind father or strong protector, for example. The Holy Spirit also appears symbolically, but more rarely.

When interpreting the two vision exercises below, use language which gently explores the concept of God, so that you don't take for granted where people are on the scale of getting to know Him. This gentle exploration can involve respectful questions using phrases like, "That's interesting – Jesus cropped up in your vision. Is that name a name you are comfortable with?", "Is the term 'God' comfortable for you?"

These two vision exercises also give you an opportunity to explore what you would say to the women as you articulate the interpretations of their visions.

## Exercise 5.4: Jo's vision story

### The context

Jo came over to the Bath café with a friend from Cardiff for a vision reading. Her friendly, upbeat personality and bright creativity struck us immediately. At the time, Jo was curious and actively exploring different types of spirituality on a search for truth.

### The vision we had for Jo

"In my vision I saw Jesus on the bank of a calm, winding river. Behind him was a rowing boat, lined with purple cushions.

"Jesus came to take Jo's hand and guide her to the rowing boat with gentleness and care. Jo reclined on the cushions while Jesus rowed the boat with Jo trailing her fingers in the green clear water of the river. A sense of ease and peace filled the scene; there was no hurry, just rest and a sense of being carried and cherished. Round a bend in the river was a low tree trunk, almost like a table. On it was a book, and from the book came shafts of dancing light. Jesus said to Jo, 'I wrote that book; it's My autobiography. It's a letter to you.' They stopped at the bank and collected the book (the Bible).

"There were two more stops on the bank of the river. Firstly to pick up a baby in a basket-weave cradle. At the third stop was a shining woman who had grown up rapidly. She was dressed all in silver, with a silver sword upheld in her right hand."

How would you interpret this vision, and handle this encounter?

### Helpful symbolism

**Boat** (positive symbol): rest, intimacy, no rush

**River** (positive symbol): refreshing, peaceful journey in the Spirit, blessing

**Tree trunk** (positive symbol): roots of life, hope, regeneration, tenacious

**Bible** (literal)

**Shafts of dancing light** (positive symbol): revelation coming from the Bible

**Baby in a cradle** (positive symbol): infant spiritual gifting (girl baby: Holy Spirit gifting)

**Young woman in silver** (positive symbol): a grown gift set which has been redeemed by the grace of God and tested, which has brought forth strength

**Sword** (positive symbol): understanding of the Word of God ("Take… the sword of the Spirit, which is the Word of God"[141]), calling to cut people free with the Word of God.[142]

Compare your interpretation with the interpretation at the end of the chapter.

## Exercise 5.5: Kitten vision

### The context

A school teacher in her early thirties brought a dream to be interpreted at the outreach café. She also asked for a vision reading.

### The vision

"I see you in my mind's eye as a tiny kitten. It looks beautiful, but it is also timid and is out in the concrete yard of a semi-detached house, watching everything with wide eyes. Next door is another house, and in my vision, God lives there (I would say 'God', because that's my worldview; I'm not sure what you would call Him). In my vision God put His hand over the wall and stroked the kitten so she wasn't scared any more. She began to relax and play.

---

141     Ephesians 6:17.
142     Hebrews 4:12.

"In the house next door was a cat basket, which was lined with a soft, blue, velvet cushion. The kitten snuggled down in the warmth."

The woman experienced the clear presence of God during the vision reading.

How would you interpret this vision, and handle this encounter?

### Helpful symbolism

**Next door** (positive symbol): close by, but on the other side of the wall

**Concrete yard** (positive symbol): hard, without comfort

**Stroked** (positive symbol): reassured and comforted

**Cat basket** (positive symbol): where cats are provided with comfort and security

Compare your interpretation with the interpretation at the end of the chapter.

We live in a society that has rapidly stopped believing in God and started idolizing celebrity. God is still world famous, yet virtually unknown. But when people hear His voice and feel His touch through dreams and visions, we often see them weep with relief, because they have come home. We see God reaching out and touching people at their point of need. Touch was important to Jesus – He often touched people, and they had a habit of getting healed when He did.

## "Run with Me" vision

*In the other religions, people always seek God. In the Christian religion, God seeks man.[143]*

During prayer, about eight years ago, I had a vision which has stayed with me and has shaped my life.

In the vision I was in a church. There was a situation going on, and the church was full of people making a fuss about a rather unimportant issue (in the dream someone had made a bad-mannered smell!). As I looked on, God took my hand and said, "Run with Me". So we ran and we ran – freely, effortlessly, and fast. Above us the sky suddenly opened,

143    Reinhard Bonnke, *Father of Lights* DVD, Darren Wilson, published by Wanderlust, 2012.

the grey-blue cloud disappeared and I saw the golden canopy of heaven – God's glory, His absolute sovereignty and salvation. And straightaway I began to see pictures, heartbreaking, soul-wrenching pictures, like calendar photographs, page after page of lost and bruised and abused people – hurting, sad and broken; relationships in turmoil, children being shouted at, men and women in tears, in agony.

And I understood what He was showing me. The vision spoke of the tendency for the people of God to be distracted with in-house situations. This contrasted sharply with the freedom of running in God's beauty, power, and presence, as well as His love and longing to reach those who are lost and hurting. People in the world around us were in great need, and, as ever, the Good Shepherd's plan was to leave the ninety-nine and run to find them, the one.

During the Syrian crisis, an anonymous church leader in ISIS-controlled territory wrote a report. In that week, three of his pastors had been shot for "running" – running children's clubs in their homes. The church leader remained resolute in the face of danger:

> Whenever we see disaster and tragedy, we run towards it. We see throughout history that it is in these alarming moments that God works. It is in times of war, not peace that history is changed… Our nets are breaking with those coming to know Jesus – despite – maybe because of these terrible times.[144]

On 9/11, in America, when the Twin Towers fell, another man was running toward the chaos. A police officer, Will Jimeno, had been helping people when the rubble collapsed, entombing him underground. Thirty miles away, news of the attack came over the radio. Jason Thomas, the son of a pastor and an off-duty US marine, was listening. He pulled over and turned his car around. While other people were running away, Jason parked his car and ran toward the danger.

The second tower had fallen, and firemen and police officers had been called off the site because the rubble was too unstable. Jason was sure there would be survivors under the wreckage: He set out on foot across the burning pile, calling, "This is the United States Marines. Is anybody there?"

---

144    Identity withheld.

Meanwhile, amid the burning red-hot metal, and ready to give up, Will had a vision. "I saw a figure in white walking toward me. I knew it was Jesus. Over Jesus' left shoulder was tall grass waving, and a scene of such peace. Strength filled me." He began to cry out, "PAPD – Officers down! Can anyone hear me? Officers down!"

On top of the rubble, the fire department were calling Jason back because they were about to hose down the burning site. But he replied in a stern voice, "We are United States Marines. We don't go backward, we go forward." And he moved on, hour after hour, calling out, "This is the United States Marines. Is anybody there? You are our mission."

Finally he heard Will's voice: "PAPD – Officers down!"

Jason jumped into the hole, with one arm already cut and disabled by the jagged burning metal. He finally distinguished Will from the rubble around him. And the rescue effort began in earnest.[145] Will came home just in time to see his second baby daughter born, because another man ran to save him.

Despite the noise and the chaos around us, we are called to run. The lost and the hurting and the forgotten, including those who look like they have it so together: they are our mission. "For the Son of Man came to seek and to save the lost."[146]

## Exercise 5.6: Cars in the darkness vision

### The context
I had this vision last summer.

### The vision
"I was leaving a cross-channel ferry. It was really dark. I drove the car out of the huge ship and drove on to the motorway. There were only a few cars going in either direction, but the cars going out had really bright headlights which shined in the darkness as pinpoints of light. On the opposite carriageway of the motorway, a few cars were coming in dribs and drabs from the darkness into the ferry. Gradually, more and more cars left the ferry and joined the few cars that were going out. As they did so, the darkness became lit up by the greater concentration of lights."

---

145     *The Lost Hero of 9/11*, CBC News Network, 11 September 2016.
146     Luke 19:10.

Interpret this vision. What is its message?

## Helpful symbolism

**Cross-channel ferry/ship** (positive symbol): in the water of the Spirit, the church

**Car** (positive symbol): personal vocation/ ministry

**Motorway** (positive symbol): journey across the nation

**Headlight** (Positive symbol): light, revelation, manifestation of Jesus

Compare your interpretation with the interpretation at the end of the chapter.

As we interpret dreams and visions for the people who come into our outreach café, we see that many of them have a very standard set of secular interests. Their dreams reflect their lives, including elements of comfort, calling, and direction from God.

But we also connect with very spiritual people from all faiths and worldviews. This group of highly colourful people are on a journey to explore spirituality. Typically, they are gifted and have a high awareness of the supernatural realm. God loves these gifted people and He wants to bring them home.

Their spiritual awakening has mostly happened entirely outside of the context of a Christ-centred worldview, they have connected with spiritual practices and influences which can be quite dark. This is reflected in their dreams and visions, so it's vital that we are comfortable dealing with people's darkness and diversity.

As we have journeyed with people from dark spiritual backgrounds, we have noticed that, broadly speaking, the people we encounter have two reactions to their dark revelation: fascination or fear. There is, of course, a third option for those of us who are involved in outreach, which is to be relaxed and secure, because, "You, dear children, are from God and have overcome them, because the one who is in you is greater than the one who is in the world."[147]

I once heard of an outstanding accolade paid to a missionary on his death. He had arrived single-handed to live on a Pacific island among people who directly worshipped demons. On his death they wrote this on

---

147     1 John 4:4.

his monument: "When he came there was no light; when he left there was no darkness." When love encounters darkness, it manifests as salvation.

During one outreach, two men came in and asked us to interpret their dreams. The dreams were all dark, but the two men had very different reactions to their own dreams. One man was terrified; the other man was fascinated. The first man came to have a series of nightmares interpreted. They were intimidation dreams using very common symbols, but I have never seen a dreamer more gripped by fear. The dreamer had an awareness of God but he was focused on the content of the dark dreams. Our job was to help him lift his gaze and to dispel the shadow cast by his dreams.

## Exercise 5.7: A series of dark dreams causing fear

In this next exercise, using the three dreams, write a redemptive interpretation which you could tell the dreamer. A redemptive interpretation is an interpretation which takes dark content and supplants it with what God is saying into the situation. First look and see if you can understand the simple message of the three dreams, and then adapt it to bring peace in the interpretation. Use language that is non-religious and culturally relevant.

Tip: this is a simple set of dreams with a clear message. Keep your interpretation short and sweet. Drawing out the three dreams with simple drawings may help you.

### Teaching point

Dreams in a series can be:

- dreams showing a developing theme;

- dreams showing a timeline about the person's life;

- dreams carrying a repeating message which needs to be heard. A repeating message highlights its importance. It's the dream equivalent of shouting.

This series of dreams show a developing theme. (If we had more time with the dreamer, we may have heard more about his life and noticed that the series of dreams were also a timeline, showing life events, which increased fear.)

## The context

This dreamer came into the outreach café for the first time, telling us, "I have lots of nightmares. I had these three nightmares in one week. I can't stop thinking about them. I'm worried about what they mean."

## Dream 1

"I dreamt that spiders were coming from two corners of my bedroom window. There was an infestation of spiders in each corner of the window."

## Dream 2

"There was an angry woman yelling at me in my bedroom. The spiders were all over the floor."

## Dream 3

"One of my boots had a hole in the sole and there were spiders inside it."

Please write a short literal interpretation for each dream to aid your own understanding. How would you interpret these dreams and handle this encounter?

Then write a redemptive interpretation, which you could say to the dreamer.

## Helpful symbolism

In this set of dreams the symbols are negative, although in other dreams these same symbols can appear as positive.

**Spiders** (negative symbol): demonic attack, deception
**Infestation of spiders** (negative symbol): compacted spiritual problem
**Shoes** (positive symbol): Ephesians 6:15
**Window** (neutral symbol): place of revelation and connection with the spiritual world (of darkness or of light)
**Bedroom** (positive symbol): place of rest

Compare your interpretation with the interpretation at the end of the chapter.

## Exercise 5.8: Chris's dreams about flying

### The context

Chris had the opposite response to his dreams. He was fascinated by the supernatural and enjoyed the thrill of the dreams, even in his fear. Dreamers who are fascinated by the supernatural tend to be bolder in personality, attracted by the feeling of power that the supernatural gives them. They are typically less sensitive, and are also under a greater degree of deception.

When Chris came into the outreach café for a meal, he asked for a dream interpretation. A "rough and ready" Glaswegian, he had frequent spiritual experiences as a young boy, which nobody had explained to him. As a child he had been very afraid.

### Tips

Heavily rely on the dream's storylines before looking at any symbols. The key to these dreams lies in the stories and what is happening. In an outreach setting, with these dreams, you, the interpreter, have a dual task:

- Interpret the dreams in non-religious language and in a way that Chris can understand.

- Use the dreams to help you understand what is happening in his spiritual journey. This understanding is broad brush; you don't need to go into detail. What do the dreams suggest about his life?

A strategy to help you interpret Chris's dreams:

- First read all three dreams and work out which are dark dreams and which are not.

- What do the first two dreams show you about his life?

- What does the third dream say about the way ahead?

- Write down what you would say to Chris.

### Dream 1

"I've had three dreams recently that mirror those I've been having for years.

"There were people after me. It was random. I was running and hiding in various familiar areas, people's back gardens, etc. Then I hid in a nice hotel.

"There were stairs down and I was aware, 'If I go down, they may come up and get me.' So I jumped out of a window. This is always dangerous. In different dreams it can be off a cliff, a bridge, a building as I jump out of the window.

"I was on a ledge, clinging on by my hands like a child on monkey bars, and I had to go along the edge, hand over hand, where there was a platform and I jumped up onto it. Sometimes I fell, but I always woke up before hitting the ground."

### Tip

You can't tell too much from this dream. Don't go too deep. Be general and broad brush. This dream sets the scene for Chris's spiritual life.

How would you interpret this dream, and handle this encounter?

### Helpful symbolism

**Being chased** (negative symbol): a sense of fear and awareness of negative spirituality

**Stairs down** (negative symbol): being wary of negative spirituality. This dreamer is lucidly dreaming and making decisions to stay safe

**Window** (negative symbol): revelation of negative spirituality where the fear of being pursued is causing the dreamer to make rash decisions

**Ledge** (negative symbol): the dreamer is in a precarious position but hasn't yet hit the ground

### Dream 2

"I was in bed – the bed was rocking. There was a sense of evil – a presence.

"This used to happen when I was a boy. I was so scared. I used to think it was like a ghost was rocking the bed when I was awake.

"But in this dream, I didn't wake up. In the dream I got out of bed and went to the window, which exploded outward. I was flying high, high above the village. I felt wind in my hair – it was lovely – then I fell into my garden, hit the floor, was blind, and couldn't see.

"I felt the glass and the side of the house for the window ledge – it was covered with glass. I found my bed – it was still rocking."

### Tip

A sense of fear came and a negative presence came into the room while Chris was recounting the dream. That didn't worry me in the slightest, it lifted when we took no notice and carried on, it just helped me to understand that this was an encounter dream. A rocking bed is a common manifestation of negative spirituality.

How would you interpret this dream, and handle this encounter?

### Helpful symbolism

**Flying** (positive symbol): spiritual giftedness
**Window** (neutral symbol): place of revelation and connection with the spiritual world
**Blind** (negative symbol): without spiritual sight
**Finding the ledge and bed** (neutral symbol): he has learnt to manage the situation

### Dream 3

"This dream is also recurring and recent.

"I was in a gunfight. Then there was a real battle, like a war, and I was fighting.

"Next scene: then I was in trouble with the police for killing people. I was running, trying to get away, and the police were after me. I knew I had to go home to Scotland, where my Dad said, 'What have you done? Take the keys to my car to get away.' I went to the drive outside the house and on it was not a car but a biplane. I got in and turned it on, and I was flying away and escaped."

### Teaching point

There is a shift as you look at the symbolism in this third dream – we have some positives appearing in the symbols. What does this tell you?

How would you interpret this dream, and handle this encounter?

### Helpful symbolism

**Gunfight** (negative symbol): accusation and criticism

**Running away from the police** (negative symbol): not entirely innocent!

**Dad** (positive symbol): God

**Keys** (positive symbol): increasing authority to overcome the things which are against you, understanding, power to bind and loose

**Biplane** (positive symbol): ability to go higher in the Spirit in safety while still enjoying that sense of freedom

Compare your interpretation with the interpretation at the end of the chapter.

In these two contrasting dream sets, we have a glimpse into the spiritual life of each of the men. Engaging with spiritual people who find their counterfeit spiritual experiences fearful is easy, because "perfect love drives out fear".148 When the peace of God settles around these encounters, people find a sense of rest. Because they recognize the darkness for what it is, the light is a welcome gift.

It's less simple dealing with those who are fascinated by darkness. The word "fascinate" means "to engross, captivate, absorb, enchant, beguile, spellbind, occupy, or compel". There is power involved here.

Higher levels of insensitivity and deception in a person's spiritual journey often indicate that people are interested in using other spiritual forces for power. Control is a dominant issue. As we get to know them we realize that there is often a need for healing in their life story. Strongholds have built up as they have tried to cope with their life on their own.

Our "serve, don't sell" ethic means that we bring understanding and language around people's spiritual journey to articulate their choices and bring light in, so that they have more choice and freedom to choose their direction and spiritual home.

> *"Hospitality… is not to change people, but to offer them space where change can take place… It is to offer freedom not disturbed by dividing lines… So that words of meaning can find root and bear ample fruit… where strangers can enter and discover themselves as created free."149*

---

148    1 John 4:18.

149    Henry J. M. Nouwen, *Celtic Daily Prayer Book 2*, HarperCollins, 2015, p. 1315.

## Esther's vision of angels with bowed heads

A close friend came to faith from a journey exploring the supernatural. One of her vision experiences illustrates a very strong and scriptural marker for weighing vision encounters of a supernatural nature. Esther had begun to walk in some dark places, but increasingly began to look for the light. Because she was used to the supernatural realm, Esther would seek enlightenment and help from angels. It was a common, almost daily, experience for her to relate to spiritual beings, but she continued on her search for God.

This jumble of spiritual experiences – sometimes unmistakeably dark and intimidating, and at other times light and uplifting – was a mixture of dark and light revelation. Esther's biggest need was for guidance and a growing discernment to know which experiences were from God.

One day Esther had a profound vision, which she tells in her own words:

"When I was searching, I used to talk to angels, but then one morning I was in my kitchen and I could feel something to the side of me, and then I had a vision:

"I saw row on row of angels facing one another, leaving a clear aisle between them. All of their heads and shoulders were bowed down in submission. I remember saying, 'What's going on here – why are they bowed down?'

"Then a voice to the left of me said, 'We can't take you any further; you have to go to Him now.' I turned and I saw a massive bright, white light, and the outline of a person sitting on a throne. I couldn't see His face because the light was so bright. And I knew it was Jesus."

Dreams and visions of angels or spiritual beings will always point the seer to Jesus if they are from God. This distinction is important as we lead people on a journey from spiritual mixture into the light, because Scripture tells us clearly that Satan masquerades as an angel of light.[150]

> *Dear friends, do not believe every spirit, but test the spirits to see whether they are from God... every*

---

150     2 Corinthians 11:14.

*spirit that acknowledges that Jesus Christ has come
in the flesh is from God, but every spirit that does not
acknowledge Jesus is not from God."[151]*

This vision marked a turning point in Esther's journey, and she began to look for Jesus. He quickly found her, and a new journey of faith began.

We have increasing numbers of spiritually gifted people from all spiritual backgrounds coming on our dreams and visions courses and signing up for one-to-one mentoring. We thoroughly enjoy meeting these colourful, sensitive, intelligent, and often highly gifted people, and sharing their journeys.

Using dreams and visions to mentor those who want to explore their spirituality is fun. We quickly realized that we needed to find new and meaningful ways to talk to those around us, because the spiritual landscape in which we live is changing with the times.

We live in a postmodern world that has morphed through three phases:

- The premodern world, where the existence of God and revelation were commonly accepted concepts; religion was the source of truth.

- The modern world, where science came to replace religion as the main source of truth and reality, where humanists and atheists have set up camp.

- Increasingly we need to engage with the postmodern world, where "my truth is my truth, your truth is your truth". Truth and reality are seen to be shaped by our own circumstances and cultures.

In the postmodern world there is an amusing and contradictory ethos: there is no absolute reality, except for the fact that "there is no absolute reality". In this age, people are largely unclear, unguided, and spiritually open. They have no reliable markers for spiritual encounters and, as such, are open to all sorts of spiritual influences without discernment.

---

151     1 John 4:1–3.

We use a model which begins to articulate that spiritual landscape in order to mentor spiritual people from all walks of life toward their destiny and to overcome the things that are holding them back.

Our three-level working model reflects Christ's experience of life and spirituality on earth: relating to God, dealing with the counterfeit and the supernatural, and impacting the everyday world to bring God's kingdom and will to Earth.

| Level 3 | The kingdom of God – seeing what the Father in heaven is doing so His will is done and His kingdom of joy, peace, cleansing, and power is really tasted on Earth. |
| --- | --- |
| Level 2 | Encountering and dealing decisively with darkness and counterfeit practices (including pseudo-spirituality in religious structures that lack His mercy and power). |
| Level 1 | Living in the everyday world. |

The spiritual people we meet have been relating to the first two levels of this spiritual landscape: the everyday world and counterfeit or dark spirituality. It's our joy to be able to introduce them to the kingdom of God. Our simple three-level chart not only gives people language to recognize their own spiritual journey, it also draws their gaze to look at God and experience His love and kindness in their lives. The process of the Holy Spirit of truth taking what is heavenly and making it known to us on earth is the premise of using dreams and visions on outreach: "He [the Holy Spirit] will glorify me, because he will take what is mine and declare it to you."[152]

It might be helpful to put some detail into this three-level working model for your own understanding. We use the word "realm", which literally means a kingdom or field of activity and interest.

---

152     John 16:14 (ISV).

| Level 3/ Third Realm | **The kingdom of God**<br>The Kingdom of joy, peace and righteousness.<br>True wisdom brings truth, clarity, unity and love.<br>There is a search for meaning.<br>A revelation of truth: <u>Jesus</u><br>"Sozo" – Power to save, heal and deliver<br>Experiencing revelation helps people to become aware of and engage with God, to "taste and see" |
| --- | --- |
| Level 2/ Second Realm | **The supernatural: counterfeit spirituality/created beings**<br>Fear, bondage and fascination<br>False wisdom brings deception, confusion, isolation/withdrawal, anger/hatred<br>A search for spiritual experience<br>Spirits use people and people use spirits for power.<br>Listening to created beings or the dead.<br>Religious spirit – Pharisaical attitude<br>Weighing spiritual experience by the plumb line of Scripture passage meditation, helps people to begin to discern the source of their experience and its fruit. |
| Level 1/ First Realm | **Living in the everyday world**<br>We experience this realm with our five natural senses, with logic, emotions and appetites.<br>But this is also the world which buds and flourishes when the revelation of God through dreams and visions flows down like rain: and instead of the thorny sharp tearing edges of our worlds, life comes in an abundance of Shalom.<br>In dreams, visions and passage meditation the revelation of God flows and help comes. |

*"The quest for spirituality [is] now a search for that coming together of heaven and earth: which is genuinely on offer to those who believe.… God wants to anticipate now by the Spirit a world put to rights – a world in which the good and joyful gift of justice has flooded creation."[153]*

---

153    Tom Wright, *Simply Christian*, SPCK, 2011.

In one-to-one spiritual mentoring, we initially use a blank template which we fill in as the mentoring journey progresses. Initially it may look something like this:

| | |
|---|---|
| **Level 3/Third Realm** | |
| **Level 2/Second Realm** | Your supernatural experience with created beings and the dead. For example, ghost walks/tarot/angel cards/ mediums/witchcraft |
| **Level 1/First Realm** | Your life story: what can we celebrate? Where is there a need for healing? |

As people are guided on a journey with led vision exercises, and through the interpretation of their dreams, they encounter God, Jesus, and the Holy Spirit. We are simply guides who interpret what God shows them as we help them to engage in a dialogue with Him.

We then begin to fill in the third level of the diagram, describing what they encounter. One mentee explained to me how they had begun to recognize the difference: "The kingdom of God brings me hope for the future, peace, joy, confidence in my destiny, and comforts me. Dark revelation brings me confusion, anger, isolation, and fear for the future".

*Everything exposed by the light becomes visible – and everything illuminated becomes a light.*[154]

And a process begins where what God is saying to them begins to transform their lives. The question we are training people to examine is, "What is the source of the revelation or spiritual experience?"

As I write this, in my garden a gardener is weeding my raspberry patch. He is distinguishing between the thorns and the raspberries. As I look out at the grass, I notice that several raspberry plants have been pulled up by mistake. There's a slight difference between the

---

154     Ephesians 5:13.

raspberries and the thorns. The thorns are a deeper green; their infant thorns are sharper and less closely packed together. They have slightly more jagged edges to their leaves. I recognize them easily because I tend my raspberries lovingly. Each summer and autumn I make the next year's jam, mothers from the street come to pick raspberries and I freeze more for the huge Christmas party pavlova. But those who are not as familiar with my plants as I am find it difficult to tell the difference in their infant form. This is what happens with people who are looking for spiritual things. In infant form, things can look very similar.

At each mentoring session we introduce different passage meditations for the mentees to use in between sessions. The passage meditations convey the life-affirming truth that there is help and care from a loving God, from Someone higher, who is actively and intimately concerned with their well-being and daily lives. Helpful passage meditations are:

> *Come to me, all you who are weary and burdened, and I will give you rest.*[155]

> *For I know the plans I have for you… plans to prosper you and not to harm you, plans to give you hope and a future.*[156]

> *For my thoughts are not your thoughts,*
> *neither are your ways my ways…*
> *As the heavens are higher than the earth,*
> *so are my ways higher than your ways*
> *and my thoughts than your thoughts.*
> *As the rain and the snow*
> *come down from heaven…*
> *so is my word that goes out from my mouth…*
> *You will go out in joy*
> *and be led forth in peace.*[157]

---

155      Matthew 11:28
156      Jeremiah 29:11.
157      Isaiah 55:8–10, 12.

When Jesus appeared to His disciples post resurrection, He not only initiated an encounter, He also opened their minds so they could understand the Scriptures.[158] This growing engagement with Scripture is vital because, as one friend pointed out, "God is warmly welcomed in the post-modern world as long as He doesn't try to play God."

## Emmaus Road-led vision exercise

This vision exercise develops into a unique encounter with Jesus for each person. As you lead someone through this vision, your questions will begin to be shaped by what that person is telling you, enabling you to facilitate their encounter with Jesus in a peaceful, easy-going way.

Simply be a guide and a companion, listening and seeing what God is doing and joining in.

The mentee can stop the vision at any time – they are in total charge of the encounter. The exception would be if an encounter begins to include negative spirituality in any way or to be a negative experience. In that event, take charge with a gentle, soft voice and say, "We are coming out of this exercise now in order to return to a place of peace." But I have in fact found this exercise to be wholly positive.

The beauty of the Emmaus vision exercise is that people are truly free to have an experience of meeting Jesus and decide on their own level of encounter. So this vision exercise fits well with our "serve, don't sell" culture.

The Emmaus Road story between Jesus and the disciples is told in Luke 24.

Stage 1: Jesus met the disciples on the road and listened to their thoughts and feelings and, in their case, confusion and sorrow. He then explained to them the journey that they had been on and warmed their hearts, bringing a level of understanding.

Stage 2: The disciples asked Jesus to hang out with them.

Stage 3: Their eyes were opened to who He was.

Stage 4: They were reconnected to their destiny and went back to Jerusalem with the message, "It is true!"

This four-stage journey mirrors the mentoring journey. People will

---

158    Luke 24:31–32.

journey as far as they want to over the course of several sessions, and then they will stop.

## Helen's Emmaus Road vision encounter

**Liz:** "I'd like you to get comfortable and relaxed in your chair. I'm going to guide you through this peaceful exercise. I'd like you to see a picture of a road. What do you see?"

**Helen:** "I see a road with Jesus standing on it."

**Liz:** "If Jesus is standing on the road, where are you?"

**Helen:** "I'm not on the road; I'm in the ditch"

**Liz:** "Is it nice in the ditch?"

**Helen:** "No, it's dark and cold. I'm wearing a big coat, hat, and scarf."

**Liz:** "I'd like you to see Jesus on the road. What do you see?"

**Helen:** "Jesus is standing on the road with a light. His face is not clear. He's wearing pink, orange-ish robes, but that might be the light, I'm not sure."

**Liz:** "What is Jesus doing?"

**Helen:** "He's offering me His left hand."

**Liz:** "Do you want to come out of the ditch?"

**Helen:** "No."

**Liz:** "I'd like you to ask Jesus why you don't want to come out of the ditch."

**Helen:** "I am questioning myself whether I can trust Him. This will represent a different life/direction and would create changes in relationships."

**Liz:** "What does Jesus say about that?"

Helen began to be tearful. "I did take His hand and He helped steady me as I took a step out of the ditch. I am next to Him on the road as I look forward."

**Liz:** "What does the road look like?"

**Helen:** "It's misty. I still can't see into the distance, but it is clearer than it was at first. The light is a pinky, orange, yellow colour. Jesus and I are stood together."

Tears came again and we finished the session with a sense of peace and rest.

**Liz:** "How do you feel now?"

**Helen:** "Anticipation, kindness, togetherness, safe, accepted. He's reliable."
**Liz:** "Ask Jesus if He's going to leave now."
**Helen:** "No, He will always be there if or where I turn to Him."

Helen chose to continue her walk with Christ and is now a valued part of a vibrant church family and loving her new-found faith.

Many of those who have been involved in mixed spirituality during their search for truth and meaning are people of peace who have rejected an aggressive experience of religion. Because of this, it's important that we are able to articulate the difference between our own religious attitudes ("God is good, you are bad – try harder"[159]) and the Holy Spirit of grace and truth.

> *I like your Christ, I do not like your Christians, they are so unlike your Christ.*[160]

I sat down to relax and watch television with my son when he flipped on a programme called *Football's Funniest Moments*. A clip of a match was shown where one manager, Phil Brown, sat his players down at half time, in the middle of the pitch, to chastise them publicly. Finger wagging, face frowning, voice obviously yelling: they were shown up in front of everyone. And then the commentator said this, "There's something of the church about Phil Brown. There's something of the born-again about him."

Worse still, everyone listening understood what the commentator meant, without him needing to add any further explanation. The general perception of the church is a world away from the Jesus who liked people and touched them to bring freedom from captivity in all its forms.

The spirit of Christ "leads us into all the truth to form Jesus within us. His Spirit changes hearts, therefore the Lord looks upon the heart of men and in them He is looking for the heart of His Son. The religious spirit changes outward behaviour but the Spirit gives life."[161]

---

159     Dr Henry Cloud (Foreword John Burke), *Soul Revolution*, Zondervan, 2008, p.7.
160     Ghandi, cited in R. T. Kendall, *Holy Fire: A Balanced and Biblical Look at the Holy Spirit's Work in Our Lives*, Charisma House, 2014.
161     Rick Joyner, *There Were Two Trees in the Garden*, Morningstar Publications Inc, 2007, p. 12.

We have to admit, though, that no matter how hard we try to live authentic lives of grace toward ourselves and others, no matter how much we genuinely respect and enjoy other people's journeys, or how earnestly we try to articulate the spiritual landscape in everyday language and terms, we still freak some people out.

People from all walks of life come along to our community events evenings, where they begin to hear God for themselves. One girl who had come to the outreach café for a vision reading returned and brought her friend, who had a strong humanist worldview. During the workshop, the friend with the humanist worldview saw a vision from God for her exercise partner. When I helped her to interpret it, the presence of God fell, in the form of a tangible and deep stillness and peace. I suggested that she might like to have an experience of the presence of God's peace which came through her picture. So she scooted over on the sofa next to her friend, into the quietness and tangible presence of God. Initially sitting happily in the rest and quietness of God, our new friend became slightly perplexed later in the evening because we had totally exploded her worldview. She had encountered a God whom she had believed could not exist. After that, it was going to go one of two ways. She never came back.

But most people don't leave, they stay and enjoy waking up to a life of spiritual reality and meaning.

One community member put it like this: "They talk compassion, they talk love, and they talk about spiritual connection with God. And they show all these attributes in the way they encounter people and by actually living that way."

## Combine harvester dream: Is your church ready for people like this?

### The context

The comfortable Christianity of our Western world has failed on many fronts to engage with the complexity of the spiritual world around us. Spiritual force must be met with Spiritual force.

We have realized that this mentoring ministry has to be rooted in prayer. Prayer is the humble recognition that the power of God achieves the will of God through the work of God: "No one can come to me unless the Father... draws them."[162]This work is a sovereign work of the Holy Spirit, and comes at the cost of a lifestyle of prayer.

Our genuine, unconditional acceptance of people on their spiritual journey needs to be matched by their encounter with the gospel of power. Otherwise, the good news of God's love will be added into the melting pot of experiences, without a radical new life that is free to enjoy and express the freedom and power of the kingdom.

A friend of mine whom we met at the outreach café and became a passionate Christ-follower told me this dream.

### The dream

"I dreamt that Jesus met Liz and they were leaning on a gate looking over a field of white wheat. Jesus said, 'You can't harvest this, can you Liz?' and Liz replied, 'No.'

"Jesus said, 'That's because you haven't got a combine harvester.'"

At first, as I weighed this rather discouraging dream, I was partly of the opinion that it might be dark revelation, until I noticed the biblical references of the gate and the field which was white for harvest.[163] It became very important to find out the interpretation of the combine harvester, because I clearly needed one.

Some months later I held a prophetic school, and asked Wes Hall from the IHOP[164] leadership team to help me. I sat listening with appreciation, as I always do when Wes and Carol minister, until one little phrase jumped out at me: "When we agree with one another and we line up and agree with God..."

Agreeing together and agreeing with God's word gives a "combination" of prayer, alignment with God, and His people which adds power to the reaping. A combine harvester's powerful reaping cylinder is much wider than the vehicle. When its function is in place, the harvest reaped is larger than the expected size of our impact on the world around us.

As we kept listening to God, it became clear that a combine harvester also carries out a number of functions. It doesn't just reap. In order to

---

162      John 6:44.
163      John 10:7; John 4:35.
164      International House of Prayer.

gather the harvest, it also threshes to free the grain from the chaff and winnows it to separate the grain from the dirt and the chaff by forcing a current of air (Greek – *pneuma* – wind, air, breath, spirit) through it to blow away its impurities.

The Holy Spirit powers a threshing process, as spiritual force meets spiritual force. And He separates out the precious grain of the person's life from the dirt.

> *For I am the Lord your God*
> *who takes hold of your right hand*
> *and says to you, Do not fear;*
> *I will help you...*
> *See, I will make you into a threshing-sledge,*
> *new and sharp, with many teeth...*
> *You will winnow them, the wind [Hebrew – ruah – wind/Spirit]*
> *will pick them up.*[165]
>
> *Rise and thresh, Daughter of Zion,*
> *for I will give you... hooves of bronze.*[166]

There is a process to go through to release people from harmful spirituality, hurts, or fear. We have found especially that those who have been active in witchcraft and the occult as practitioners need an experienced level of specialized deliverance.

Hurting and unhealed places in people need healing as we bring in the light of God's truth. Our most helpful learning curve came in recognizing that unchecked soulish behaviour – using the power of the will to control, dominate, and overwhelm others – was a big part of the story. We had to discern which part of each scenario was soulish behaviour and what was actually demonic. We learnt how choices and behaviour link with empowering the demonic, and how Scripture and discipleship (discipline) link with freedom. Our threshing is becoming sharper in line with the combine harvester dream.

When interpreted, the dream was far from discouraging; rather, it sharpened our vision. It gave us a humility, a prayer, discipleship, and deliverance strategy which began to change the nature of the ministry.

---

165    Isaiah 41:13, 15–16.
166    Micah 4:13.

It reminded me of a vision we were given at the outset of our ministry: "I see a dilapidated, deserted house. We went inside it and did it up, and lights appeared all over the house. From there we went out to talk to people, who came back in with us. After a while these same people went out and began to gather other people in."

God is bringing His prophetic people home – sheep that are not of [our run-of-the-mill] sheep pen."[167]

After turning away from dark spirituality and choosing to follow God, one of our new friends tried to attend a church. Her sad testimony was that whenever people encountered her and discerned the darkness, they would instinctively take two steps backward.

Another man, who had literally been dedicated to darkness at birth, recently asked a Christian community for help. He moved into their home for several months. Their home then experienced some difficult and dark dynamics spiritually, even after he had left. I came into the picture when they talked to me about how to bring the spiritual atmosphere in the house back to peace and purity. I was told that one of the questions he had asked the Christian community was, "Is your church ready for people like this? Because I can bring them to you."

Quite honestly, it's a good question. My observation is that we are still getting ready, and our task is to help equip the church with the skills to reach and welcome home these gifted people and help them to transition to walking in the light.

But as Geoffrey Bull put it:

> *It is not a matter of missionary method. The most vital factor is a way of living. It is the straightening to that life of the Master which is described so adequately in the taunt, "This man receiveth sinners and eateth with them." It means a life, which is of such purity and love, that to touch the leper no longer means defilement, but the beginning of his cleansing.*[168]

It is a life to which I aspire.

Jesus' guidelines for ministry were to see what the Father is doing

---

167     See John 10:16.
168     Geoffrey T. Bull, *When Iron Gates Yield*, Pickering & Inglis Ltd, 1960.

and then to carry that out. Dreams and visions are being released in a pouring stream, and in this season we are being called back to authentic discipleship and Christ's pattern for ministry. Empowered by the Spirit of Christ, we are called to fulfil the commission of Christ.

Some years my raspberries fruit so plentifully I don't have time to gather them all, and the fruit rots on the plants for want of picking. I see the same around me in the ministry – fruit literally asking to be picked, mentored, and discipled, sometimes rotting on the vine.

> *The harvest is plentiful but the workers are few. Ask the Lord of the harvest, therefore, to send out workers into his harvest field.*[169]

We have, within our reach, a unique portion of the harvest:

> *Jesus came to them and said, "All authority in heaven and on earth has been given to me. Therefore go and make disciples of all nations, baptising them in the name of the Father and of the Son and of the Holy Spirit, and teaching them to obey everything I have commanded you. And surely I am with you always, to the very end of the age."*[170]

## Teaching points from chapter 4

Dreams and visions mirror the way Jesus dealt with people – joining in with what God was showing Him. We need to find new and innovative ways to communicate with people using relevant language. Jesus longs to touch and gather those who are hurting and lost.

- Serve, don't sell. Find out what God is saying and doing through the dream or vision and join in.

- To speed up the interpretation of dreams and visions on outreach, drawing out the dreams and visions cartoon-style, with stick men, is a helpful aid to interpretation.

- Write any feeling words next to the cartoon.

169    Matthew 9:37–38.
170    Matthew 28:18–20.

- Develop an understanding of the spiritual landscape into which you are interpreting dreams and visions on outreach:

    – Use culturally relevant language.

    – Look at application of dreams, not simply the interpretation.

    – Become secure with interpreting dark revelation.

    – People are either afraid of or fascinated by the darkness.

- Dreams in a series over several nights, or with a series of scenes in the same dream or vision can be:

    – showing a repeating or developing theme;

    – showing a timeline of the person's life;

    – carrying a repeating message highlighting the importance of that message, which needs to be heard.

- Overcome dark revelation with light. There is a model we can use to help people weigh the source of their dreams and visions and the source of their spirituality:

| **GOD'S KINGDOM** |
|---|
| Heavenly realm |
| • An understanding and awareness of God's kingdom, through dreams and visions. |
| • Meeting Jesus' love, power, and authority. |

| **THE REALM OF THE SUPERNATURAL AND COUNTERFEIT SPIRITUALITY** |
|---|
| Dark revelation, created spiritual beings, counterfeit practices – including pseudo-spirituality in religious structures. |

| **THE EVERYDAY WORLD** |
|---|
| Developing language to see beyond the physical and rational world and to see the goodness of God come into the everyday, through dreams and visions, prayer and passage meditation on Scripture. |

- Teaching people to be aware of this model helps them to develop an effective model of spirituality and to seek God.

- A Pharisaical religious attitude is as much at odds with the teaching of Christ who loved the world, as other false teachings are.

- We journey with people of all faiths and none. Guided vision encounters make a safe place where they can meet with God personally and hear His voice for themselves at an intimate level.

- Passage meditation continues to articulate truth and meet people at their point of need.

- God is bringing His prophetic people home. There is a need to train people in the skills to reach and receive them well.

- Prayer is the humble recognition that the power of God achieves the will of God through the work of God. This work is a sovereign work of the Holy Spirit and comes at the cost of a lifestyle of prayer.

- Interpreting their dreams, guiding people through vision exercises, and introducing Scripture passage meditation is a fruitful way to help people encounter God.

- The discipleship process is fun, vibrant, and intense, but very rewarding as we learn to engage with spiritual people on a journey.

# CHAPTER 4: ANSWERS AND INTERPRETATIONS

## Exercise 5.1: Patrice's supermarket dream

### The dream

"I was shopping in a supermarket, choosing things from the shelves, when a guy came along who I liked, but wasn't in love with. He was really into me, and grabbed me and kissed me. But I wasn't that into him."

**About:** Patrice.

**Type:** Life-processing dream with elements of revelation.

**Protocol:** Interestingly, the interpretation of this dream is for the minister, and not for Patrice.

**Sense of the story:** I'm OK with the guy, but I'm not that interested.

### The interpretation

Patrice is discerning the evangelistic zeal which the outreach minister feels for her. She is interested and looking for what she wants, but isn't that keen on what he has to give yet. The interpreter might say to the young male evangelist, "You may want to go with that and relax your attitude and approach a little. Serve Patrice and her choices. The passion you feel can be poured into prayer for her to find her way."

## Exercise 5.2: Completely full lavatory dream

### The dream

"It was night time and I was in a camp, looking for somewhere to go to the toilet. I found a toilet in a shed, but it was full of solids, right up to the brim, so I couldn't use it. I searched round the camp again and found another toilet in a small hut. It was scruffy and ill-kept. I opened the lid but again it was full to the brim and I couldn't use it."

**About:** The dreamer, in the context of their work.

**Type:** Life-processing dream with elements of revelation to bring understanding, correction (cleansing), and direction.

**Protocol:** Interpret gently.

- Record your interpretation for future reference.

- Work in a team.

- Be general, not directive.

- Ensure the seer knows the weighing procedure for weighing your interpretation.

**Sense of the story:** The dreamer can't find a place to process because everything is unclean/unflushed.

### The interpretation

The interpreter might say, "I would imagine that you may have been feeling a little vulnerable lately, and that you have some emotions to process which have been upsetting you. The dream tells me that even though you have been trying to do that diligently, it hasn't been possible or successful to do that because of the condition of your surroundings.

"This dream shows that you need to process some things in order to experience a sense of well-being; it suggests the current location isn't meeting your needs. You may want to talk to someone about that.

"The giver of the dream (I would say God) seems to have seen what you've been through and wants to help you deal with that."

A conversation may develop from this point about how inner healing can help as a type of counselling, leading them to healing prayer.

## Exercise 5.3: Singing a love song dream

### The dream

"My partner started to sing a song. It was a love song, but he couldn't remember the words. So he stopped halfway through. I was disappointed. Then a young man in his thirties came in. I knew he was a family member, although I didn't have anyone like that in my family. He began to sing the love song to me. He looked directly into my eyes and sang this amazing song – it was beautiful."

**About:** The dreamer.

**Type:** Revelation dream from God with some life-processing elements.

**Protocol:** Interpret freely, carefully defining who is singing the love song in order to avoid the misunderstanding that the dream is foretelling a new romantic attachment for the dreamer.

**Sense of the story:** Your partner has forgotten how to sing, but your family member sang beautifully.

### The interpretation

The interpreter might say, "This dream suggests you may have been feeling disappointed in your relationship, and wanting more of a sense of love than there is. But it also carries a message of being shown how much you are loved by the figure in the dream, who loves to sing over you. I'm interested as to why two frequently seen cultural symbols are cropping up in your dream. Firstly, the man in his thirties who is a family member, is not a literal man, but a symbol of the type of love which loves unconditionally, without wanting anything in return.

"In addition to that, he is singing a love song, and it reminds me of a passage meditation: 'He rejoices over me with singing.' The image in your dream suggests that the giver of the dream wants you to know you are loved unconditionally. He is with you, even when your partner is finding it hard to love.

"The cultural reference refers to Jesus, which is interesting, because if that is not your worldview, you don't use that cultural reference, which underwrites that the dream is coming from outside yourself. You may find it helpful to meditate on the passage meditation which this dream refers to. I will write it out for you… [Paraphrase: "God is with you, He is a hero who saves you, He takes delight in you and sings over you. He will comfort you with His love" Zephaniah 3:17.)

"He has seen your needs and come in this dream to sing over you."

## Exercise 5.4: Jo's vision story

### The vision we had for Jo

"In my vision I saw Jesus on the bank of a calm, winding river. Behind him was a rowing boat, lined with purple cushions.

"Jesus came to take Jo's hand and guide her to the rowing boat with gentleness and care. Jo reclined on the cushions while Jesus rowed the boat with Jo trailing her fingers in the green clear water of the river. A sense of ease and peace filled the scene; there was no hurry, just rest and a sense of being carried and cherished. Round a bend in the river was a low tree trunk, almost like a table. On it was a book, and from the book came shafts of dancing light. Jesus said to Jo, 'I wrote that book; it's My autobiography. It's a letter to you.' They stopped at the bank and collected the book (the Bible).

"There were two more stops on the bank of the river. Firstly to pick up a baby in a basket-weave cradle. At the third stop was a shining woman who had grown up rapidly. She was dressed all in silver, with a silver sword upheld in her right hand."

**About:** Jo.

**Type:** Revelation – edification, encouragement, comfort, and calling dream from God.

**Protocol:** Use neutral language to express this beautiful vision. Don't add anything – simply communicate God's heart for Jo and the sense of the journey it contains.

**Sense of the story:** You are invited on a lovely journey with God.

### The interpretation

The interpreter might say, "That's an interesting vision. It's not common for Jesus to turn up in vision readings. Are you comfortable with that name? The vision is sent to encourage you. It's beautiful. You are being called on a restful, peaceful journey with Jesus, to discover the flow of His life, where you are loved and cherished.

"The journey leaves behind the trying and heaviness of the journey which you've been on, to be carried along in rest. There's no rush. It includes an unveiling of your destiny in three easy stages, beginning with being carried and cared for in a place of rest. It suggests that the journey progresses with an encounter, with revelation coming from reading the Bible, which later will become a sharp tool for cutting people free as your gift matures quickly."

### Real-life story: application

Jo began on a journey of one-to-one mentoring through our mentoring school. This dream sets the pace: it's relaxed, there's no hurry, and the feeling is of coming into something caring and supportive. Because it's highlighted in the vision, passage meditation and gift training will also be part of the journey for this new and delightful friend who will be such fun to work with.

We had the joy of baptizing Jo recently into her new-found faith.

## Exercise 5.5: Kitten vision

### The vision

"I see you in my mind's eye as a tiny kitten. It looks beautiful, but it is also timid and is out in the concrete yard of a semi-detached house, watching everything with wide eyes. Next door is another house, and in my vision, God lives there (I would say 'God', because that's my worldview; I'm not sure what you would call Him). In my vision God put His hand over the wall and stroked the kitten so she wasn't scared anymore. She began to relax and play.

"In the house next door was a cat basket, which was lined with a soft blue velvet cushion. The kitten snuggled down in the warmth."

**About:** School teacher.

**Type:** Edification, encouragement, and comfort/calling.

**Protocol:** Use neutral accessible language. Serve, don't sell.

**Sense of the story:** There is comfort and support for a scared kitten.

### The interpretation

The interpreter might say, "This vision suggests that although I can see you look very together, you don't always feel like that. This picture has the kitten without comfort and suggests that you may even feel a little left out sometimes.

"The vision has a message that God (if that's a term you relate to) wants to bring you to peace and to a place where you are relaxed and cared for." As we spoke, a sense of love and deep acceptance surrounded us and communicated a deep peace.

"From this vision, you seem to have two choices: you can receive God's help and calm from time to time, or you can choose to 'go and live in His house' and receive that care in a much closer relationship."

### Real-life story

Having just experienced the sense of love and peace of God's touch, this lovely teacher said that she would like to talk about what it meant to go home to God's house. We discussed how that would happen. And she gave her life into God's care.

## Exercise 5.6: Cars in the darkness vision

### The vision

"I was leaving a cross-channel ferry. It was really dark. I drove the car out of the huge ship and drove on to the motorway. There were only a few cars going in either direction, but the cars going out had really bright headlights which shined in the darkness as pinpoints of light. On the opposite carriageway of the motorway, a few cars were coming back in dribs and drabs from the darkness into the ferry. Gradually, more and more cars left the ferry and joined the few cars that were going out. As they did so, the darkness became lit up by the greater concentration of lights."

**About:** The cars.

**Type:** Revelation – edification, encouragement, and comfort from God.

**Protocol:** Interpret freely. Convey the sense of encouragement and comfort.

**Sense of the story:** You are leaving the comfort of the ship and going into the darkness.

### The interpretation

The interpreter might say, "You are carrying the light into the darkness. You are at the start of a move out from the place of the church into the world to carry the light. It can seem a lonely journey, but there are others, and as you come back into the church for rest and refreshment to share your stories, others will go out into the darkness. As they do, the light will grow brighter and outweigh the darkness."

## Exercise 5.7: A series of dark dreams causing fear

### Dream 1

"I dreamt that spiders were coming from two corners of my bedroom window. There was an infestation of spiders in each corner of the window."

### Dream 2

"There was an angry woman yelling at me in my bedroom. The spiders were all over the floor."

### Dream 3

"One of my boots had a hole in the sole and there were spiders inside it."
**About:** The dreamer.
**Type:** Dark intimidation dream.
**Protocol:** Trump the dark message with God's light revelation.

- Record your interpretation for future reference.

- Work in a team.

- Ensure the seer knows the weighing procedure for weighing your interpretation.

- Don't interpret the dream.

- Restrict the amount of information you give according to the level of relationship you have with the dreamer.

**Sense of the story:** There is an infestation of spiders.

## Literal interpretations which should not be articulated

### Dream 1

"You are under demonic assault from deception and intimidation which may be causing fear when experiencing spiritual things."

### Dream 2

"You are being accused and intimidated and it is affecting your place of rest."

### Dream 3

"The active intimidation is continuing to disrupt your sense of peace and comfort which in turn affects your spiritual walk."

### Redemptive interpretations

As an interpreter, you need to lighten the situation with your words, but maintain enough authority to bring peace. The interpreter might say, "Wow – aren't nightmares horrible?! These are simply intimidation dreams with nothing interesting to say. I'd imagine you sometimes have thought patterns which may not be peaceful. That can be really tiring. We've found a great way to settle our nights down to peace –

would you like to hear a bit more about that? We've found that it stops nightmares."

Use Compline from Appendix 1 and bless the dreamer with peace.

### Teaching point

If we had a place of pastoral responsibility for this dreamer, we would begin to look at what was causing the fear in his life and how to help him begin to walk increasingly in confidence and joy. As a dream interpreter, though, what you can do is bring this sense of confidence and joy into the moment of interpretation.

## Exercise 5.8: Chris's dreams about flying

### Dream 1

"I've had three dreams recently that mirror those I've been having for years.

"There were people after me. It was random. I was running and hiding in various familiar areas, people's back gardens, etc. Then I hid in a nice hotel.

"There were stairs down and I was aware, 'If I go down, they may come up and get me.' So I jumped out of a window. This is always dangerous. In different dreams it can be off a cliff, a bridge, a building as I jump out of the window.

"I was on a ledge, clinging on by my hands like a child on monkey bars, and I had to go along the edge, hand over hand, where there was a platform and I jumped up onto it. Sometimes I fell, but I always woke up before hitting the ground."

### Dream 2

"I was in bed – the bed was rocking. There was a sense of evil – a presence.

"This used to happen when I was a boy. I was so scared. I used to think it was like a ghost was rocking the bed when I was awake.

"But in this dream, I didn't wake up. In the dream I got out of bed and went to the window, which exploded outward. I was flying high, high above the village. I, felt wind in my hair – it was lovely – then I fell into my garden, hit the floor, was blind, and couldn't see.

"I felt the glass and the side of the house for the window ledge – it was covered with glass. I found my bed – it was still rocking."

## Tip

A sense of fear and a negative presence came into the room while he told the dream. That helped me to understand that this was an encounter dream, with a specific presence.

## Dream 3

"This dream is also recurring and recent.

"I was in a gunfight. Then there was a real battle, like a war, and I was fighting.

"Next scene: then I was in trouble with the police for killing people. I was running, trying to get away, and the police were after me. I knew I had to go home to Scotland, where my Dad said, 'What have you done? Take the keys to my car to get away.' I went to the drive outside the house and on it was not a car but a biplane. I got in and turned it on, and I was flying away and escaped."

## The interpretations

**About:** Chris's life and spirituality.

**Type:** The first two dreams are dark dreams. The third is a revelation and calling dream from God. This series of dreams shows a pathway of developing spirituality toward more freedom.

**Protocol:** Interpret the dreams to help Chris have insight and understanding into his own journey, to help him take charge of his spiritual life.

**Sense of the story:** In the dreams Chris is being chased. He escapes through windows, which are dangerous, and finally finds out how to fly safely.

• What does each dream say about Chris's life and journey?

The interpreter might say, "These dreams are about your spiritual experience and journey. They show a progression in your life."

## Dream 1 interpretation

"There is a sense of intimidation and fear here. You recognize that you need to take action, and it shows me that you are trying to make good decisions, doing your best to deal with it. You show awareness that going down will make you vulnerable, and you head toward a place of revelation. You are beginning to demonstrate discernment. But at the moment you can't find a solution. So there's a problem with intimidating forces."

### Teaching point

The three dreams flow together, and the interpreter might link their interpretations by saying, "Let's have a look at your other dreams. They explain to us more about those negative forces and how you can deal with them."

You are leading Chris on a journey of increasing awareness of what is happening spiritually in his life. Use the dreams like stepping stones.

## Dream 2 interpretation

"This is a very different dream. This dream suggests to me that you have been experiencing negative spiritual energy since you were a young boy, when it must have been very scary, because even then you were spiritually aware.

"This dream has you flying, which shows me you are spiritually gifted and part of you loves the spiritual side of life, because you were made for it. But it shows me a problem: something negative is coming through that gifting, bringing fear and intimidation, and in this dream you got hurt. The window is a common symbol for spiritual revelation, but instead of more vision and more understanding, there is a blindness which signifies that, although you are spiritually gifted, you lack true understanding. You jump at apparent solutions, but risk losing safe control. The dream suggests that there is a need for light and safety, and a place of rest, in order to enjoy the feeling of flying in your gifting. The question for me as an interpreter is how we get you flying freely, without being prevented."

## Dream 3 interpretation

"In dream 3 we have the same themes: chasing, more fighting, and the new themes of accusation and blame. But this dream is very different: instead of trying to solve this yourself and getting cut, being blinded, or falling, you have an inner awareness of where to go for help: to a safe place, home to your Dad, the person who created you and loves you unconditionally, in spite of anything you may have done. You are maturing and learning. And you were given keys to access power to fly freely in your spiritual gifting, with more power, and a greater sense of fun and freedom."

Ask Chris a question, "Chris, does your Dad have a plane?" Answer: "No." These are symbols.

The interpreter might say, "This dream is to give you an invitation to go home to a higher power – a Father who loves you (I would say God), the giver of the dream, who will give you power and authority to leave behind the things that are against you, even those things you may have been blamed for – and you may even have done some of them. A higher level of giftedness and freedom will come with it from all that is negative. These dreams are about freedom, and the giver of the dream is giving you a way out of the past into a whole new area of freedom and flight, because you were born to fly."

### *Real-life story*

We had a conversation with Chris, and in this sort of conversation we often give follow-up literature in the form of the book *Run Baby Run*, the story of Nicky Cruz. Nicky's story is initially very spiritually dark, but charts a journey into freedom and productivity.

*Chapter 5*

# DREAMS AND THEIR USEFULNESS IN MODERN CHURCH LIFE

*The one who prophesies edifies the church.*[171]

The real-life stories in this chapter are examples of times when God spoke through a dream or a vision to a specific church. They show how He cared about their journey and how He guided or affirmed them.

In a church or ministry which is prophetically literate, dreams and visions chronicle what is happening. Like a mirror, they can help the leadership to slow down and observe the dynamic of the situations in which they are caught up. They bring direction, correction, encouragement, and counsel. If they are interpreted and presented well, they provide a status report on the church and contain a fresh perspective to help the leaders.

Dreams and visions can also inform effective prayer on behalf of the church and the leadership.

> *By wisdom a house is built,*
> *and through understanding it is established…*
> *those who have knowledge muster their strength.*
> *Surely you need guidance to wage war,*
> *and victory is won through many advisors.*[172]

---

171      1 Corinthians 14:4.
172      Proverbs 24:3–6.

Leaders are often judged by those who have the benefit of hindsight. It wasn't supposed to be that way: revelation helps the leaders work with foresight.

If the relationship between the church leaders and the prophetic leaders, and the prophetic process itself, are working well, the revelation sent in dreams and visions will be effective. These two factors are key in using revelation in the church context: firstly, team – the way the leadership team and the prophetic team relate; and secondly, the maturity of the prophetic process so that it can receive, weigh, interpret, and present revelation well, to be understood and considered by the leadership. This life-giving process drops helpful revelation into situations and brings light. With training and support, this ministry is steadily growing across the body of the church.

On occasion we are called into a church situation where real examples of accurate high-level revelation have been misunderstood or ignored. Sadly, the consequences that this has had in the life of those individual churches has been extreme and life changing. Those consequences are an expensive learning curve, which itself opens the eyes of the church to the value of weighing revelation well.

> *Good judgement is the result of experience, and experience is the result of bad judgement.*[173]

But dealing with revelation well takes time, lots of time. C. S. Lewis titled his paper on theological biblical criticism, "Fern-seed and Elephants". In it he talks about the danger of minutely dissecting the biblical text "between the lines", so that people miss the elephants of teaching on the lines. I love the simplicity of Lewis's symbolism, because as busy leaders, we often miss important truth because our detailed attention is elsewhere.

Borrowing Lewis's terminology and reapplying it more generally to modern-day church life, I have noticed that most leaders are caught up with herding elephants – those everyday important pastoral, preparation, building, and management matters that are essential to the running of a good church or ministry. We frequently don't have

---

173    Mark Twain, available at https://www.goodreads.com/quotes/162381-good-judgement-is-the-result-of-experience-and-experience-the (accessed 23 August 2017).

time to process the fern-seed of revelation. But the Gospels of Matthew, Mark, and Luke all emphasize that seed's power, and the importance of hearing, understanding, retaining, and applying revelation so that it can bear fruit.[174]

During five years on a senior leadership team of a large, busy resource church, it amazed me how many hours were eaten up with staff meetings, people management in my department, and wider meetings over lunches and coffees. It was especially surprising when my responsibility area was prayer and the prophetic. I was continually pulled into other things. Now I have moved to concentrate on a more missional model of ministry, to teach and train wider afield in the prophetic and run the growing prophetic outreach communities, I am still continually accosted by elephants, necessary elephants that fill my lines. But over time we've had to learn to push past these leadership and ministry distractions, and one of our main values has become to centre on prayer and listening to God. Unless we continue to do this, we would fail to plant the fruit-bearing seed for the plethora of elephants, wasting both our time and other people's resources to little effect.

We have a team who are very fruitful in bringing an accurate flow of dreams and visions about the ministry. They alert us to developing situations, and it is a huge help. I collect, collate, interpret, and apply this revelation with my team.

Church and ministry leaders need support like this from competent prophetic people who are there to support and serve them, both in a wider network of trusted relationships and as part of a functioning in-house team. These people hold the corporate prophetic memory of the church – remembering key pieces of revelation and identifying themes that are coming through.

Our task is to equip those teams to be highly prophetically and biblically literate, to truly understand the prophetic process in the context of church, and to encourage them to spend time standing in God's counsel. As they do, we find that their fruitfulness overflows into the church, strengthening the leadership and encouraging the ministry.

---

174      Matthew 13:1–23; Mark 4:1–20; Luke 8:1–15.

But we've also seen the real need to support these in-house working relationships through times when relational difficulties, internal politics, and misunderstandings undermine or explode this fruitful communication system. Without external support, the relationships tend to fail in the melee of challenges, but with support, covering, and some help to understand the common pitfalls that occur during the journey, trust is built and "the whole body, joined and held together by every supporting ligament, grows and builds itself up in love, as each part does its work".[175]

> *If there is no wise authority capable of protecting and validating them, most prophetic people... are almost always "torn to pieces."[176]*

This support system can provide stability, encouragement, and strength as churches seek to understand, develop, and realize the life-giving potential of using dreams and visions within the complex demands of church life.

As I deal with different churches I have noticed some of the ways which dreams and visions prosper the church.

> *"Listen to me, Judah and people of Jerusalem! Have faith in the Lord your God and you will be upheld; have faith in his prophets and you will be successful."[177]*

## Case study 1: Empty water tank vision

Dreams and visions will find the things among people that keep God from moving on their behalf – and will do it redemptively.

### The context

Sitting with one church leadership team while they went through a mid-week retreat, God gave me a vision.

---

175     Ephesians 4:16.
176     Richard Rohr, *Falling Upwards*, John Wiley & Sons, 2011, p.12..
177     2 Chronicles 20:20.

## The vision

### Scene one

"Each team leader was working hard in their own department and they came and put a huge saucepan full of water in a large round corrugated iron water tank (the church). As they continued to pour their water in, the tank remained empty. No matter what they did, no matter how hard they worked, it made no difference. As a result, those leaders had become disappointed and discouraged. Although there was living water and fruit in the separate departments, the church wasn't growing or flourishing.

"As I looked at the vision, God showed me the walls. The corrugated iron walls inside the tank were like sections of pie, dividing the staff in the vast container of the church. He started to cry. His teardrops fell on the walls and they melted like sugar crystals. And suddenly water filled the tank."

### Scene two

"And I saw the rain from heaven fall to the earth to flow into the rivers, on into the sea, and evaporate back up to fall on the earth again. It was an effortless cycle of life and fruitfulness. A verse flashed before my eyes: 'As long as the earth endures, seedtime and harvest... will never cease.'[178]

"And I heard an instruction: 'Don't stop the cycle.'

"Suddenly I saw each person in the leadership team under an umbrella of offence, protection, retaliation, hopelessness, and rebellion, arising from judgment of one another. The umbrellas were stopping the rain (positive) from soaking them.

"And again came an instruction, 'You stopped the cycle, but prayed for rain. I can cover you – I'll cover you – it's OK to be you.'

"God was encouraging them to let go of their fears, offences, and dashed hopes because He was able to protect them.

"I saw a rainbow of promise rising and God's healing wings outspread to bring protection."

---

178    Genesis 8:22.

### Interpretation and application

This vision was a passionate insight into God's heart for this church and the team. They had retreated from one another in pain, anger, and fear, retaliating with control and aggression. This was grieving God.

> Surely this is what Jesus meant when He said you could tell a good tree from a bad one, "by its fruit".[179]

> Inside of "life-energy", a group or family will be productive and energetic: inside of "death-energy" there will be gossip, cynicism, and mistrust hiding behind every interaction.[180]

The vision had literally found those things that were keeping God from moving in the church. It provided a *Kairos* moment of opportunity for the team to begin to deal with their offences, receive healing and forgiveness, to see the redemptive effortless cycle of life, and see fruitfulness return to the church.

## Case study 2: Praying for a young man's hands vision

Dreams and visions involve us in loosing God's purposes on the earth.

### The context

In pre-meeting prayer for a big conference, I was standing by the wall. Suddenly the Lord spoke to me: "Bang on the wall three times."

There were many people I didn't know at the meeting, and I wasn't keen to behave in an unusual way, so I gently and furtively banged on the wall behind me. Again I heard the instruction, "Bang on the wall!" I repeated my timid gesture.

The command came a third time; this time it was a firm command: "Bang on the wall!" I turned around and banged on the wall.

### The vision

"Above me in the wall, in an open vision a double window opened outward and a figure leant out. He told me, 'Go and pray for the hands

---

179     Matthew 7:20.
180     Rohr, *Falling Upwards*, p. XIV.

of that boy on the other side of the room.' I looked up to see a very young man whom I had never seen before. Interested, and somewhat apologetic, I went up to the boy and said, 'I think the Lord asked me to come and lay hands on your hands and pray for them.' He put out his hands and said, 'I'm the drummer [for this evening].'

During the meeting, the young man played the drums. As he did, the meeting came to a standstill. It was an awe-inspiring sound of joy and command. I saw angels fly out from behind his drums, in answer to a prayer that was being prayed for the prodigals to return home. Angel after angel was dispatched to the sound of the drums. Afterward he came to find me and said, 'I can't play the drums like that!' He was amazed at what God had done for him."

Working with God's revelation helps us to take part in what He is doing. I love that He shows us what He wants us to do and graciously involves us in the process.

## Case study 3: Prayer castle cream

Dreams and visions guide and facilitate prayer.

### The context

God is raising prayer castles all over the UK, where He shows us His will through dreams and visions and we pray it back to Him in a fruitful cycle of intercession, which joins with Jesus' present-day ministry of intercession with authoritative prayer: "Thy will be done, Thy kingdom come."

> *A man of noble birth went to a distant country to have himself appointed king and then to return. So he called ten of his servants and gave them ten minas "Put this money to work," he said, "until I come back."*[181]

The "minas" were a large amount of money. This parable has often been applied to using our gifts and talents, but money can also symbolize favour, influence, and authority. When Jesus told His disciples to "ask me for anything in my name, and I will do it",[182] He gave them access to all three. There are times in our lives when we need to put our "minas" to work.

---

181    Luke 19:12–13.
182    John 14:14.

At the time of writing, both the UK and America are coming in to a time of transition. In the UK, the vote to leave the European Union has taken place, we have a new prime minister, and other radical changes face us in the next decade. The United States has a new president and is going through some turbulence. And there will be those of us who are in, or who know people in our neighbourhoods who are in their own transition. It is at times like these that wisdom in prayer is especially needed.

Prayer castles are places of strategic prayer, of strength, refuge, and community.

In the eleventh century, the king, William the Conqueror, embarked on a programme of building a series of regional castles, as he was getting older, to prepare the nation for transition. Transitions are vulnerable times. The local castles were a sign of the king's presence. They provided security and kept order in their region. They steadied the country and brought the rule of peace to the area under their care. These prayer castles raised the people's eyes to the stability, surety, and security of the throne.

Isaiah lived in a time of transition and uncertainty. In prayer, he saw the Lord:

> In the year that King Uzziah died, I saw the Lord, high and exalted, seated on a throne; and the train of his robe filled the temple… [He saw the seraphs] calling to one another:
>
> "Holy, holy, holy is the Lord Almighty; the whole earth is full of his glory."[183]

The vision of heaven and earth was ringing with God's power and His goodness. And Isaiah was gripped with a desire to serve God's purposes.

As we engage with our dreams and visions they open our eyes to see what God is seeing. They provide specific revelation about specific areas of God's will. They allow us to be highly strategic, accurate, and effective in our prayers.

---

183    Isaiah 6:1–3.

## Sarah's dream

### The context

The dreamer was a faithful intercessor. "You" is her church leader.

### The dream

"I had a dream… You and I were standing on the ramparts of a castle with crossbows. A demonic army was heading toward this fortress on what looked like horses; they were a vast army. You were in command and took the first section. I was second-in-command and took the next section. I could see other individuals but they had no faces; however, I was aware of them fighting as well. Every so often you would write answers down on a list. I remember reading them and carrying out the instructions. The demonic army were not in battle positions but just heading toward us. We were shooting arrows at them and I was hit on the breastplate by one, and you asked me if I was OK. I replied that I was and carried on fighting. Then I woke up."

### The interpretation

Sarah's dream highlights six points about effective intercession:

- the church as a place of rule and refuge;
- the strong union of the intercessors and leaders working together;
- the leader is receiving insight from God which informs intercession;
- the intercessors are backing up the leaders with prayer;
- the intercessors are protected by the righteousness received from Christ;
- the leaders are covering and watching out for the intercessors.

When the body of Christ picks up the dreams and visions that are given to promote prayer, the church carries on the work of Christ, modelled by His pattern of intercession.

## Case study 4: Vision honouring a church

Dreams and visions bring affirmation and commendation.

### The context

Visiting one mid-sized church in 2016 to do prophetic training and preach at the Sunday service, I had the following vision.

### The vision

"I saw the scene from the book of Esther where Mordecai is rewarded for service to the king by being clothed in royal robes and being led through the streets by an official crying, 'This is what is done for the man who the king delights to honour.'"

### The interpretation

God had sent me there to honour and affirm the church. He wanted me to honour them for their service to Him.

> *"What honour and recognition… [have they] received for this?"[184]*

### Application

Let's take a moment to honour King's Church, Chesham, Buckinghamshire, for the way they love those in their care and seek to love God with their whole hearts.

## Case study 5: Church leader's dream

Dreams and visions bring conviction, correction, and vindication.

### The context

This leader ran a church which was staffed with strong, gifted, and somewhat competitive people. As is the case in most organizations, be they medical, educational, or a church institution, there was sometimes considerable tension and misunderstanding between those engaged in "ministry" and the administrative function of the house. The ministry teams didn't fully appreciate or understand the difficulties of the administrative function. A previous dream had highlighted the fact

---

184      Esther 6:3.

that the ministers took the administrative team totally for granted. The bad feeling had a historical root.

The church leader had this dream which brought to light another part of this increasingly tense scenario.

## The dream

"I was making a movie. I stood and watched as people I knew chased a woman away down a corridor. She hid in a shed, and I didn't see her again until I saw a poster which advertised the fact that she was appearing in an A-list movie."

## The interpretation

The key to the interpretation of this dream is, "Who does the woman represent?" Because she wasn't identifiable, the initial interpretation was general. It was put like this, "You are standing by and watching a process which you have the authority to shape. Someone is being driven down a corridor of transition from the church into a temporary outpost of refuge. You will see them again, but not for some time."

But nine months later, one of the prayer ministers (who had resigned after finding the unsupported relationships in-house very unhelpful and negative) came back to see the leader. He had literally just prominently appeared in a top-grossing A-list movie as a movie extra, just as the dream had foretold. He was the symbolic woman, and he had been forced out by those unpleasant in-house dynamics.

The dream shone a spotlight on the situation which God was highlighting. It was sent to bring understanding and conviction. It also brought vindication for the young man who had been badly treated.

He was symbolized by a woman in the dream because:

- The mystery identity of the person had raised interest and discussion about the dream. Curiosity means that people pay attention to the dream, and when it comes, the interpretation has more "punch".

- The woman symbolizes a Holy Spirit ministry of the church in the prayer department.

# Case study 6: Ocean vision with different levels of interpretation

Dreams and vision interpretation releases God's truth into everyday reality.

## The context

This vision was given in a church meeting. It was beautifully spoken, and the presence of God stilled the room. As the seer interpreted the vision with an initial interpretation, the confirming presence of God lifted, until Edmund, one of the few prophets that I've met, gently came forward and took the microphone. As he interpreted the vision, the presence of God settled upon the congregation to confirm God's message.

## The vision

"I see maps in atlases, with currents flowing through the oceans of the world, in purple. Then the picture changed, and I saw these oceans at the level of the surface – with storms and waves and gulls fishing. The waves were big and overwhelming, and it was if God took the 'camera' down underneath the sea and I saw the current, purple and flowing inexorably and continuously, in the direction God had set in place."

## The seer's own interpretation

"There is a call to us to dive down deeper and escape the turbulence, the waves and the gulls picking us off like fish. God is saying, 'Take My hand and dive down deeper into the current of My purposes and love.'"

## Edmund's interpretation

"Peter says that the royal way is the way of love. I feel the Lord showed me that purple is the colour of royalty. And it's His kingdom that is based in love. Despite all the turbulence, the kingdom is progressing; nothing discounts it, nothing slows, nothing changes the inexorable process of His kingdom, and that's true in the world 'underground', as it were, and in our individual hearts. When you are knocked about by the strains, the royal way of the kingdom is still proceeding with you. Deep down where you may not be aware of it, there's a sense of God saying He is committed to you. His kingdom is being built up in you and His kingdom is moving forward in the world – that is the purple current."

The immature interpretation made a suggestion that people trust God. It reports biblical fact. The first interpretation was true – it wasn't complete or wholly accurate. The authority of God did not come and confirm the words.

> "I am Yahweh... who confirms the words of His
> servant, and performs the counsel of His messengers."[185]

Mature interpretation achieves the purposes of God and extends the rule of His kingdom. The mature interpretation lifted the stress from the church. A deep awareness of and appreciation for the kingdom of God came. Security, gentleness, and faith rose in the room. The people grew in strength and in the knowledge of God as the reality of His kingdom came among them. The sense of the purple current rose, held, and carried them, as God's love was released. An overwhelming sense of rest and confidence came over the congregation.

## Case study 7: A dream bringing a pastoral mandate

Dreams and visions help to bring clarity, as we pastor the individual people of the church.

### The context

The dreamer, Deborah, is a natural pastor. She had a dream about Jenny, who had been through a really rough time with a relationship which had turned bitter, leaving Jenny vulnerable and isolated. The same relationship had drawn Jenny away from the steady and life-giving relationships that she had formed in her church small group.

### The dream

"I saw Jenny in the living room. It was dark and there were all these shadows sitting down in the room. Jenny was talking to them. There was a coin suspended from the ceiling. It was an upside-down pentagram (used in occult practice). And in the middle of the coin was the face of a specific creature, half man and half goat, who represented Satan.

---

185     Isaiah 44:24, 26 (WEB).

"I started to back out of the room and I heard a voice saying, 'Jenny is running the risk of turning her back on God.'"

### The Interpretation

This dream revealed a deeper issue than Jenny's pain at losing her new friend. It highlighted the temptation that Jenny was undergoing, owing to her feelings of being isolated and discouraged.

It suggests that Jenny was vulnerable to being drawn back toward her occult roots and facing inner struggle. Deception was creeping into the gap that had been filled by positive and life-giving friendships in her small group.

The dream highlights Jenny's deep need to walk in a loving faith community. The dream, along with the context, suggests that there are three issues that could benefit from pastoral input:

- how to help Jenny recognize the unhelpful nature of isolation from a loving source of friendship and support;

- how to offer Jenny the chance to re-engage with that loving source of support;

- a counselling and ministry agenda to identify any hidden "lies" Jenny was believing at that time, relating to the occult world.

The dream brings into the light hidden issues which need to be talked through for Jenny to develop a strong success strategy for her walk with God and her sense of community. It reveals a deception that still has power to influence her life. Simply re-engaging with the group would not have dealt with all these issues.

## Case study 8: A strategic revelation dream

This demonstrates the need for a mature level of interpretation at leadership level as dreams and visions expose hidden strategies of the enemy that are hindering the purposes of God.

> *...in order that Satan might not outwit us. For we are not unaware of his schemes.*[186]

---

186     2 Corinthians 2:11.

## The context

The curate of a lively established church, an experienced and committed woman, had this dream. Several months after the dream had occurred, the church was experiencing the threat of a split. Sides were forming around a doctrinal issue and there was resulting disagreement and pain.

The situation had begun when a senior and well-respected churchwarden sent out an unannounced letter to the congregation about his strong disagreement with the vicar and leadership team on a matter of doctrine. People began to take sides and the situation became extremely heated.

Recognizing the parallels between her dream and her church situation, Jo (not her real name) brought it to me.

## The dream

"I saw dark clouds roll in and underneath the clouds were winds. The clouds and the winds were between God's throne and the earth. They were hindering what God was releasing from heaven from being received on the earth. Both the clouds and the winds were negative and I knew the dream was about the church. In my dream I understood the clouds represented clouds of darkened understanding. The winds were the winds of doctrines."

## The interpretation

The curate had correctly interpreted the dream as a foretelling and warning dream, saying that a situation was blowing in where clouds of darkened understanding and winds of false doctrines would be an issue. But that factual interpretation was simply the beginning of the meaning of the dream. There were key elements in that concise dream which had a much deeper symbolic message, providing a solution, as God continued to reveal His will and provide a comprehensive prophetic perspective on what was going on spiritually in the church.

This process of mature interpretation is sometimes called "round tabling". Mature leaders and prophetic people look at the dream in the presence of God, asking the Holy Spirit to lead the process to bring understanding. They look at the revelation in the context of the real-life situation, and in the light of the whole counsel of Scripture. This deeper level of interpretation is important, so the message of the dream can be comprehensively dealt with.

## *The dream in the context of the real-life situation*

The symptoms of darkened understanding began to show up as Jo talked about the church. The congregation were beginning to get confused. Some key members were thinking about leaving as discord was escalating. The leaders were being judged by those who lacked a full understanding of what was happening and began to feel angry.

In the swirling winds of false doctrine, the issue was turning people against one another.

There were two strategies which needed dealing with: the issue of discord and the issue of false doctrine. The issue of discord is one of the most common strategies we see coming against churches. It was not for nothing that one of Jesus' last prayers for His disciples before going to the cross was for unity.[187] Unity comes when the Holy Spirit's wisdom pervades the whole, joining people together into one body. But when darkened understanding (false wisdom) comes, disorder comes with it.[188]

## *The dream in the light of Scripture*

The church was experiencing a level of attack. As the leaders waited on God, He began to highlight a story in 2 Samuel 10, where Israel faced just such an attack. Ammonites and the Arameans (their hired foot soldiers) declared war on Israel after a misunderstanding.

Israel's commanders, Joab and his brother Abishai, each took a contingent of men and came up with a strategy which is very effective, both in the Bible story and in the modern-day church context in the face of attack:

> *"If the Arameans are too strong for me, then you are to come to my rescue; but if the Ammonites are too strong for you, then I will come to rescue you."*[189]

Brother stood with brother in unity in the face of battle. As they did, the king came out to help them rout the army.

But how is the strategy in this story helpful in the case of Jo's church?

---

187      John 17.
188      James 3:16.
189      2 Samuel 10:11.

The symbolism in the names is important: "Joab" means "father", representing the leader of the church – in this case, the vicar. "Abishai" means "gift of God", representing, in this case, Christ's grace gifts to the church listed in Ephesians 4 which strengthen the people of the church against being blown about by winds of false doctrine: "So Christ himself gave the apostles, the prophets, the evangelists, the pastors and teachers, to equip his people... so that the body of Christ may be built up... until we all reach unity... Then we will no longer be infants... blown here and there by every wind of teaching."[190]

The application of this revelation is that the five-fold grace gifts need to operate next to the vicar, who has the apostolic role as father to the house. The team can help to **pastor** individuals, to bring calm, authoritative **teaching**, and what God is saying **prophetically** to the people, to stabilize the church. The **evangelistic** gift also needed to come in to help the pre-Christians in the community who were seeing the discord in the church and were becoming confused and disillusioned.

It is interesting to note that the armour of God has no "back plate", because this is where your "brother" stands. As these men and women came to stand with the vicar, their functions protected both him and the people.

### Real-life story

As we explained the spiritual angle of what was happening around them, the leaders graciously recognized any discord, anger, and self-righteousness rising in their own hearts and they began, in a place of repentance – breaking agreement with the divisive strategy at work – to focus on God.

The vicar took the interpretation to heart and applied it. The teamwork meant that, although the strategy had done a certain amount of damage, it hadn't taken the team or the church down. The leader of the church in question is a calm, strong, apostolically gifted man, with an unusual openness to the prophetic and an equally strong value for the integrity of the Scriptures. He is committed to five-fold team.

The raid wasn't without cost, however; the churchwarden resigned and took several church members with him.

---

190     Ephesians 4:11–14.

In this particular church, the interface between the prophetic and the leadership was developed and effective. The trusted relationships between literate prophetic voices and leaderships are what make dreams and visions fruitful in the church context.

## Developing as an interpreter: How are you relating to your current church context?

In our own location there is a process of developing true relationship, a track record for accuracy and trust, which builds naturally over time, although God, being God, can bypass that in a moment, giving favour in an instant where He chooses to use someone. It always amuses me where He does and doesn't choose to fast-track this process, and I often glance upward with a smile and a "What are you up to now?" question in my eyes.

To use dreams and visions fruitfully, in any sphere, there needs to be a synergy between your gifting and the people in that context. There are four sequential steps which will help you to develop that place of healthy interaction: Affirm, Confirm, Influence, and Counsel.

As you read this section, ask yourself:

- Which of the four sequential steps am I currently welcome to work in, in my own church/group?

- Am I faithfully seeking to love and serve with my gift, through affirmation and confirmation?

- Have I built up trusting working relationships?

- Do I need to engage in more training to gain credibility in using dreams and visions accurately in my sphere?

## Affirmation: Revelation which strengthens, encourages and comforts[191]

Some years ago I was booked to speak to a room full of senior pastors and ministers. God gave me only one thing to say: a small and rather obscure verse from 2 Timothy 4:13: "When you come, bring the cloak that I left with Carpus with Troas..." Paul was in a damp cell. He was

---

191     1 Corinthians 14:3.

cold. That was the sum total of the revelation God gave me. That was it. And in front of me was a ballroom full of senior leaders waiting for me to speak.

As I shared, it emerged that I had men and women with me who had cancer, men who had family problems, marriage troubles, and ministry challenges. The leaders were just people and many of them were "cold". They stood in need of God's comfort, affirmation, and encouragement. I watched as the walls came down and they began to comfort and affirm one another and pray together in that safe environment.

This ministry of God's love toward the leaders and the people of the church builds a foundation of relationship and trust. Without that, everything else you say is "just noise".

> *If I speak in the tongues of men or of angels, but*
> *do not have love, I am only a resounding gong or a*
> *clanging symbol. If I… can fathom all mysteries and all*
> *knowledge… but do not have love, I am nothing.*[192]

Our task is to serve Christ by loving His people.

> *God is not unjust; he will not forget your work and the*
> *love you have shown him as you have helped his people*
> *and continue to help them.*[193]

> *The believer who yields himself wholly up to Christ*
> *for service in the spirit of a simple childlike trust will*
> *assuredly bring forth much fruit.*[194]

---

192     1 Corinthians 13:1.
193     Hebrews 6:10.
194     Andrew Murray, *Abide in Christ*, Whitaker House, 1979, p. 161.

# DREAMS AND VISIONS EXERCISES
# EXERCISE SET 6: QUESTIONS TO UNLOCK AN INTERPRETATION

## Exercise 6.1: Affirmation vision – rooms, stars, and wells

### The context

This small vision was given to a church which had a successful history as a resource church. It had been through a time of restructuring and preparation to re-engage with that call. The people were gifted and committed, and the leadership was hungry for more of God.

### The vision

### Scene 1

"I saw a large room in heaven and I knew it belonged to your church. It was pure white and completely empty, like a vast hall. It was beautiful, warm, inviting, and full of God's presence."

### Scene 2

"I saw a black sky, and one by one stars lit up as bright lights in the sky."

### Scene 3

"I saw a well which had been stopped up, being uncovered."

A supporting Scripture was given with the visions which contained the same imagery:

> "I will make your descendants as numerous as the stars
> in the sky... and through your offspring all nations on
> earth will be blessed"... Isaac reopened the wells that
> had been dug in the time of his father Abraham...
> Isaac's servants dug in the valley and discovered a
> well of fresh water there. But the herdsmen of Gerar
> quarrelled with those of Isaac and said, "The water
> is ours!"... Then they dug another well, but they
> quarrelled over that one also... He moved on from there

*and dug another well, and no one quarrelled over it. He named it Rehoboth, saying, "Now the Lord has given us room and we will flourish in the land."... That night the Lord appeared to him and said, "I am the God of your father Abraham. Do not be afraid, for I am with you; I will bless you and will increase the number of your descendants for the sake of my servant Abraham."[195]*

What do these visions mean? Answer the questions to unlock the vision:

• Who or what is this affirming vision about?

• In the vision three symbols were used to speak about the church: a room, stars, and a well.

• Read the supporting Scripture and look at the context of these symbols.

• What is the vision saying to the church? Write an interpretation which you could give to them.

Compare your interpretation with the interpretation at the end of the chapter.

## Confirmation: "Every matter must be established by the testimony of two or three witnesses"[196]

In this second season of your development, interpreting dreams and giving visions will begin to confirm the things that God is already saying to the church and to those around you. "Every matter must be established by the testimony of two or three witnesses."[197]

This process not only builds trust and relationship; it also develops your credibility as your accuracy begins to be recognized. It establishes an accurate track record in hearing God.

Confirmation is often not shared publicly. It is a gift to encourage and affirm individuals or leaders of families, businesses, organizations, or churches. As you go through this process, it tests the heart and

---

195    Genesis 26:4, 18–22, 24.
196    2 Corinthians 13:1.
197    2 Corinthians 13:1.

maturity with which you give the revelation. It also highlights the need for a secure base to work from where you have affirming relationships, which are independent from the people whom you are serving, so that you aren't dependent on public recognition for your own affirmation.

If this invisible process of serving tests your heart and maturity levels, that's not a bad thing; it's a human thing, which gives you permission to grow into wholeness. The freedom and maturity you find when you go through this stage of growth will allow God to use you for more public ministry in the future, because it will highlight any unmet needs which might cause you to share what you see unwisely or inappropriately.

Your private aim in this season of confirmation is to grow in accuracy, seeing in the Spirit and interpretation, and into greater maturity and freedom. Being trained and mentored during this process will prepare you for the freedom and power of service to Christ, rather than the celebrity of church, which would distract you.

If you are called to minister or function in the church, this is a lesson you will learn in one of two ways: by being rooted in and taught by a people who are devoted to Christ, or by the lessons of church life. Francis Frangipane discovered, "To inoculate me from the praise of man, He baptised me in the criticism of man until I died to the control of man."[198] I respectfully suggest that you want to beat God to this one, and work this lesson out before He works on it for you.

## Exercise 6.2: Confirmation vision – sailing ship

### The context

This picture was given to a church which broadly contained three groups of people:

- an old guard, who had cherished the vision of the church and held dear a piece of symbolism from years before – a ship with the caption, "Not a pleasure cruiser but a warship";

- the new generation of enthusiastic younger members in their twenties and thirties;

- the pastor who is hungry for the move of the Holy Spirit.

---

198    Francis Frangipane, *The Shelter of The Most High*, Charisma House, 2012.

## The vision

"I see a tall, beautiful, stately sailing ship moored in the harbour beside the quay. It hadn't just come from the sea; it had been put in the harbour ready for relaunch. It carried the king's flag and was secure, steadfast, graceful, and at ease."

What does the vision mean? Answer the questions to unlock the vision:

- Who or what is this vision about?

- What type of vision is it and what is its source?

- What type of protocol do I need to apply to interpret this type of vision?

- What is the sense of the story?

## Helpful symbolism

**Ship** (positive symbol): large church
**On the water** (positive symbol): the things of the Spirit
**Sailing** (positive symbol): called to catch the things of the Spirit and go with Him
**King's flag** (positive symbol): authority and protection

Use the sense of the story, the answers to the questions, and the helpful symbolism list above to write an interpretation of the vision that you would give to the seer.

Compare your interpretation with the interpretation at the end of the chapter.

# Influence: Impacting the world around you through dreams and visions

Once affirming relationships and your credibility are established, through the process of affirmation and confirmation, God can increasingly use you in different situations. There's a reason why people will begin to listen to you.

In 2 Kings 9 Elisha chose a man from among the company of

prophets and told him to go and anoint Jehu, commander of the army, as king. But the instruction included a command to do it in private. The prophet summoned Jehu from among his friends, anointed him, and gave him a mandate for kingship:

> *"This is what the Lord, the God of Israel, says, 'I anoint you king over the Lord's people Israel.'"… Then he opened the door and ran.*
>
> *When Jehu went out to his fellow officers, one of them asked, "Is everything all right? Why did this maniac come to you?"[199]*

In the course of telling them what had happened, Jehu begins with this statement: "You know the man and the sort of things he says."[200] Jehu directly referred to the man's credibility and track record.

> *They quickly took their cloaks and spread them under him [Jehu] on the bare steps. Then they blew the trumpet and shouted, "Jehu is king!"[201]*

The prophet had enough credibility in both his own character ("you know the man") and in the accuracy of his ministry ("the sort of things he says") to speak for Elisha and to speak for God. He influenced the situation and established the specific agenda for Jehu's actions in dealing decisively with Ahab and Jezebel, on whose behaviour God had called time.

This level of influence needs to be used carefully, and the next two dreams will help you understand the need to develop wisdom and discretion as you interpret dreams and visions in the church context with increasing influence.

## Exercise 6.3: Using influence with wisdom and discretion – two dreams which work together

These two dreams were sent to me by different dreamers within a three-week period from one of the ministries with which I have relationship.

---

199    2 Kings 9:6, 10–11.
200    2 Kings 9:11.
201    2 Kings 9:13.

At the time of the dreams, the first dreamer, Jeremy (not his real name) is the associate pastor of a large youth church in Europe. He is looking for a change in context after becoming increasingly frustrated with his present job. Jeremy's dream is processing his feelings but also contains encouragement and direction from God. It helps Jeremy to navigate what is about to happen: events in his life are about to move very quickly and he would be leaving his job within a matter of weeks.

The second dreamer, Tony, is his junior assistant and "right-hand man". Tony knows precisely nothing about how Jeremy has been feeling. Despite this fact, Tony has a foretelling dream from God, which details what is about to happen.

Your task in this exercise is to read both the dreams and understand the situation. Then adapt the unedited interpretation of the second dream to come up with a wise interpretation which will prepare that dreamer (Tony) for what is to come.

First, read Jeremy's dream and its interpretation. It will explain to you more about what is about to happen.

## Dream 1: Jeremy's dream

### The dream

"I was on the street, ministering with a church ministry team. A senior woman leader was there. We were taking it in turns to give our testimonies over a PA system. By the time it came round to me again, I got frustrated. I remember saying, "Well this isn't working," and just started asking people as they walked by if they wanted healing, using words of knowledge, etc. Some ignored me, and some responded and got touched by God. Dave Tomberlin, a 'Fresh Fire' associate, was with us and he and I were ministering together.

"Then we were in the room in the same place and my small son was there. And suddenly two other guys ran out of the room, saying that Dave Tomberlin had been killed. I asked them what I should do because I was looking after my son, and they said just bring him with me.

"Then I was in a large building (all still in the same place) in a car on the top floor. I had people in the car with me (I don't know who), and I was trying to get out of the building. I saw what looked like an elevator, but I wasn't sure I could get the car in, so I kept looking. I saw some other routes out which were like helter-skelter slides and stuff, came back to the elevator, got the car in, and the lift shot down really fast. It came to a stop and I drove out."

### Interpretation of Jeremy's dream

As a senior leader in relationship with us, we interpreted Jeremy's dream freely, because it flowed in with a frank, ongoing conversation we had been having about these things.

The dream suggests that in his present context, Jeremy has been giving all that he has to give, but is frustrated with platform ministry and its results.

Dave Tomberlin represents the aspirations and dreams Jeremy had for his current context: miracles, people healed, and many coming to know God. But those hopes have died. There's a call to move on and a reassurance that Jeremy's family will be fine. Others, for whom he is responsible, will go with him.

There will be several opportunities to leave, but some will be hasty and chaotic. One opportunity will be planned and ordered, and it will happen quickly. The headline of the dream is, "Slow down; don't panic. Change is coming for your ministry and family of an importance which will bring heaven to earth (the lift) and it has its own momentum."

A few weeks after interpreting Jeremy's dream and understanding that he was about to leave, and leave quickly, Jeremy was offered an outstanding and challenging ministry opportunity. In a mature way, he and his wife considered the matter before God. At that point, Tony, his "right-hand man", who had been told nothing, emailed us his dream for interpretation.

Your task is to use Tony's dream and its unedited interpretation as if you were giving the interpretation to Tony. How much will you decide to tell Tony?

### Tony's dream

"I was at my house and suddenly remembered that I was supposed to be at Jeremy's house (the associate pastor) before 4 p.m. But time had passed really quickly, I had completely forgotten about it, and I was annoyed about it because I really wanted to go and I was supposed to be there. I felt like I had been cheated because time had gone so quickly, quicker than normal. I went to the housing estate and was walking along toward the church building. Lots of people were walking past me in all directions and I just walked in a straight line toward the church building. I looked down at my feet and saw Jeremy's car keys on the floor. I knew that they were his car keys and I knew he had lost them. They didn't look like real car keys; they looked more like a TV remote with a big red button on the front that would unlock the car. So I thought I'd better go to his house to give him the keys, even though it was past 4 p.m.

"But when I got there, Jeremy's family had decided to move house for a while and the house was empty. When I returned to my car, I had kids in the back. As it turned out, later I went with the Jeremy to the new house and everything was fine."

### Unedited interpretation

In Tony's dream, there is also an urgency around a change of season (the number four). His feelings were upset. He felt cheated and annoyed at the sudden unexpected change.

The dream suggests Tony will inherit the associate pastor's role with responsibility for the young people, but he will miss Jeremy and his family. At some point, Tony will then join Jeremy and his wife in their new ministry and feel reconnected, settled, and content.

### Headline interpretation

Jeremy is leaving; it's going to take you by surprise; you will feel cheated and upset. You will run the ministry, before leaving the job to join Jeremy in his new ministry.

The above interpretation is unwise and unedited. It is both foretelling and directional. There is very little of this that you can legitimately tell Tony. Jeremy's situation is confidential; his own family have yet to be told.

As an interpreter, your job is to orientate Tony and fulfil the purpose of the dream. Your job is to bring him peace and to raise faith, to prepare him for what is to come, without betraying Jeremy's confidences.

> *"I have told you these things, so that in me you may have peace. In this world you will have trouble. But take heart! I have overcome the world."*[202]

---

202    John 16:33.

Write down what you would say to Tony.

Compare your interpretation with the interpretation at the end of the chapter.

Influence is a place of spiritual authority. It causes things to happen as a result of your prophecy or interpretation and people begin to recognize the grace of God upon your life. And when people begin to recognize the grace of God on your life, in gifting and wisdom, they begin to seek out your counsel.

## Counsel: Speaking truth to power

> *Those esteemed as pillars [leaders], gave me and Barnabas the right hand of fellowship when they recognised the grace given to me.*[203]

Some years ago God gave me a vision about working with leaderships. It was of pillars – rows of pillars – and over the top of them was a prophetic canopy of peace and prayer. It was a picture of one of the functions of the prophetic – to be a place of shelter for the leaders. In turn the pillars held up the covering, and together it provided a safe haven that drew people in from the world.

I saw rain begin to fall, and people heard the sound that was made when the Word of God hit the tent roof [the prophetic], which was held up by the pillars [the leaders]. This joining made a relational structure that the world ran into for refuge and shelter.

When the two ministries joined together, the structure was really powerful.

We have referred several times to the pivotal verses in Ephesians 4:11–13; as the different gift sets work together, the body of Christ is joined and held together by every (relational) supporting ligament to be filled with the fullness of Christ.

The imagery reflects that used in the Old Testament, in Ezekiel 37, where the dry bones of the body are joined together with (relational) tendons, to be filled with the breath of God. Into this picture of the body coming together, the Lord gives Ezekiel a command:

203    Galatians 2:9.

*"Son of man, take a stick of wood and write on it,*
*'Belonging to Judah and the Israelites associated with*
*him.' Then take another stick of wood, and write on it,*
*'Belonging to Joseph (that is, to Ephraim) and all the*
*Israelites associated with him.' Join them together into*
*one stick so that they will become one in your hand."*[204]

The consequences of that blending together are recorded in the rest of the chapter as: unity, cleansing, obedience, peace, increase, and the sanctuary of God among the people:

*"Then the nations will know that I the Lord make Israel*
*holy."*[205]

The symbolism of the representative names is interesting. Judah (Hebrew), meaning "prince with God" – key leadership. Ephraim – the son of Joseph, the dreamer and prophetic leader who stood beside Pharaoh and brought interpretation and counsel from God to help Pharaoh (the key leader) fulfil his mandate.

When the prophetic leaders bring counsel, stand with, and serve the church and ministry leaders, fruitfulness results in the world. Territory is taken. Order and life comes.

## The rise of the prophetic in team

### David's razor blade dream

David is a highly gifted seer. He is in part time "tent-making" employment but is also a trusted member of a thriving, vibrant church. He was part of the wider leadership community in the church.

### The dream

"I went into a shop to buy razor blades. I picked up a packet of really quality razor blades. The lady at the till told me that they would cost £43,000. I thought that was expensive, but the blonde lady manager came out of the office and said, 'No, they cost £34,000.' I thought that still costs a lot, but it's not the huge price that I had been asked before."

204     Ezekiel 37:16–17.
205     Ezekiel 27:28.

## Helpful symbolism

**Razor blades**: cutting edge prophetic words
**Quality**: to do it well is costly
**Till lady**: the authority of man exacting a high price
**£43,000**: a high cost has been demanded of David in the past for his giftedness, because of human thinking and religious attitudes

- 4 (in the negative): a recurring number symbol representing, in this context, the wisdom of man

- 3 (in the negative): representing religious tradition

**Shop manager:** the Holy Spirit
**£34,000** (positive): a recurring number symbol representing, in this context, the naming of a son

## The interpretation

"This dream shows your commitment to pay a high cost to use God's word at a high level. In the past you may have encountered difficulty because of other people's soulish or religious attitudes toward you, which was a high cost for you to pay. The Holy Spirit is now intervening on your behalf. There is a cost on your life for your gift function – it's expensive, but not as high as it had been. "34" symbolizes 'the naming of a son' – you are in a time of positioning."

## The application

David was clearly ready to be set in place (named as a son) as having a formal role in the prophetic team. After talking to the leadership of the church where I was having some input, they set David in place into a leadership function, with responsibility for the prophetic. David James Armstrong's name means, "He who supplants with a strong arm", and in naming this "son" as a part of the leadership, his role was released with greater authority in the sphere of the church community. In Romans 8, those who are led by the Spirit of God are sons of God.[206] The Greek word for son is Huios – it is a word representing a mature son, not an infant. Those who shave (razor blades) have come to maturity, and use the word with deliberation and precision.

---

206 Romans 8:14.

The naming of this son facilitates far more than a new leadership position. The application of the dream is for the church leadership to be enhanced in two ways:

- the completion of an already effective leadership team;
- the addition of a team member with a specific mandate to overthrow the enemy's influence.

> *The creation waits in eager expectation for the children of God to be revealed.*[207]

David's dream encourages and provides a vision for the prophetic to work with the church using the cutting edge of God's word to bring God's kingdom to earth. To stand in the place of counsel is an unseen task. It requires us to walk closely with God, and to stand beside others and serve the purposes of God in that particular season. In some seasons, those purposes are hidden behind the scenes and are very precise. They can easily be misunderstood and judged by those looking on, who know a tiny part of the story. In this way you will sometimes share in the sufferings of Christ, if you are called to minister at times of difficult leadership issues.

In its local expression (which is far harder than the trans-local role), the role of "counsel" can be extremely difficult because of politics, competition, misunderstandings, and spiritual attack. It can be hard to navigate the rivers of ministry, which John Wimber's mentor counselled him were "treacherous waters to row through".[208]

In partnership with the group of churches that I serve, who are my home base, we run the Prophetic Mentoring School to raise the prophetic in all its spheres. As we do, we realize that part of our role is to support and guide people as they serve the church. And to be a healing community for them if the journey has been a hard one.

To quote C. S. Lewis, "nothing [including the church itself] is yet in its true form."[209] We belong to a church and a people in process. It has, like any family, its great strengths and its weaknesses.

After one particularly difficult meeting, involving strong male leaders butting heads with one another, I was weary of the game. Running

---

207    Romans 8:19.
208    Carol Wimber, *John Wimber: The Way it Was*, Hodder and Stoughton, 1999.
209    C. S. Lewis, *Till We Have Faces*, Geoffrey Bles, 1956.

different employment options through my head, I picked up my son, who was three at the time. Out of the blue as we were driving home, from his car seat in the back of the car, Jonathan started to prophesy. The words he said cut through my discouragement: "Mummy, Jesus washed people's feet [serving the disciples]. He rode on a donkey [God's code word to me about immature ministries]. He died on a cross [laying down His life]." He paused for a minute or two and then continued, "Mummy, let's build a church." Needless to say, I stayed at my post.

The reason for this chapter is to help you navigate the occasionally choppy waters, so you can successfully work with God's revelation within the sphere of the church when you do. As you seek to serve the church, it will help you if you understand that there is a wisdom about tables and servants, which defines Christlike ministry. You get to choose which "table" you sit at, and your choice defines your ministry.

When Daniel was taken to sit at the table of the Babylonian king to work in revelation, dreams, and visions, he made an interesting decision when he recognized that the court of the king was a political environment with seductive and deceptive currents.

> *The king assigned them... food and wine from the king's table. They were to be trained for three years and after that they were to enter the king's service...*
>
> *But Daniel resolved not to defile himself with the royal food and wine.*[210]

I wonder, did Daniel, a devout Israelite, take note of Solomon's written warnings of hundreds of years before?

> *When you sit to dine with a ruler,*
> *note well what is before you...*
> *Do not crave his delicacies,*
> *for that food is deceptive [misleading].*[211]

Jesus picks up the table symbolism when a dispute arose among [the disciples] as to which of them was the greatest: "Who is greater, the one

---

210      Daniel 1:5, 8.
211      Proverbs 23:1, 3.

who is at the table or the one who serves? Is it not the one who is at the table? But I am among you as one who serves."[212]

Jesus then He gives a remarkable promise directing the disciples' gaze to a higher table in a higher kingdom: "You are those who have stood by me in my trials [the fellowship of His sufferings]. And I confer on you a kingdom, just as my Father conferred one on me, so that you may eat and drink at my table."[213]

There's a choice here: we need to decide whether to sit or to serve at the table of man, and that decision determines whether or not we sit at God's table of authority and counsel.

This is, of course, a heart decision, not a job description. There are times when we are called to the table of leadership to complete a specific task in a specific season. We need to know when to sit at the table and when to turn the tables over.

But it's at those times when we, like Daniel, need to be alert to the seductive quality of some of the food that can be served at those tables, so that we can be heard on high. Daniel's integrity shone like a beacon in a political court. At great cost to himself, he refused to play politics or curry favour. It gave him a high level of authority and influence both in heaven and on earth. When Daniel prayed, heaven moved:

> "Do not be afraid, Daniel. Since the first day that you
> set your mind to gain understanding and to humble
> yourself before your God, your words were heard, and I
> have come in response to them."[214]

This place of mature, pure, prophetic authority can be lacking in our Western churches.

> "Which of [us] has stood in the council of the Lord to
> see or to hear His Word?...

> "Is not my word like fire," declares the Lord, "and like a
> hammer that breaks a rock in pieces?"[215]

---

212      Luke 22:27.
213      Luke 22:28–30.
214      Daniel 10:12.
215      Jeremiah 23:18, 29.

## Heaven's court is in session vision

One day I was preparing to lead a residential retreat when God showed me a vision.

### Scene 1

"I saw a court. God began to speak to me about leaders standing in His council: 'My people are dying and leaders search for their own glory. Walk in heaven's courts. Court is in session and they have been distracted by the things of man. Circumcise your hearts.'"

### Scene 2

"I was led to a flower-filled meadow to sit at God's table. The command came, 'Feed the hungry. It's time for the oil.'"

"At God's table, I saw rows of oil in jars which were to be given away. People were then given this dangerous oil to radically change their situations. 'This oil is given to others for their provision, life in all its fullness, and for the joy of their children. It's dangerous oil – it comes from the anointing oil given to you. In the place of cleansing, you will also find a place of anointing.'"

As we stand in God's counsel, we begin to be dangerous dreamers, distributing dangerous oil. A cleansing is taking place across the body of Christ, as our hearts come into alignment with His purity of purpose: Christlike sincerity and truth.

## Exercise 6.4: Your own table vision

There are different tables in Scripture:

- Psalm 23:5: The table of provision – "You prepare a table before me in the presence of my enemies."

- Luke 24:30–31: The table of the revelation of Christ – "When he was at the table with them, he took bread, gave thanks, broke it and began to give it to them. Then their eyes were opened and they recognised him."

- Revelation 3:19–21: The table of cleansing – "Those whom I love I rebuke and discipline. So be earnest and repent. Here I am! I stand at the door and knock. If anyone hears my voice and opens the door, I will come in and eat with that person, and they with me. To the one who is victorious, I will give the right to sit with me on my throne, just as I was victorious and sat down with my Father on his throne."

- Luke 22:29–30a: The table of authority – "And I confer on you a kingdom, just as my Father conferred one on me, so that you may eat and drink at my table in my kingdom."

### The exercise

Step 1: Ask the Lord to show you a table. Write down what you see.

Step 2: Ask the Lord which table you are sitting at. Write down what He shows you.

Step 3: Ask the Lord what the message of the table is for you at this time in your life. Write down anything He shows you.

Take time to interpret your vision fully, and ask God about the application of your vision. Share this interpretation and its application with a trusted friend, which will give you a context to talk about it and further apply it into the context of your life.

## Using and administrating dreams and visions in church gatherings

I have a particular love for Amos. He describes himself as "one of the shepherds of Tekoa",[216] a small town just south of Bethlehem. He understood the context and the times he lived in, and his visions were important enough to be written down as a lasting and living message to God's people. Amos makes three statements that speak to us today, firstly by being one of the people, not a priest or a courtier. Yet he made a significant contribution. He also tells us, "Surely the Lord does nothing without revealing his plan to his servants the prophets."[217] If Amos is right, and history suggests that he is, then leaders in churches, ministries, and pastorates can benefit greatly from their accurate

---

216    Amos 1:1.
217    Amos 3:7.

foresight. But Amos also asks us the question, "Do two walk together unless they have agreed to do so?"[218]

Our observation is that when no one has a fully functioning awareness of the process by which the prophetic and leadership walk together and there is a disconnect at best, this can easily become a frustration. There is a need to clearly define how dreams and visions work in the church meeting setting. It allows the leaders and prophetic people to work together with enjoyment and peace.

If the church and prophetic leaders don't define how dreams and visions work in church meetings, either someone else will define it or it will be both unfocused and unclear. But when the leadership and the seers understand that revelation brings help through safe practice into the church, it becomes helpful. Both parties begin to settle down and work together.

A mature prophetic leader can help to shape the prophetic in the church by working with both leaders and people to understand and benefit from the prophetic process. Without clear prophetic processes in place, the sense of how to operate and administrate prophecy, dreams, and visions is obscured, and expectations can clash.

I visited one church where the prophetic people were faithfully copying the twenty-five-year-old traditional use of the prophetic in the church. This now large church had grown from a tiny church which met in somebody's living room, where it had been easy and important for everyone to bring words they had received prophetically from God for each meeting. This model of church is described by Paul in 1 Corinthians 14:26: "When you come together, each of you has a hymn, or a word of instruction, a revelation, a tongue or an interpretation. Everything must be done so that the church may be built up."

The older members of this congregation told me that in those days people could hardly wait to get to church to see what God would show them. They had a high value on prophecy. The church had, at that stage, been a congregation of thirty, then fifty people. But now, as a church of more than 850, no one had updated their protocol. The people kept on reproducing what they had always done, bringing a continuous stream of visions, dreams, and prophecy to the leaders to be given on Sundays

---

218    Amos 3:3.

in the meeting. Both the people and the leaders were expressing frustration. The people were confused, wondering why their individual revelation wasn't shared, and the leaders didn't realize that the church, having grown and matured, needed a maturing prophetic protocol.

When the prophetic was being released in the form of visions and dreams, no one recorded, interpreted, weighed, or applied the revelation. A growing disconnection between the people and the leadership was the result. Important revelation was falling to the ground. The church had begun to despise revelation; no one quite knew what it was for any more. The leaders had fallen into playing the role of "grown-ups" and the prophetic people had become "children" to be humoured or contained.

> *Do not quench the Spirit. Do not treat prophecies with contempt but test them all; hold on to what is good.*[219]

Paul's instructions in 1 Corinthians 14 bring a godly balance into larger corporate settings so that dreams and visions can be useful:

> *Therefore my brothers, be eager to prophesy... but everything should be done in a fitting and orderly way.*[220]

> *Two or three prophets should speak, and the others should weigh carefully what is said.*[221]

We can therefore learn:

- There was a need to give a clear lead to the people in the church, to bring unity and a common understanding and practice to the church. The fact is that everybody still gets to play, but at a more mature level, bringing the right revelation in the right way to the right place so that it can bring fruitfulness to the church.

- If the leader doesn't define this, everyone will have a different agenda. A lack of clarity brings confusion. And prophetic

---

219    1 Thessalonians 5:19–21.
220    1 Corinthians 14:39–40.
221    1 Corinthians 14:29.

people don't work well with confusion – they were made for revelation and clarity.

- A basic understanding of prophecy and prophetic literacy for both the people and the leadership needed to be taught. This framework or "order", as Paul puts it, is a support for the abundant growth of the prophetic in the garden of the church.

- As the seers in the church are taught to use dreams and visions effectively, it enables them to dovetail revelation neatly into individual church meetings.

Bringing revelation during a church meeting works smoothly when everyone understands that the meeting leader will be asking themselves several things:

- Does the topic of the vision or dream fit in with the sermon?

- Does it complement the worship?

- Is there going to be a planned ministry time into which the revelation will speak?

- How much can we fit into the time constraints of this meeting?

In this way, seers become mature people who work alongside and behind the scenes, with and for the leaders of the meeting. That communication and unity brings strength and peace. The seers will begin to weigh their own dreams and visions because they understand that there is an intelligent order to the meeting time, with certain articulated criteria for publicly shared revelation, so that they can be at peace.

The prophetic people, when trained, will already be asking:

- Who or what is the revelation about?

- What type of revelation is it? And what is its source?

- What is its message and does it line up with Scripture?

- To whom does the revelation need to be given? Is it for me, for another individual, or for the church? To answer this question, ask yourself, "Who might need to apply this revelation, and in what timing? Is it a 'right now' message?" If not, it can wait.

- Edification, encouragement, and comfort dreams and visions may relate to the season that the church is in, or may be for an individual or a group within the church.

- Exhortation and cleansing revelation may well fit in with the sermon topic. God may be using them to confirm the sermon with a repeating message.

- Direction and foretelling messages are usually to be recorded privately and weighed and applied in a wider context by the leadership. If these messages are initially spoken out, then momentum can be dissipated in a moment of "thrill" and then forgotten. They have a more strategic use which isn't fulfilled by quickly sharing them in a public setting.

- Dreams showing areas for prayer need to be received and applied, to prosper the church: "seek the peace... of the city [church] to which I have carried you... Pray to the Lord for it, because if it prospers, you too will prosper."[222]

- Dreams and visions which reveal ministry or healing words may be for the whole meeting, if a time of ministry is planned. Or God may be wanting to minister into specific people's situations, where the interpretations are delivered to an individual or to a pastor who will deal with them in a separate conversation.

We need to have an individual church protocol for messages from dreams and visions, which are given one to one. If they are more than encouraging messages, the protocol of running them past a mature prophetic point person first, or a pastoral contact, brings added safety.

---

222     Jeremiah 29:7.

I recently sat in a church gathering where the pastor of the church stood up and said a very sweet but incompetent sentence: "I have just seen this… and I know Jesus is talking to us about it, but I don't know what it means." And then the meeting moved on. Their team clearly wasn't working well. There was no one to whom this church leader could turn in that moment to interpret his vision.

A mature weighing team, to whom visions and dreams are sent during the week, can help leaders. It can relate to and give feedback to the prophetic people and call them to pray in response to revelation when necessary, and filter words for the leadership, so that the headlines of revelation can be communicated to the leaders where necessary. This focused summary can fuel, inform, and confirm the leadership agenda.

Chapter 6 includes a detailed exercise which takes you through this mature weighing process, to give you experience of producing a summary of revelation which is flowing to an individual church, and then present it in an accessible and helpful way to church and ministry leaders.

This maturity comes with training and good practice, as people become aware of the immaturity of presumptuous interpretation and they begin to weigh, wait upon God, and recognize the purpose of what He is showing them. In this way the prophetic becomes a fruitful place where God's voice rings out with clarity and truth to galvanize, heal, and hearten His people.

> *Even in the case of lifeless things that make sounds…*
> *how will anyone know what tune is being played unless*
> *there is distinction in the notes? Again, if the trumpet*
> *does not sound a clear call, who will get ready for*
> *battle?… Since you are eager for the gifts of the Spirit,*
> *try to excel in those that build up the church.*[223]

To excel takes training for both people and leaders. A dose of common sense and security is needed in the interactions between those who see and those who are asked to lead. Grace and security means that the leaders and those who see dreams and visions don't have to get it right 100 per cent of the time.

---

223     1 Corinthians 14:7–8, 12.

When I was just starting out in ministry, God showed me one Sunday that He wanted to touch people who had been disappointed. The speaker that morning was a well-known international speaker. The meeting leader was of course keen to give them as much time to minister as was possible, so decided not to use any ministry words that morning. Halfway through the preach, the speaker stopped, changed tack, and said, "I have a strong sense that God wants us to stop and minister to anyone who is carrying disappointment." Forty people streamed forward.

You see, it is God who is in charge, not us. Everybody can relax. Our job is simply to be faithful to what He has shown us in dreams and visions. Not only faithful, but good-humouredly faithful. God will take up the responsibility to sort it out if necessary.

> "Because you have been trustworthy in a very
> small matter, take charge" [of more resources and
> responsibilities].[224]

## Exercise set: Weighing dreams and visions for a church meeting

For the sake of this exercise, you are being given the position of weighing dreams and visions before they are shared at a Sunday church gathering. You have been given these four dreams and visions by members of the congregation, shortly before the meeting begins. Crucially, you have also been told that the sermon topic for that Sunday meeting is, "Our impact upon the world". The worship songs have been chosen to reflect that topic. Your task is to interpret each dream or vision and decide whether each message should be shared publicly at the meeting or not, before comparing your conclusions with the answers at the end of the chapter.

The context of these four dreams and visions is that they were brought to the weighing team by different members of the congregation of a large church shortly before the Sunday morning gathering. The seers were submitting them in order that they could be shared during the meeting.

---

224      Luke 19:17.

## Exercise 6.5: The eagles of intercession vision

### The vision

"I saw a landscape in my vision. The landscape was arid and desert-like, sandy with dusty stones, no water or vegetation. Riding along was a single-file line of dark horsemen. I knew they were the enemy.

"Suddenly eagle after eagle began to fly in overhead from the east, until the sky was dark with eagles. They completely blocked out the watery sun. As the light darkened, the horsemen got smaller and smaller and weaker and weaker. Springs of water began to bubble on the earth, gathering into pools. Around the pools it became green. As the enemy lost his power, the people began to get stronger and to overcome the things that were against them. I saw some of them being physically sick."

Interpret the message of the vision. Then decide if it should be shared at the meeting. Answer the questions to unlock the vision:

- Who or what is this vision about?

- What type of vision is it and what is its source?

- What type of protocol do I need to apply to interpret this type of vision?

### Helpful symbolism

**Desert** (negative symbol): barrenness, infertility, temptation, trials, place away from God

**Horsemen** (negative symbol): conquest, spiritual warfare, authority

**Eagle** (positive symbol): royalty, seer, Spirit of revelation, strength, swift, lifted by the Spirit, victorious

**(Watery) sun** (negative symbol): false light (revelation)

**Springs of water** (positive symbol): Holy Spirit, the word of God, cleansing prayers, the water of the Spirit

**Physically sick** (positive symbol): being freed from oppression

Use the answers to the questions to come up with an interpretation and answer the question: would you ask the seer to share this vision at the church meeting?

Compare your answer and interpretation with those in the interpretation set at the end of the chapter.

## Exercise 6.6: Andrew's window dream

### The context

Andrew worked in a ministry, ministering to those who lived on the streets.

### The dream

"I was sitting in a comfortable chair in my ground-floor office, looking out, positioned by a huge window. As I was sitting there, gradually cardboard boxes were put inside over the window – piled up high. So the window was covered and cluttered. The boxes were accumulating. There were voices outside and I knew people were waiting to come in."

Interpret the message of this dream. Then decide if it should be shared at the meeting.

What does the vision mean? Answer the questions to unlock the dream:

- Who or what is this dream about?
- What type of dream is it and what is its source?
- What type of protocol do I need to apply to interpret this type of dream?

### Helpful symbolism

**Comfortable** (positive symbol): settled, at rest, in a place of peace; (negative symbol): too comfortable and unaware of the situation around you

**Office** (positive symbol): position in an organization

**Head office** (five-fold) (positive symbol): God's "Head Office", authority; (negative symbol): structure removed from the substance of real life

**Huge window** (positive symbol): place of revelation, flow of the Spirit, fresh air

**Boxes** (negative symbol): confined or restricted, "boxed in", "boxed up" – put on one side, limited thinking

**Significant words or phrases:** Covered, cluttered

Use the sense of the story, the answers to the questions, and the helpful symbolism list above to write an interpretation of the dream that you would give to the seer.

Compare your interpretation with the interpretation at the end of the chapter. Would you ask this seer to share this dream at the church meeting?

## Exercise 6.7: Big ship dream

### The context
This dream was shared at a dreams and visions course which we did with a local church. The dreamer lived in a small village, surrounded by other small villages. He was an insightful, caring, pastoral person.

### The dream
"I dreamt of a big sailing ship on a stormy sea. It was in full sail and the waves were tossing it around. People were trying to hold on to ropes on the deck, but some were falling into the sea. But the big ship kept on going. A flotilla of smaller ships were picking up the people who had fallen into the sea."

Interpret the message of this dream. Then decide if it should be shared at the meeting.

What does the vision mean? Answer the questions to unlock the dream:

- Who or what is this dream about?

- What type of dream is it and what is its source?

- What type of protocol do I need to apply to interpret this type of dream?

### Helpful symbolism
**Big ship** (positive symbol): large church, large business, strength, voyage, passage

**Small boat** (positive symbol): small church, personal ministry, business, support

**Stormy sea** (negative symbol): angry voices, difficult circumstances, lack of peace

These questions will also help you:

- What would a big ship normally do with its sails in a storm?

- What do the big ship and the small ships represent?

- Does the attitude of the dreamer appear in the dream?

Use the sense of the story, the answers to the questions, and the helpful symbolism list above to write an interpretation of the dream that you would give to the seer.

Compare your interpretation with the interpretation at the end of the chapter. Would you ask this seer to share this dream in the meeting?

## Exercise 6.8: "Thy kingdom come" vision

### The vision

"I saw us going out into the community and we had what I thought were stakes. As we prayed and prophesied we were like stakes embedding the truth of God's word into the community. When surveyors are plotting new sites, they put stakes to mark the layout. I saw our estate and these stakes being driven hard into the ground. They had writing on them like 'hope', 'love', 'joy' – but they sat there, almost like seed markers, but nothing was growing up. And then I saw what looked like very thin strands starting to join up all the stakes. It wasn't going point to point, in order; there was a fluidity; it was as if it was living. Then I realized the strands were very thin flames of the Holy Spirit, alive, literally dancing from one stake to the next. All the strands were joining the words spoken, the actions of love, the prayers that had been staked into the estate over the years, and making a massive golden awning. It rose higher and higher, providing shelter and protection. It was God's kingdom on the estate. A tent cover, there was a sense that anything not of God couldn't stick without getting destroyed."

Interpret this vision. What does the vision mean? Answer the questions to unlock the vision:

- Who or what is this vision about?

- What type of vision is it and what is its source?

- What type of protocol do I need to apply to interpret this type of vision?

Write an interpretation of the vision that you would give to the seer.

Compare your interpretation with the interpretation at the end of the chapter. Was there anything you missed? Would you ask this seer to share this vision at the church meeting?

As a teenager I came upon my Father's Bible open on his desk. He had underlined some words written by Paul: "I have a daily burden of my anxiety about all the churches."[225] It was a glimpse into his heart about the welfare of the church that he pastored, led, and taught.

I married a man who also holds within his own heart a dream about the church, "that a group of people can live together according to beatitudinal values, shining Christ's light into the world". It's a dream we consider worth fighting for.

In around AD 95, John the apostle had a vision: "Write on a scroll what you see and send it to the seven churches."[226] The Book of Revelation contains the seven letters written to those seven churches. Each one had different things for which Jesus commended them, including their service, love, faith, purity, hard work, and perseverance. He saw their needs, afflictions, and difficult circumstances, and even when He corrected their failures – lack of spiritual awareness, compromise, immorality, or hypocrisy – He always laid out a path to restoration with the promise of a reward for those who travelled it.

Earlier in the New Testament, Paul writes that the prophetic gift is one that Jesus has given to the church to help it mature, to help bring the knowledge of God and to grow into the unity He prayed for.[227]

Our job is to help the churches we serve to go on that same pathway to restoration and fruitfulness.

---

225     2 Corinthians 11:28 (ISV).
226     Revelation 1:11.
227     Ephesians 4:11–13.

## Teaching points for chapter 5

- Dreams and visions chronicle the life of the church. They are a mirror image of what is going on and can inform the leaders so that they can prepare for what is coming.

- Leaders find it helpful to have clear, credible prophetic seers who can collate, weigh, and present a summary of the revelation which is coming to and from the church.

- Training, mentoring, and support will help both these seers and the interface between the seers and the church to be effective.

- Dreams and visions will expose the hidden things and expose the enemy's strategies to hinder what God wants to do.

- Dreams and visions will find the things among people that keep God from moving on people's behalf, and will do it redemptively.

- Dreams and visions bring affirmation and commendation.

- Dreams and visions will help you personally and corporately to know and to realize what God has called you to do.

- Dreams and visions bring conviction, correction, and vindication.

- Dreams and visions involve us in loosing God's purposes on the earth.

- Dreams and visions inform effective intercession.

- Dreams and visions release the purposes of God into church gatherings.

- Dreams and visions will expose the hidden strategies of the enemy, which hinder the purposes of God.

There is a sequential process by which an interpreter grows in relationship and credibility within a church context:

- Affirm: with pure motives and a giving heart.

- Confirm: a hidden stage where your heart is tested and you mature and grow. Seek training and mentoring in this season to prepare you for the next season.

- Influence: use this influence wisely. You will see more than you are able to say. The key here is to work with the purpose for which God is sending the revelation.

- Counsel: with credibility and a track record of effective influence comes an increasing role of sought-out counsel.

- Leaders benefit tremendously from a fresh perspective on their situations. But a seer walks with God, not leadership, at a heart level, maintaining a neutral, dispassionate stance with a heart fixed on God's perspective.

- We have found that key prophetic people working in church at the local level need support and training to do this, because of the different personality types, politics, and competition that can often creep into any organization.

- External affirmation and counsel help seers to maintain an unbiased point of view and prevent them being destroyed by, or caught up in, internal church dynamics.

- Mature interpretation is a voice which facilitates what God wants to do at any given time.

- In church gatherings, commonly articulated and mutually understood protocol draws leadership and prophetic people on to the same page, so that the gift can mature in the house.

- Working together under one set of literate guidelines matures both the seers and the leadership in the use of revelation. It enables them to work in peace and unity.

- There is a vast difference between protocol for a small gathering and a large church gathering, because of the practical dynamics.

# CHAPTER 5: ANSWERS AND INTERPRETATIONS

## Exercise 6.1: Affirmation vision – rooms, stars, and wells

### The vision

### Scene 1

"I saw a large room in heaven and I knew it belonged to your church. It was pure white and completely empty, like a vast hall. It was beautiful, warm, inviting, and full of God's presence."

### Scene 2

"I saw a black sky, and one by one stars lit up as bright lights in the sky."

### Scene 3

"I saw a well which had been stopped up, being uncovered."

### The interpretation

**About:** The church.

The interpreter might say, "This vision carries a message of assurance and hope. The messages in the vision repeat in the accompanying Scripture [Genesis 26:4, 18–22, 24]. This repeating message highlights its importance. The individual members of the church will light up, bringing God's light. The church will be fruitful in bringing new people to Jesus. The revelation suggests you have known some testing and difficulties, but you are coming into a time of fruitfulness. And God is giving you room to flourish, a place that is uniquely yours, which no one else will occupy or remove."

## Exercise 6.2: Confirmation vision – sailing ship

### The vision

"I see a tall, beautiful, stately sailing ship moored in the harbour besides the quay. It hadn't just come from the sea; it had been put in the harbour ready for relaunch. It carried the king's flag and was secure, steadfast, graceful, and at ease."

### The interpretation

**About:** The church.

**Type:** Confirmation – repeating messages highlight the importance of the message of the vision.

**Protocol:** Interpret freely.

**Sense of the story:** There is a beautiful vessel which is ready for a journey.

The interpreter might say, "This vision speaks of the church and its call to move in the things of the spirit, with a high ability to catch the wind. The sense of a stately vessel which is at ease and full of grace shows the secure and statured quality of the church. This vision shows who you are made to be, and those hallmarks are hallmarks of the Holy Spirit's ministry. The authority and protection of the king's flag speaks of dignity, affirmation, and security, all of which you are invited to walk in. There is a new journey about to begin, but it's in His grace and charge, in the Spirit and not in the dry things of the flesh."

## Exercise 6.3: Using influence with wisdom and discretion – two dreams which work together

### The dream

"I was at my house and suddenly remembered that I was supposed to be at Jeremy's house (the associate pastor) before 4 p.m. But time had passed really quickly, I had completely forgotten about it, and I was annoyed about it because I really wanted to go and I was supposed to be there. I felt like I had been cheated because time had gone so quickly, quicker than normal. I went to the housing estate and was walking along toward the church building. Lots of people were walking past me in all directions and I just walked in a straight line toward the church building. I looked down at my feet and saw Jeremy's car keys on the floor. I knew that they were his car keys and I knew he had lost them. They didn't look like real car keys; they looked more like a TV remote with a big red button on the front that would unlock the car. So I thought I'd better go to his house to give him the keys, even though it was past 4 p.m.

"But when I got there, the Jeremy's family had decided to move house for a while and the house was empty. When I returned to my car,

I had kids in the back. As it turned out, later I went with the Jeremy to the new house and everything was fine."

### The interpretation

The interpreter might say, "This dream is about your ministry in the church. It seems to suggest you may feel a bit surprised by some of the things that are happening in the ministry, which seem a bit of a muddle.

"But this is a great dream. Your own personal ministry will be growing in responsibility and God will be giving you all the keys you need. God has sent you a personal and direct message in this dream. It's your headline for the coming season. It's a season of change, and God is reassuring you in the dream that everything is going to be fine. You may want to go with that and aim to be very assured during any changes ahead, because the dream clearly says that it will work out in a really good way. God seems to be reaching out to you giving you reassurance, authority, and an upgrade. There is an inherent commendation in the dream that God trusts you, Tony, enough to give you more authority."

## Exercise set: Weighing dreams and visions for a church meeting

## Exercise 6.5: The eagles of intercession vision

### The vision

"I saw a landscape in my vision. The landscape was arid and desert-like, sandy with dusty stones, no water or vegetation. Riding along was a single-file line of dark horsemen. I knew they were the enemy.

"Suddenly eagle after eagle began to fly in overhead from the east, until the sky was dark with eagles. They completely blocked out the watery sun. As the light darkened, the horsemen got smaller and smaller and weaker and weaker. Springs of water began to bubble on the earth, gathering into pools. Around the pools it became green. As the enemy lost his power, the people began to get stronger and to overcome the things that were against them. I saw some of them being physically sick."

### The interpretation

**About:** The prophetic seers.

**Type:** Revelation prayer dream from God.

**Protocol:** Interpret clearly.

**Sense of the story:** The eagles can limit the power of the enemy and free the people.

This vision calls in the prophetic intercessors to work together to influence both territory and the landscape of people's lives. Their operation in a situation will weaken the enemy, rob him of authority, and strengthen the prophetic people, bringing a level of deliverance to the areas which have been affecting their lives, so that the land will become fruitful again.

This vision is for the church intercessors and prophetic seers. It is a corporate message which should be shared at the church meeting. It confirms the message of the sermon: "Our impact upon the world".

The vision and its interpretation can both be shared, but there is also a strategic application for this vision: to lead the intercessors to decide how they can work together to fulfil the function that they are given in the vision. The leaders and the intercessors need to take this vision and shape a strategy to fulfil the call given through this revelation.

## Exercise 6.6: Andrew's window dream

### The dream

"I was sitting in a comfortable chair in my ground-floor office, looking out, positioned by a huge window. As I was sitting there, gradually cardboard boxes were put inside over the window – piled up high. So the window was covered and cluttered. The boxes were accumulating. There were voices outside and I knew people were waiting to come in."

### The interpretation

**About:** Andrew.

**Type:** Revelation dream from God.

**Protocol:** Be clear but relaxed in your observations.

- Record your interpretation for future reference.

- Work in team.

- Ensure the seer knows the weighing procedure for weighing your interpretation.

- Be general, not directive.

**Sense of the story:** If this goes on, soon you won't be able to see.

This dream is sent to protect the effectiveness of Andrew's gift which is being boxed in and increasingly made ineffective by things which are being put around him.

The interpreter might say, "This dream suggests that you may feel very comfortable in your role at the moment. It also speaks about your abilities to work in revelation and to be aware of others and their needs. There is an interesting hint that you may be a little 'boxed in' and that your once-clear dream of what God is doing has become obstructed in a way that could affect your ministry and your awareness of what He is showing you."

This dream is for the dreamer, not the church meeting.

## Exercise 6.7: Big ship dream

### The dream

"I dreamt of a big sailing ship on a stormy sea. It was in full sail and the waves were tossing it around. People were trying to hold on to ropes on the deck, but some were falling into the sea. But the big ship kept on going. A flotilla of smaller ships were picking up the people who had fallen into the sea."

### The interpretation

**About:** The church situation in the locality.

**Type:** Elements of revelation, prayer, cleansing, and life-processing dream.

**Protocol:** Interpret clearly to facilitate intercession.

- Record your interpretation for future reference.

- Work in team.

- Ensure the seer knows the weighing procedure for weighing your interpretation.

- Be general, not directive.

**Sense of the story:** People need rescuing.

Unedited interpretation: "The dream suggests that a church has been through some stormy seas which may be having a knock-on effect on people in the church, because of bad sailing. The dream indicates that there has been some disregard for how to manage the storm's effects on the people involved. Smaller churches appear to be more aware and are coming alongside to care for those who are being badly affected and lost from the church congregation, again through no fault of their own.

The dream suggests that the dreamer may be feeling cross about that careless and inept sailing, especially when they see the effect it has had on others."

This dream should not be given in the meeting. A carefully worded interpretation could be given to the leaders and the church intercessors: "A dream has been sent in that suggests the church may be sailing through some waters which may be hard to navigate. It suggests a need for prayer and care so that people don't get separated from the church body. There may even be some people who have been lost and need a level of rescue and protection."

### Teaching point

This dream uses a big ship to represent the church. Other familiar symbols representing the church are: mother, coach/bus, big plane, train, a pride of lions or a family, although the list goes on and is of course dependent on the context of these symbols, which gives them meaning.

## Exercise 6.8: "Thy kingdom come" vision

### The vision

"I saw us going out into the community and we had what I thought were stakes. As we prayed and prophesied we were like stakes embedding the truth of God's word into the community. When surveyors are plotting new sites, they put stakes to mark the layout. I saw our estate and these stakes being driven hard into the ground. They had writing on them like 'hope', 'love', 'joy' – but they sat there, almost like seed markers, but nothing was growing up. And then I saw what looked like very thin strands starting to join up all the stakes. It wasn't going point to point, in order; there was a fluidity; it was as if it was living. Then I realized the strands were very thin flames of the Holy Spirit, alive, literally dancing from one stake to the next. All the strands were joining the words spoken, the actions of love, the prayers that had been staked into the estate over the years, and making a massive golden awning. It rose higher and higher, providing shelter and protection. It was God's kingdom on the estate. A tent cover, there was a sense that anything not of God couldn't stick without getting destroyed."

### The interpretation

**About:** The church and the community.

**Type:** Revelation from God, bringing encouragement and edification.

**Protocol:** Interpret freely.

**Sense of the story:** We are impacting the community in what we do.

It is an encouragement to persevere, to be utterly bold, and to pray extravagant prayers to speak out words, and to push outward with ministries, and to pray protection for what is to come. The whole thing is about us impacting the land for God. The tent is a place of transformation because of the Holy Spirit covering. More than that, it is a place of celebration and joy, because it is like a wedding marquee.

As we intercede, the ground very slowly starts to seed as we work with the Holy Spirit, through revelation and praying back the promises of God.

This vision is an encouragement to the whole church. It should be shared at the meeting by giving both the vision and the clear interpretation. It echoes both the sermon topic and the message that came in the eagles of intercession vision. The church will benefit from hearing the repeating message, but the leadership will also benefit from having their attention drawn to the repeating theme of the link between prayer and their desire to impact the community.

# Chapter 6

# THE MATURE USE OF REVELATION: MAKING IT REAL

*What is seen was not made out of what was visible.*[228]

Once I had learnt to interpret visions and dreams, I began to realize the huge fun that was to be had when people would bring those little pieces of revelation which had bubbled up into their lives and we would see them bear fruit and change things. I watched Jesus doing it again: reaching down to set people free, speaking the Jubilee which was first expressed in Leviticus: "Proclaim liberty throughout the land to all its inhabitants."[229] Every fifty years slaves were released, belongings were restored, and people came home.

In Luke 4, Jesus proclaimed the spiritual Jubilee when He quoted the words of Isaiah 61, announcing 'the year of the Lord's favour',

> "*The Spirit of the Lord is on me,*
> *… he has anointed me*
> *to proclaim good news to the poor…*
> *to proclaim freedom for the prisoners*
> *and recovery of sight for the blind,*
> *to set the oppressed free,*
> *to proclaim the year of the Lord's favour.*"[230]

---

228     Hebrews 11:3.
229     Leviticus 25:10.
230     Luke 4:18–19.

And it is this same Jubilee which we have seen echoed in the words of Isaiah 55, when revelation is dropped from heaven, on to the landscape of our lives:

> *"You will go out in joy*
> *and be led forth in peace;*
> *the mountains and hills*
> *will burst into song before you,*
> *and all the trees of the field*
> *will clap their hands.*
> *Instead of the thorn-bush will grow the juniper,*
> *and instead of briers the myrtle will grow."*[231]

As Isaiah's "instead" comes into play, we become inhabitants of a land that was once overrun with briers and thistles.

Dreams and visions from God are an invitation to find that same freedom being spoken over our own lives: to be more free, to heal, to be at peace, to laugh,[232] to pray. Waves of God's mercy begin crashing over us and we catch those waves of revelation by applying what they say to our lives:

> *Deep calls to deep*
> *in the roar of your waterfalls;*
> *all your waves and breakers*
> *have swept over me.*[233]

The creative power of the Holy Spirit forms something that began in the unseen will of the heavenly Father, so that people can partner with what God is doing, move out of the cul-de-sacs of their lives into the rhythms of His grace, overcoming any schemes of the enemy.

As well as that exciting moment of interpretation and application, it is, of course, the beginning of a journey for people as they choose to live in the good of that and continue in positive change.

For you, moving from accurate interpretation to bringing renewal takes experience (practice), anointing (prayer), and maturity (time).

---

231  Isaiah 55:12–13.
232  Proverbs 31:25.
233  Psalm 42:7.

In this chapter you are asked to go beyond the interpretation of the revelation, to come up with a strategy and a time frame which applies it to the real-life scenario given to you.

## The maturing skill base

| Revelation | Interpretation | Application | Timing |
|---|---|---|---|
| Seeing what God is showing you through dreams and visions. | Asking questions: <br>• Who or what is it about? <br>• What type of revelation is it and what is its source? <br>• What does it mean? Look at the sense of the story, its important symbols and statements. <br>• Run its message through a scriptural filter. <br>• Use the filter of team, especially for correction, direction, foretelling, or warning revelation. | • Into which situation does the interpretation apply? Understanding the context of the real life situation will help you considerably. <br>• Use good protocol: how much of the interpretation is to be shared, in what way, and with whom? | • Applying it in the right place at the right time. <br>• "*Kairos* is a moment in time when a portal is opened between time and eternity so an event can take place in its fullness, as appointed by God."[236] <br>• Living a life focused on God and listening to His still, small voice will position you to respond to these pivotal moments. |

From left to right, this diagram lays out the stages we go through to interpret and apply each dream or vision. It also lays out the maturity continuum of an interpreter.

234    Faisal Malick, *The Destiny of Islam in the End Times*, Destiny Image Publishers Inc., 2007.

Timing is the last piece of the interpreter's skill base to emerge. When that shift happens, God will trust you with time-critical dreams and visions. You only need to miss the timing once or twice to wake up to its importance and to be prepared never to miss it again. That, too, is part of your natural development.

The key with timing is to hold a file of significant revelation on one side if you are not sure where it fits. That file can be mental, digital, or practical, to be ready to access at the moment when that window of time opens in front of you, so you can reach back and slot it into place. It's much like suddenly noticing a hole in a jigsaw and realizing that you have exactly the puzzle piece that fits. As time goes on you will begin to be ready to apply revelation to events that are yet to happen.

The use of a systematic approach will help you avoid the presumption that is the pitfall of inexperienced ministry. One of the most unsettling passages of Scripture I have ever read comes in 1 Corinthians 1:17: Paul writes that he was called to minister "not with wisdom and eloquence, lest the cross of Christ be emptied of its power".

We can do that? We can empty the most powerful breakthrough that happened on earth of its power? That Scripture alone is enough to keep us rightly humble, thorough in our good processes and safe practices, and healthily dependent on the Spirit of God:

> *If any of you lacks wisdom, you should ask God, who gives generously to all.*[235]

Because this chapter is about applying dreams and visions to achieve their purpose, we will handle each revelation set differently, and take time to explore the content and matters they raise. Each exercise set requires you to find time to put aside the "elephants" in your life, to listen deeply. As you do, you will hear the voice of God and encounter His grace.

## Dreams and visions exercise set 1: Finding the real-life Application and actions arising from dreams and visions

The dreams and visions in this set are strategic in caring for the person to whom the revelation is given. God is watching over their well-being.

---

235    James 1:5.

An elderly lady called Irene in one of my discipleship groups once brought us a poem:

> *Wash my feet, Lord, wash my feet,*
> *As I stand at the Mercy Seat.*
> *I've been walking on the world's highway,*
> *My feet need cleaning at the end of the day.*

Jesus washed the feet of His disciples in a radical countercultural move to demonstrate servanthood. As He did so, He also taught them to receive from him.

We've noticed that Jesus continues to care for the feet of His modern-day disciples. The condition of our feet is symbolic of our well-being.

> *The way is slippery and your feet are feeble*
> *But the Lord himself will be your guardian.*
> *He will keep your feet from faltering so that you do not defile*
> *your garments or wound your soul.*
> *He will keep your feet from wandering so that you do not go*
> *into the path or error or ways of folly.*
> *He will keep your feet from swelling and blistering because of*
> *the roughness of the way.*
> *He will keep your feet from wounds.*
> *Your shoes will be iron and brass so that even if you tread on*
> *the edge of a sword or deadly serpents, you shall be safe.*
> *He will also pluck your feet out of the net.*
> *You shall not be entangled by the deceit of crafty foes.*
> *With such a promise as this, let us run without weariness and*
> *walk without fear.*
> *He who keeps your feet will do it effectively.*[236]

Each exercise demands an action and application to keep the person safe and well.

### Helpful symbolism

Shoes:

- Preparation and protection of the gospel of peace, authority,

---

236   Charles Spurgeon, www.spurgeon.org

the authority of a child of God; and co-heir with Christ.

- Sons wear shoes; slaves do not.

## Exercise 7.1: Nancy's shoes dream

### The context

Nancy is a key leader for one of the outreach cafés. Returning from the mission field, the family continue to be radically involved in front-line ministry.

### The dream

"I was walking down the pavement with some friends (I think it was the outreach team). I was barefoot and I stepped in a muddy puddle. I couldn't see the bottom and I stepped on a parasite which went up into the ball of my foot. I couldn't walk properly and I was distressed. I couldn't keep up with my friends. I went home and went to bed. Soon my friends turned up and they had brought a doctor with them. He was a kind old man and he said, 'Your friends have told me about your troubles. It sounds like you may need quite a serious operation. Can I take a look?' He looked straight at my foot and said, 'Oh, this is easy,' and took the parasite straight out. He looked me in the eye and said, 'Don't go anywhere dangerous without your shoes on again.'"

### Helpful symbolism for the context of this dream

**Parasite** (negative symbol): hidden spiritual attack
**Foot** (positive symbol): balance, ministry of bearing good news, messenger
**Muddy puddle** (negative symbol): unclean spiritually, obscured from vision
**Doctor** (positive symbol): God
**Friends** (positive symbol): place of loving community, love covers
**Shoes** (positive symbol): preparation and protection of the gospel of peace

- Interpret the dream using the template at the beginning of the chapter to increasingly guide you toward the mature use of dreams and visions.

- Suggest a real-life application of the dream and its time frame.

- Compare your interpretation and application with those in the interpretation section at the end of the chapter.

## Exercise 7.2: A pair of shoes dream

### The context

At the time of this dream the dreamer was working in the leadership team of a church which held a lot of conferences at which she played a "starring" role. The church leader and his wife were her best friends – supporting the dreamer and her brother as they left to go abroad on mission.

The dreamer interpreted this dream at one level, applying it diligently by later supplying shoes to hundreds of impoverished children in Africa. Movingly, she washed each child's little feet before fitting the shoes, the first many of them had ever owned. In doing so the dreamer answered the question, "Who or what is the dream about?" as being about the children in the slums who were literally without shoes.

In this exercise I would like you to do a second level of interpretation in which this dream is about the literal dreamer.

### The dream

"My older brother and I were walking round a toy shop [we were children]. He was saying, 'We have to buy you a "Buzz Lightyear".' I tried to tell him that I did not need one, but he kept on persisting... Finally we found one... he handed it to me.

"Instantly I found myself standing in a dirty little slum house. In front of me, my mother was standing, screaming at me, but I had no idea what for. I was scared and confused and felt that my life was in danger. Suddenly she pulled out a metal stick and began beating me with it... if I did not escape I was going to die. I ran out of the house, down the little dirt road... I could hear her footsteps coming up behind me; I knew that if I did not keep running that she would catch me.

"[I ran]. My body ached with exhaustion and with each step I felt weaker... I felt a sharp pain in my foot. I started to stumble and I fell.

"I grabbed my foot... I saw that the soles of my feet were infected and maggots were crawling out... as I sat there, staring at the soles of my feet... the footsteps of my mother came closer. In fear I shouted, 'I told you I didn't need a Buzz Lightyear. I just needed a pair of shoes.'"[237]

### Helpful symbolism

**Older brother** (positive symbol): church leader
**Buzz Lightyear** (negative symbol): flashy toy which couldn't fly
**Transported** (negative symbol): change of location
**Metal stick** (negative symbol): rod, judgment, dominion
**Mother** (negative symbol): Jezebel spirit
(We also see this particular spiritual attack appearing in dreams and visions as a beguiling young woman, a witch, or an old evil woman.)
**Feet** (positive symbol): balance, ministry of bearing good news, messenger
**Maggots** (negative symbol): feeding on the flesh
**Shoes** (positive symbol): preparation and protection of the gospel of peace

- Interpret the dream using the template at the beginning of the chapter to increasingly guide you toward the mature use of dreams and visions.

- Tip: What did the dreamer need from her home context?

- Suggest a real-life application of the dream and its time frame.

- Compare your interpretation and application with those in the interpretation section at the end of the chapter.

## Exercise 7.3: Genevieve's vision

### The context

Genevieve is a sensitive, prophetic intercessor. She was given this vision by a visiting prophetic minister.

### The vision

"I saw you walking barefoot on a pathway made of blue chips of broken

---

237     Nicola Neal, *Journey into Love*, River Publishing, 2013, p. 16.

glass. You were determined and resolute and you had a cloak of suffering wrapped around you. It covered your head, but you did not give up.

"Beside you was a meadow of grass and flowers. Jesus came and took the cloak of suffering from you and led you into the meadow. He took you to a crystal-clear stream and bathed your sore feet. He kissed them and you ran freely in the soft grass.

"In the middle of the field was a circle, and in the middle of the circle was a pair of shoes. I was expecting to see a pair of strong boots to guard you against the shards of the journey. But in the middle of the circle sat a thick-soled pair of flowery flip-flops."

### Helpful symbolism

**Flip-flops** (positive symbol): light-hearted footwear, giving a feeling of freedom and holiday, open and free from restraint

**Thick sole** (positive symbol): substantial protection to protect your feet on the pathway ahead

**Circle** (positive symbol): covenant, circle of friends, spiritual space

- Interpret the dream using the template at the beginning of the chapter to increasingly guide you toward the mature use of dreams and visions.

- Suggest a real-life application of the dream and its time frame.

- Compare your interpretation and application with those in the interpretation section at the end of the chapter.

## Exercise 7.4: Vision exercise – washing your feet

**Freedom**

*He wants to befriend my failure, walk with me through every weary place,*
*Wash my feet, and take me with Him, on a journey to High Places with gladness as my only clothing*
*My shame drops off like the dust that He wiped from my feet.*
*And He laughs, until finally I can laugh with Him.*
*That's what being a pilgrim is all about.*
*I make a journey with Christ as my companion. I ask Him to*

> *Walk with me through all the ordinary days, and realise He*
> *Already was waiting for me there.*[238]

We need to understand who Jesus is. Jesus is not the forced Sunday morning smile after a difficult week; He is not the Sunday shirt, pressed and ironed. He left that clean and shiny place and came to us, down here. Not in spite of our mess or to force us to clean it up, but because of our mess: to show us a better way, "the most excellent way".[239]

Jesus "loved them to the end... he got up from the meal, took off his outer clothing, and wrapped a towel around his waist... he poured water into a basin and began to wash his disciples' feet, drying them with the towel which was wrapped round him."[240]

Not only were the disciples dusty, but also their hearts were contentious; they had just been bickering about who was the best, but still Jesus rose and stooped and loved and served.

## Vision exercise

In this exercise some of you will have visions and some of you little pictures and some of you will need someone to lead you through the exercise so that can see. You may like to do it in a group with a reader. Don't rush your gift; let it grow as you journey. It's like a muscle – as you use it, it becomes more elastic; it has further reach, nourishment flows to it, and it grows in strength.

**Step 1:** Sit quietly in all your dust, soiled by your journey.

You may hear your dust, your fear, or your pride talking: "I am too filthy, too proud, too independent, too unworthy." Dust is afraid of light because it will be washed away by love. Its voice will be rendered irrelevant by His higher truth.

**Step 2:** Just sit, and as you sit, picture yourself among the disciples.

Jesus is three disciples away from you. One man, head bowed, is submitting to having his feet washed – humbled but warmed. Then the next disciples meet Jesus' gaze and hold it as tears fill his eyes. And now Jesus is next to you. In your mind's eye, see Jesus as He kneels in front of you. It's He who is in charge. See and then write down what happens next. Give it time to develop.

---

238    Andy Raine, *Celtic Daily Prayer Book Two*, HarperCollins, 2015, p. 1469.
239    1 Corinthians 12:31.
240    John 13:1, 4–5.

**Step 3:** As he washes your feet, there will be things you lay down.
What are they? You may know as it happens or you may like to ask
Jesus. Write them down.

**Step 4:** There may be things that you receive.
Write them down.

**Step 5:** In your picture, what does Jesus say to you? Or tell you
silently through meeting your eyes. Write down what you see and what
happens.

Share with someone you know how that vision went for you,
especially if you had a powerful encounter.

## Dream and visions exercise set 2: Applying correctional revelation

## Exercise 7.5: Channel Island dreams

### The context

These two dreams were given to the wife of a minister (she appears as
"you" in the dream). Her husband Michael is the minister of a little
church in the Channel Islands. They have four children. Michael's
elderly mother lives with them too. The dreams were sent to them
along with a very stern letter about the correction which they bring as
a message from God.

## The dreams

### Dream 1

"I was coming home from the beach. As I came into St Peters Port, your
family were buying crepes from a market stall. I came up and smiled
to you all to say hello, but Michael was busy: he was buying crepes for
everybody, except me. I wasn't hungry but I was upset by Michael's
attitude because he did not buy me a crepe."

### Helpful symbolism

**Crepe** (positive symbol): nice treats, Spiritual provision
**Money** (positive symbol): favour, power, investing in something

**Market stall** (positive symbol): place of provision
Key statement: "I was cross."
Hint: The key to these dreams lies in the type of the dreams.

- Interpret the dream for the minister using the template at the beginning of the chapter to increasingly guide you toward the mature use of dreams and visions.

- Suggest a real-life application of the dream and its time frame for him.

- Compare your interpretation and application with those in the interpretation section at the end of the chapter.

### Dream 2

"We were in your home, eating dinner before midweek children's church. The whole team had arrived unexpectedly, so the portion you served me was smaller than I would have expected. I felt cross, because before we arrived you had already served out your own meals, which were bigger.

"Then I looked into your kitchen, where a lady looked up at me and smiled warmly. She beckoned to me and gave me food from a large dish which she had brought along."

### Helpful symbolism

**Dining table** (positive symbol): communion, fellowship, provision
**Your home** (positive symbol): the church
**Serving food** (positive symbol): providing spiritual food
**Lady in kitchen** (positive symbol): Holy Spirit
Key phrase: "You put your family first."

- Interpret the dream for the minister using the template at the beginning of the chapter to increasingly guide you toward the mature use of dreams and visions.

- Suggest a real-life application of the dream and its time frame. What should he do following the interpretation of the dream?

- Compare your interpretation and application with those in the interpretation section at the end of the chapter.

## Exercise 7.6: David's vision

This small vision is a profound piece of revelation which was brought to one of our prophetic schools by one of our mentoring school trainers. David interprets with great depth and maturity.

His interpretation is included at the end of this exercise, when we will spend time applying its message, but I'd like you to do the exercise first to the depth that you can.

The vision is a modern-day parable, using wasps and bees.

I suggest that you google a small overview about each. Common sense and practical knowledge are also part of wisdom. Knowing facts about real-life symbols can help us to understand them.

### The vision

"I saw the eagle of revelation over the prophetic school. This time it shook out its feathers and I saw people receive the feathers as wings. I saw people receive the feathers and some became bees and some became wasps."

Helpful hint: contrast the bee and the wasp.

- What is the function of each?

- What are their homes made out of?

- What is the perceived nature of each?

- What happens when they each sting?

Write an interpretation and application of David's vision before comparing it with David's interpretation below, as we apply the issues raised by the vision to our own lives.

### David's interpretation

David said, "This vision is about the prophetic people who are given revelation. They fall into two categories: wasps and bees. Bees make honey, which represents sweet, nourishing revelation. Their home and the place they do their honey-making is made of perfect hexagons which represent order. It is also the place where they raise their bee babies.

"This speaks to the prophetic people providing revelation to nourish others but also having order, both in their homes and ministries, with healthy protocol and accountability.

"The wax that is used to build this ordered and protected environment comes from their own bodies so it is the prophets who have the responsibility to build a healthy structure if nothing exists for them.

"They are attracted to flowers, which is the potential for fruit. Our prophetic ministry should be something that helps turn potential into reality. Bees do have a sting, but it costs them a lot to use it. It should cost us a lot to bring correctional rebuke. Sometimes we have to do it, but it's not something to take lightly.

"Wasps don't make honey, and their homes are made from paper. It speaks of having the word – the letter of the law – but not the Spirit that brings life. They can build a structure but it doesn't come from the life they have within them.

"They do have a sting but it doesn't cost them anything to use it. It's not a big deal for them to bring criticism or condemnation. They can spend much of their time looking for rubbish to feed off, not looking for flowers to pollinate. And people are afraid to go near the rubbish bins because of being stung. For some people the culture that they create of criticism and condemnation can create a culture of fear that stops people from dealing with their issues and getting the rubbish out of their lives. Wasps are known to attack bees, and there are people who have been hurt by wasp ministries and need healing."

During these exercises, we are reading and interpreting dreams and visions. Sometimes it's good to pause and let the dreams and visions "read" our lives.

> *My word... will accomplish what I desire and achieve the purpose for which I sent it.*[241]

### Application 1: David's vision

Am I a wasp or a bee?

- Do I search out the nectar of God's presence and His Word?

---

241     Isaiah 55:11.

- Is there order, life, and peace in my home?

- Do I have a safe place where I can co-exist with others?

- Are goodness and blessing the mark left by my ministry to bring others to their full potential, or do my words sometimes sting?

Which of the four areas above need your attention in order to let the cleansing wave of the revelation flow into your life?

### Application 2: Redeeming the wasps

Wasps are useful predators. They feed on garden pests. Their aggressive nature is rooted in a real purpose. Tempered with maturity and love, that feisty nature is used against the real enemies of the garden so that crops will flourish. Wasp ministries are often strong teachers, ministers, or intercessors who are working in the flesh rather than the Spirit, or for whom a disappointment has brought a bitter twist to their ministry. Their yellow and black stripes indicate a level of intellectual pride and judgment which is empty of the honey of God's grace.

If we recognize these traits in ourselves, there is a mandate here to stop right now, repent of these qualities, and ask ourselves:

- Have we been feeding off the rubbish of a situation instead of drinking in the nectar of God's word?

- Have we been hanging out with wasps and picking up the accent?

- Have we truly forgiven those who hurt us?

If we have pastoral responsibility, we need to see the potential in a wasp and be able to bring loving but very strong boundaries to help them to handle their negativity and to fulfil their true purpose. The shift into grace and mercy is a critical step of maturity for an interpreter. When people bring you their own dreams, or dreams and visions about what is happening in a church or organization, you will see inside the action and motives of men's hearts – "the secrets of their hearts are laid bare".[242]

---

242     1 Corinthians 14:25.

There are times when we find ourselves called next to people who are engaged in wrongdoing great and small. And at those times, we will make a sound, the wasp-like grating of the judgment and criticism of humanity, or the sound of faithful leadership firmly bringing healthy biblical boundaries in the spirit of grace.

### Application 3: Have you ever been stung by a wasp ministry?

David's revelation pointed out that there are people who have been on the receiving end of a "wasp" ministry and who need healing.

Jesus dealt firmly with wasps. He came upon a scene once which happened from time to time in the temple courts. On this occasion Jesus sat down to teach the people when:

> *The teachers of the law and the Pharisees brought in a woman caught in adultery... and said... "Teacher, this woman was caught in the act of adultery... Moses commanded us to stone such women"... But Jesus bent down and started to write on the ground with his finger... he straightened up and said to them, "Let any one of you who is without sin be the first to throw a stone at her."[243]*

We would say that He "drew a line in the sand". "Again he stooped down and wrote on the ground."[244] Leaving His words to hang in the air. One by one they slunk away.

Having made a safe space for the woman:

> *Jesus... asked her, "Woman, where are they? Has no one condemned you?" "No one, sir," she said. "Then neither do I condemn you," Jesus declared. "Go now and leave your life of sin."[245]*

In the face of the wasps, Jesus protected the woman and called her to a new life, a new beginning. Jesus was used to wasps around His ministry.

---

243    John 8:3–7.
244    John 8:8.
245    John 8:10–11.

They can be seen around the edge of any ministry.

I found a moving account of John Wimber's high-profile life by his wife, Carol. Carol writes about the stings that were inflicted upon John:

> *He explained to anyone interested about his convictions*
> *concerning how to deal with criticisms and assaults...*
> *To "turn the other cheek", to "settle a difference with*
> *a brother by going to him and working it out", with a*
> *strong awareness that our brother is never our enemy...*
> *[But], I think a bullet to the head would have been*
> *kinder and quicker than the constant slandering and*
> *unending hatred.*[246]

The stings clearly took their toll.

It is my experience that much of what is said against people is simply ignorance. When Nehemiah was rebuilding the wall around Jerusalem, accusation came against him fierce and fast.

> *It is reported among the nations – and Geshem says it*
> *is true – that you and the Jews are plotting to revolt,*
> *and therefore you are building the wall. Moreover...*
> *you are about to become their king.*

Nehemiah had a spectacularly simple and effective approach:

> *I sent him this reply: "Nothing like what you are saying*
> *is happening; you are just making it up out of your*
> *head."... But I prayed, "Now strengthen my hands."*[247]

Nehemiah prayed because he recognized that constant criticism can have a weakening effect. But, "the eyes of the Lord range throughout the earth to strengthen those whose hearts are fully committed to him".[248]

I recently saw a talented black choir, full of men and women whose faces were lined and told of long and challenging journeys. They were singing, "Those who wait upon the Lord will renew their strength." The

---

246      Carol Wimber, *John Wimber: The Way It Was*, Hodder and Stoughton, 1999, pp.170–71.
247      Nehemiah 6:6–9.
248      2 Chronicles 16:9.

shining example and strength in their lined faces, as much as their song, was proclaiming: "We made it – the strength and the healing is real. Jesus is really with you on the journey and He really will strengthen you to fulfil the potential of your life."

Rest from your journey. You see, Jesus is the "bee", bringing the potential of your heart and life into full fruit.

God loves human beings. They don't have to be perfect, or finished, or clean – He just loves them. And many of them, especially the ones who knew they weren't perfect, noticed this about Jesus and loved Him right back.

Of course, it stirred up a wasps' nest of murmuring when one day a woman came to Him, and, with her tears falling on his feet, she wiped them with her hair and poured perfume over them.[249]

And then the buzzing began in earnest.

I saw Jesus' words from this passage repeated at a conference recently when a young minister, who had been attacked by a different ministry (which was working in a high degree of judgment and presumption), received a prophecy from the high-profile speaker. The speaker's voice rang out clear and strong: "Leave her alone; she poured perfume [the knowledge of God] on my body."

In our community, we have two people who have been badly stung by "wasps". To see them beginning to trust us after their difficult journeys is a delight as they realize they are really loved here.

We need to understand this dynamic of Jesus's ministry. He defends those who have been stung, and He makes a safe place for them in healing communities.

If you have been stung yourself, Nehemiah's strategy remains the best one I've seen. He puts a strong boundary, a line in the sand around his spiritual space: "Nothing like what you are saying is happening; you made it all up out of your head."

You may want to talk to someone about putting in some boundaries, maybe temporarily, around any familiar wasps, so that you can keep your spiritual space soft and pure and retain the identity and destiny of a bee.

If there are those who have trespassed into your spiritual space by accusing or judging you, turn them around and release them out of your

---

249     Luke 7:37–38.

spiritual space by forgiving them and putting down your boundary. It's usually their sheer ignorance.

It's very reassuring that Jesus told us to forgive our enemies. When He did that, He recognized that sometimes people will harm us. It happens. It's part of the deal.

Picture yourself forgiving and releasing them from your circle and letting them go, blessing them as you do. If you have trouble doing this or don't want to let go, you have some processing to do with a trusted counsellor. When you do, God's strength can stream back in and heal you.

Finally, find people of peace, those whose song is soft, consistent, and life-bringing. The thing about bees in real life is that they dance – they dance a pattern to one another about where the nectar can be found. And the world needs your dance, to show it where the sweet things of God are to be found, to pollinate the garden, and to store up the good things of God for others to feast on.

And right now I'm dancing; I'm dancing out the pattern of the journey which so many bees have been on, so you can find a way through, past any wasps and their murmurings, right through to the goodness, freedom and kingdom of the living God. Dance with me.

## Developing as an interpreter: How and when a bee ministry brings correction

There are still times when "bee ministries" are called to deal with highly complex or serious issues. If we have been given positional influence in people's lives, in churches, and in organizations, we are called to be a "bee" ministry – stinging and bringing correction only where absolutely necessary.

There will be a reason why God called you in to deal with what He's given you to deal with: because He trusts you. It's important for you to remember that, especially when the wasps who gather around the rubbish of a situation, circling and buzzing like wasps do, with a low and persistent threatening drone, are using their stings in judgment.

Correctional revelation is one of our "behind-the-counter medications". The rule of thumb is that you bring correction to the level of relationship or responsibility which you carry in a situation.

Otherwise you pass it up the chain to those who carry positional responsibility, and cover it in prayer.

I've seen God deal comprehensively with situations when He decides to bring discipline, in a moment. I was once visiting a council of leaders and God said to me, "There is going to be an execution." I was concerned, and asked God if He wanted me to do something. He told me, "I am going to execute My judgment". During that council, one person was taken out of ministry who refused to address a major issue of immorality.

The biblical protocol for correction is exercised where there is a genuinely serious issue which has become apparent to more than one person. We're not talking about wasps buzzing around and interfering in everyone's business. There are occasional weighty issues which arise where we have professional responsibility for a work or ministry area – a family, a child, or an organization.

Moreover, when other people bring us their dreams and visions, we get behind-the-scenes insight into what is going on. I am sent a lot of dreams and visions from different people about the different organizations in which I serve. I see a glimpse into behind-the-scenes stuff. Much of it is confirmed by different people who are involved themselves, as they share their own stories.

The dreams and visions from different people in the same organization reveal and confirm the situations about which the individual seers have no clue. And I gradually see a picture about what's going on. My responsibility for correctional revelation is limited to the level of my positional responsibility in that situation and my relationship to that person or organization. I see far more than I say in situations where I am simply an observer, although I may speak to a senior leader about it.

If it is one of the churches that I cover, my family, or my ministry, then I have full positional and relational responsibility. If it concerns one of my close friends, I have full relational responsibility. But even then I need to seek the biblical wisdom about how to deal with that situation.

The process of biblical protocol is very useful. In addition, we recommend that it is essential to also run the revelation of the situation past some wise counsel (not the type with whom we frequently "share for prayer" – meaning to share the juicy details), someone well travelled in both revelation and dealing with organizations and people. I'm fortunate to have men and women of international standing who advise at these times.

Biblical protocol reflects the redemptive heart of God. Matthew 18:15–17 has a progressive pattern of engagement for correction:

- just between the two of you
- take somebody with you
- tell it to the church.

"Tell it to the church" (verse 17) doesn't mean that we stand up in front of packed pews and expose people, although I have seen that done, but rather that we quietly bring the matter before the relevant authorities who are responsible for the organization.

This progressive approach to correction is reflected in Revelation 2:21: "I have given her time to repent... but she is unwilling."

This approach is primarily redemptive – to restore people to peace and right relationship with God and with others. But it also recognizes that people have free choice, and sometimes there is a limited amount that we can do, and sometimes God calls "time". This is tragically sad, but even in the worst of situations it's not the end of the redemptive love of God but the beginning of a new story.

Including the Matthew 18 protocol in this chapter may have given the impression that dreams and visions interpretation can be terribly serious. But in twenty years of ministry, among what must be thousands of interpretations, including some correctional visions and dreams, I've only dealt with one correctional issue which had to go all the way through to the end of the process outlined above. As a "bee", working with the relevant authorities, it cost me dearly to use my "sting".

## Dreams and visions exercise set 3: Applying family dreams and visions

Some dreams and visions have an obvious application because God raises an issue that needs to be addressed. It can be a matter of healing of the heart or a previously hidden issue at work in a family.

It's important for you to be aware that these issues can be felt very deeply. If they are carelessly raised in an interpretation it can destroy a person's ability to cope.

Even simple matters like breaking a curse need to be handled very carefully. We once had a delightful young woman at the outreach café who was living under a word curse, which had been spoken by her best friend, a girl who had spoken with venom and a high degree of control. Her pronouncement had been savage and had stayed with our guest and become part of her life. As she told me her story I offered to give her a blessing, and while doing it "broke off anything that anyone had said about her that didn't agree with what God said about her", in the name of Jesus.

Tash forgave her friend, and then I blessed her. We didn't see her for six months, but she came back to visit and told me that her life had been completely different since we blessed her. As someone who didn't have a Christian worldview she was very grateful and somewhat astonished.

I didn't tell Tash that there had been a curse operating over her life, because I would have induced fear, not faith. She just shared with me what had been said and how it had affected her. These matters need to be handled very carefully. Our heart compassion for the person in front of us must be balanced by our genuine ability to deal with their need.

It is important to be aware of the two levels of interpretations for ministry dreams and visions:

**Level 1:** raise the area to be ministered into in a general, non-emotive way. For example, "This revelation speaks about the areas of various hurts from childhood. God seems to really care about that and has a time of healing for you. You may want to talk to someone about that, who can walk with you on that journey."

**Level 2:** interpreters can deal with the issue after realistically assessing:

- the level of relationship with the person;
- the experience and expertise on the issue raised;

- whether you have time to deal with it at the time of interpretation, and the commitment to deal with it on what may become an ongoing basis. (There may be an appropriate place of referral.)

## Exercise 7.7: Selja's dream

### *The context*

This dreamer came to the prophetic school in Norway just before her son's twentieth birthday. She had cried out to God one month earlier that He would bring her son closer to himself, so, "I was in desperate prayer for him, and now God gave me this dream."

### *The dream*

"In my dream I was in a hospital visiting a young man I didn't know. He was about twenty. Even though I didn't know him I felt compassion from God for him and I gave him a hug and kissed him. Then I was told by someone in the hospital that this young man was sick with a red rash on his body, but it was like a child's disease. It wasn't a grown-up person's disease. I woke up.

"When I woke up I was wondering why I had wanted to visit this man even though I didn't know him."

### *Helpful symbolism*

**Childhood rash** (negative symbol): something that afflicted him in childhood

**Hospital** (positive symbol): place of healing

**Man** (positive symbol): who do you think the man represents?

- Interpret the dream using the template at the beginning of the chapter to increasingly guide you toward the mature use of dreams and visions.

- Suggest a real-life application of the dream and its time frame.

- Compare your interpretation and application with those in the interpretation section at the end of the chapter.

# Exercise 7.8: A mother's and a daughter's dreams which work together

### The context

The mother and the rest of the family are away on holiday. The adult daughter was at her university. Both women have a Christian worldview. Both women had the dreams on the same night, which were then sent to me.

### Daughter's dream

"The whole family were on holiday, including me, and Mum was being really stressy and rude to everyone, and so everyone was in a bad mood and tiptoeing around. She can get stressed but this was like tenfold; everyone just wanted to leave. Then I was at my parents' house while the family was on holiday and then they arrived home the day after saying they were all too ill to stay on holiday."

### Helpful symbolism

### Mother's dream

"Last night I dreamt there was lots of gunfire and screaming at our holiday park. I looked out of the window and saw that everyone was putting their lights on and going outside. I turned our lights out so it would look like no one was there. It was Islamic state. Also Abbie was in labour and I was talking to her on the phone and she was crying and wanted Becky with her. I also popped into some little church for a service and lots of my relatives were in there. I also dreamt about people who had loads of money and who were just talking about all the things they had."

### Helpful symbolism

**Labour** (positive symbol): in a critical phase bringing something into being

**Islamic state** (negative symbol): threat

**Gunfire and screaming** (negative symbol): spiritual warfare

**Money** (positive symbol): provision and resource

**Little church** (positive symbol): place of safety with God

- Interpret each dream using the template at the beginning of the chapter to increasingly guide you toward the mature use of dreams and visions.
- Suggest a real-life application of the dreams and their time frame.
- Compare your interpretation and application with those in the interpretation section at the end of the chapter.

## Exercise 7.9: A mother's traumatic dream

### The context

At a dreams and visions course, this mother gave me the following dream about her daughter who had been taken in to foster care in her early teens.

### The dream

"I dreamt I was walking along a road and I saw my thirteen-year-old daughter lying dead in a ditch."

How would you interpret this dream for the mother? What is the application of the dream? I am particularly interested in your protocol.

### Helpful symbolism

**Ditch** (negative symbol): place of refuse, depression
**Road** (positive symbol): life's journey

- Interpret the dream using the template at the beginning of the chapter to increasingly guide you toward the mature use of dreams and visions.
- Suggest a real-life application of the dream and its time frame.
- Compare your interpretation and application with those in the interpretation section at the end of the chapter.

## Exercise 7.10: Josh's dream

### The context

Josh is a thirteen-year-old boy and Esther is his twelve-year-old cousin. Esther does not live next door to either of Josh's parents or to his grandmother. The family have a Catholic heritage, which may help you when you decide how to give the interpretation.

### The dream

"I was in Granny's house and in the room were loads of werewolves; they were getting bigger and bigger so then I had to climb out the window, slide down a pole (guttering). Esther was there. We jumped over a wall to the neighbours and Esther brought out hot chocolate. We sat in their garden drinking it."

Question the dreamer: what's Granny's house like? Is it a peaceful place to sleep? Answer: "Yes."

Granny's house is not literal.

Your task here is to work with revelation to produce an interpretation and plan which will fulfil the purpose of this dream, and you must do this while using good protocol which takes into account the age of the dreamer.

Jesus was selective in the revelation He gave at any one time. He told the disciples, "I have much more to say to you, more than you can now bear."[250]

Do two interpretations: the interpretation you would give to Josh if you did not know him and his family well, and the interpretation you would give to Josh if you were in a trusted relationship with Josh and had his parents' approval.

### Helpful symbolism

**Werewolves** (negative symbol): impactful level of fear

**Granny's house** (positive symbol): secure place in the family; (generational symbol): generational symbols sometimes provoke the question, "Have the issues that are dealt with in the dream been experienced in previous generations on some branch of the family tree?"

> *Take up the shield of faith, with which you can extinguish all the flaming arrows of the evil one.*[251]

**Window** (positive symbol): place of light and revelation, a way out
**Guttering** (positive symbol): channel of the Holy Spirit

---

250    John 16:12.
251    Ephesians 6:16.

**Esther** (positive symbol): the Holy Spirit
**Wall** (positive symbol): boundary
**Hot chocolate** (positive symbol): words spoken in love, palatable

- Interpret the dream using the template at the beginning of the chapter to increasingly guide you toward the mature use of dreams and visions.

- Suggest a real-life application of the dream and its time frame.

- Compare your interpretation and application with those in the interpretation section at the end of the chapter.

## Dreams and visions exercise set 5: Preparing a prophetic bulletin

Dreams and visions bring understanding and inform action. As we listen to revelation which is coming in dreams and visions that are sent to us, we sometimes notice sets of revelation from independent sources, repeating promises, dreams, and visions which highlight a particular issue or which confirm one another.

Just like recurring dreams and visions in one person's life, repeating messages from a group of people underline the importance of a message. Interpreting them together can bring light into a situation.

Writing an effective prophetic summary can provide a prophetic and biblical roadmap to help the people involved toward a new season of promise, or bring direction, correction, affirmation, or comfort. It can also equip people to deal with what is happening or what is about to happen, even if that event is negative. If skilfully communicated, it can help to inoculate people, or unite them, against a common spiritual strategy, or raise faith to meet a coming challenge.

It's very important to use a faith lens and focus on what God is saying, and why He is saying it, rather than on the problem; and to be very discerning about how much we disclose and to whom, otherwise badly communicated summaries can draw immature people into fear, or to focus on the enemy and his schemes.

Time is spent waiting on God, in knowing the Scriptures, and honing the gift. It's this commitment we saw in the prophet Habakkuk:

> *I will stand at my watch*
> *and station myself on the ramparts;*
> *I will look to see what he will say to me...*
> *The Lord replied:*
> *"Write down the revelation*
> *and make it plain on tablets*
> *so that a herald may run with it."*[252]

The exercise below is time-consuming, but it will help you to learn to "write down revelation and make it plain", producing a headline so that people can partner with what God is doing.

A prophetic summary bypasses the need for mature prophetic literacy on the part of the person to whom it is sent. It enables them to access key prophetic messages without putting in the time to collate and interpret revelation.

Bulletins need to:

- use clear language, translating symbolism using straightforward vocabulary;
- avoid an emotive or poetic style; be concise and factual;
- biblically filter and interpret the message the revelation presents.

For a bulletin to be both accessible and comprehensive, it can be presented in three parts.

**Page 1:** using bullet points:
- outline why the summary was made
- include one short headline paragraph about the total revelation
- include any confirming situations or scriptures which backup the revelation, in a brief paragraph.

**Page 2:** a brief summary of each individual piece of revelation and its headline interpretation.

---

252    Habbakuk 2:1–2.

**Page 3:** a page detailing each dream or vision and its full interpretation.

Most readers or leaders never read beyond page 2; some never venture beyond page 1, but it is important to include the contents of page 3 in case they are needed. It is wise to only produce this lengthy summary if it has been specifically asked for in a real-life situation. Otherwise it is unlikely to be read at all.

## Exercise 7.11: Produce a prophetic bulletin for the dreams and visions set below

This exercise is more fun if you can do it together with a team of prophetic peers. Follow these steps systematically.

- Read each piece of revelation and its interpretation.

- As you read them, write a short headline interpretation from each dream or vision on a blank page, either as a series of bullet points or as a spider diagram. This page will become page 2 of your prophetic bulletin.

- Use that page to bring together one headline message that sums up all the pieces of revelation in one paragraph (no more than 10 sentences long). This summary will become the front page of your bulletin.

- Present your prophetic summary following the template given below:

# A TEMPLATE FOR YOUR PROPHETIC BULLETIN

*Prophetic Bulletin/Date* ...............................................

...............................................................................

### Page 1

- There has been a flow of revelation about........................, coming from.........................................................
- The headline message from these corroborating pieces of revelation is.................................................................
- The real-life situations which back this up are....................
...............................................................................
- Include any relevant Scriptures which corroborate or explain what you are seeing (use no more than three references).

### Page 2

- A brief headline interpretation paragraph from each dream or vision.
- A list of the people who have presented the dreams and visions on this subject. (A time scale would usually be added at this point, but for the purpose of this exercise you do not have and do not need this information.)

### Page 3

- Each full piece of revelation and its interpretation. In our exercise this is provided for you in the text so you don't need to present it in this exercise.

## Dreams and visions set: An infestation of crocodiles

Over a period of time one summer, people were sending me dreams and visions. This is not unusual. My inbox always has requests for interpretations from the people I know. But there was something interesting about these particular dreams. They all contained a common theme and a common symbol, five of which are included in this exercise. They were revelation dreams about crocodiles that were invariably negative.

That is, until the last two pieces of revelation that arrived, which included the solution to the apparent plague of crocodiles.

Crocodile symbolism in these dreams and visions represents spiritual lies, verbal attack, twisting of truth, vicious influences, misunderstanding bringing relational attack or accusations, the twisting and confusion of thought and of the mind, things from the past that drag you down.

## Crocodile dream 1: Natalie's dream

### The context

This short dream was sent to me for interpretation. Before interpreting it I checked back in with the dreamer and asked her how the relationships around her were going. She told me that there was lots of relational discord around her in the school in which she taught.

### The dream

"I dreamt that I was in a swamp in the water. Just under the water were loads and loads of crocodiles. It was swarming with them."

### Helpful symbolism

**Swamp** (historically a negative image): stagnant place where pests and insects thrive; where undergrowth covers hidden predators

### The interpretation

This dream speaks of discord in the dreamer's workplace. It highlights a hidden attack against her which is causing conflict. The situation is impacted and significant. It may have an effect on both her job role and her peace of mind.

## Using the annotation method of interpretation

We will look at the next few dreams using the annotation method. Annotating the story can help you pick out the relevant details for the interpretation.

## Crocodile dream 2: Joseph's dream – corporate attack which has an effect on the dreamer

### The context

Joseph is a lay minister in a large church.

### The dream

"My dream was bright and vivid and colourful, but it was also disturbing."

| The dream | Notes |
|---|---|
| I remember getting an invite to this volunteer celebration party with my friend for a local voluteering organization which I used to help out at. | Included. |
| We were given certificates which were colourful and beautiful. | Celebrated and affirmed – well done. |
| Then we were on top of this cliff looking down at the water where lots of other volunteers were swimming. | Place of high anointed revelation. |
| Everyone was having fun. Then all of a sudden we spotted one or two crocodiles and we were alarmed as our friends were in the water. | Identifying the attack |
| We didn't know whether we should warn them, or even how to do this without alarming them. | Those involved in ministry are coming under attack. |
| Then we realized the water was infested with crocodiles. Our friends didn't have a chance. | Feelings of alarm, and helplessness. |

| The dream | Notes |
|---|---|
| This was the really traumatic bit as we watched our friends being eaten by crocodiles. It was really gory and violent. Everyone was outnumbered. | Dreamer is exposed and involved. Vicious and widespread attack. |
| Then I remember being moved that some of the people had other people on their backs to look after them and protect them. Particularly men with women. | A level of protection for some. |
| Then the scene changed and the cliff fell away and we were in the water, but it was different water. It was a fast-flowing stream. | |
| I remember being terrified about crocodiles but no one else seemed to be afraid. | Highly spiritually aware. |
| Then we made it back to the volunteer office which was actually my old school. I remember mourning for the volunteers who died, but no one seemed to care or be aware. | A place of learning and some sadness and grieving. |
| Then I remember being cocooned up somewhere in the dark while everyone else was worshipping. | Needing comfort and healing – "cocoon" – a place of transition. |

## The interpretation

The dream suggests there has been a spiritual attack on the church which is causing widespread misunderstandings, gossip, and verbal attacks. There has been a level of covering but the situation has caused some damage, and the dreamer himself has been deeply affected. He is now in a place of rest, safety, and learning for the next part of his journey.

# Crocodile dream 3: The shaking

### The context

Christen is a worship leader in a local church.

### The dream

"The dream was of a ship near the shore of some water. There were people on the ship and people swimming in the water. The sun was shining and everybody was happy and enjoying the nice weather. Then a big grey monster with short legs came along the bottom of the water. It sneaked up and no one noticed, then it disappeared under the ship. A little later the whole ship shook and everybody ran for the shore."

### Helpful symbolism

**Ship** (positive symbol): church
**Water** (positive symbol): things of Spirit
**Sunshine** (positive symbol): place of blessing and revelation
**Monster with small legs** (negative symbol): crocodile
**Shore** (positive symbol): place of safety where people could become beached

### The interpretation

This dream is a revelation dream about the local church. It suggests that there may be something which is spiritually initiated which will shake the church, even though it is now in great shape and in a place of blessing. The shaking will be felt by individuals and it could cause people to leave the church because they don't feel safe, at which point they will become "beached".

### Dreams 4 and 5: How to outwit a crocodile

These dreams hold some protective keys to overcome this type of spiritual attack.

# Crocodile dream 4: John's dream

### The dream

"I dreamt I was going to a solemn meeting but I was the wrong colour.

I was yellow and attracted lizards so I spat on my hands and rubbed it on my knee. As I did I changed colour to white, which was a lizard repellent."

### Helpful symbolism

**Yellow** (negative symbol): intellectual pride or fear
**Knee** (negative symbol): stubborn and unyielding; (positive symbol): humility worship and prayer
**Spit** (positive symbol): washing off
**White** (positive symbol): the Spirit of the Lord, holy power

### The interpretation

This dream suggests that there may be some attack on communication spiritually to twist the truth and damage relationships. The dreamer's own heart attitude will help immeasurably, because the dream speaks of areas of pride, fear, or unyielding attitude (soul power). Diligent cleansing away of these issues when they appear will help the dreamer to move in the purity and power of the Holy Spirit, which will overcome any attack.

## Crocodile dream 5: An eight-year-old girl's dream

This eight-year-old had this vision after she had been to her Sunday school that morning where the children were looking at the armour of God in Ephesians 6.

### The dream

"I saw lots of squares of lots of different colours. Then a lizard came – a fierce one. He saw that I had the helmet of the hope of salvation on my head and he left me alone."

### Helpful symbolism

**Squares** (negative symbol): straight lines, legalism
**Colours** (positive symbol): creativity and variety of the Spirit of God

### The interpretation

This child has grown up in an atmosphere of legalism which has led to strain around her and within her, to get things right. Problems with fearful thoughts have built on top of that structure, but when she learns to have hope and confidence instead of fear, she will be able to repel those thoughts. The dream shows that the helmet of the hope of salvation will help guard people against the Leviathan spirit.

### Preparing your prophetic bulletin

Use the above five dreams and their interpretations to prepare your prophetic summary. Compare your prophetic bulletin to the pattern of the sample bulletin given in the interpretation section at the end of the chapter.

As we harness the messages given to us in dreams and visions and apply them, we begin to overcome. And the redemption of God flows powerfully. We hear and know more of who He is.

> "You will know that I, the Lord, am your Saviour,
> your Redeemer, the Mighty One of Jacob.
> Instead of bronze I will bring you gold,
> and silver in place of iron.
> Instead of wood I will bring you bronze,
> and iron in place of stones.
> I will make peace your governor
> and well-being your ruler.
> No longer will violence be heard in your land,
> nor ruin or destruction within your borders,
> but you will call your walls Salvation
> and your gates Praise."[253]

More and more people are discovering the route to freedom through the use of dreams and visions.

Yesterday I had a pastoral phone call with a powerful young woman who ministers to girls who have known abuse. Talking over recent difficult events, I had a vision of her as a hot-air balloon, with the canopy spread out on the ground. Clothes pegs scrunched up various sections of the canopy so that it couldn't be filled and fly freely. The clothes pegs represented individual events which disappointed and distracted her

---

253      Isaiah 60:16–18.

to stop her rising up and living joyfully. As we talked, Maisie applied this picture by refusing discouragement from the specific challenges. And as she did so she took those "clothes pegs" off her life, which were holding her down.

I went to bed after our phone call and had a dream about Maisie. My dream had two scenes which were a timeline of her life. The first scene showed Maisie's past: she had known what it was like to be a wartime barrage balloon. The one I saw was grey and tethered to the ground by ropes which drew enemy fire as she protected other people.

But scene two of the dream showed Maisie's future. I saw her as she is made to be: a bright red hot-air balloon – made to fly high so that others see and realize what freedom looks like.

The vision I had earlier that afternoon while we talked together described how she is to take flight, refusing to be distracted and limited – practically rooting the dream in her reality.

God loved the world "thus", proclaims John 3:16 in the direct translation from the original Greek, that He gave extravagantly. He still loves like that today, pouring out a life-giving stream of revelation. And God uses us to realize its potential in people's lives: "They will rebuild… and restore… they will renew."[254]

We have a mandate right there, to impact the world we live in. Jubilee is our mission.

I love to study the lives of the biblical prophets and seers. Elijah is perhaps my favourite, "a human being like us".[255] He was, to me, a pioneer. Through times of famine, God fed him; in places of lack, he gained such experience and knowledge of God's goodness that he was able to provide for both himself and others supernaturally. He stood calmly confident in his God while the priests of Baal were lashing themselves in a futile attempt to get counterfeit spirituality to beat the Lord of heaven and earth in a contest of power. And then he prayed for his nation, to break the famine in the land: praying seven times – completely – until he saw the deliverance and redemption of God. Elijah prayed until he saw a cloud with his own eyes, because, having previously perceived what God was doing, he had already told the king,

---

254    Isaiah 61:4.
255    James 5:17 (NRSVA).

"There is the sound of heavy rain."[256] And his prayer was the application that made it real.

The Holy Spirit has been loosed in the world. People are seeing visions and dreaming dreams.

God's Word is falling to water the earth through dreams and visions, the famine in the lives of those around us can be broken. I hear the sound of heavy rain.

When you hear it, make it real.

---

256      1 Kings 18:41.

## Teaching points for chapter 6

- We interpret dreams and visions to open a door to the transforming power of God in people's lives.

- Application is the bridge from merely understanding dreams and visions to releasing the potential of their messages into people's lives.

- Timing is the last piece of the prophetic skill set to mature.

- Using a systematic process looking at detailed interpretation, application, and timing will help you to avoid presumptuous and ineffective interpretation.

- This systematic process releases the dynamic life-giving properties of revelation.

- There is a way of collating pieces of revelation from a group of people or on a certain repeating theme, which builds a picture of what God is saying.

- It allows people who are not prophetically literate, or who don't have the time to engage in the process, to access the messages which we find in revelation.

- The prophetic process takes time.

- Ministry dreams raise issues of healing to be addressed in people's lives.

- The revelation can inform a ministry plan for people's healing.

- Simple issues are dealt with simply.

- Deeper issues need "behind-the-counter" ministry, often over time in a safe environment by people with experience.

- This is not usually a matter for an interpretation situation. In which case, be general and suggest that the seer talks to someone they trust.

- Revelation dreams and visions sometimes diagnose problems and are the equivalent of a word of knowledge. The whole counsel of God, in the form of Scripture, brings the prescription to form a ministry plan for their use.

- Two tests of your protocol are found in this chapter, in the mother's traumatic dream and Josh's dream.

   If you went beyond the guidelines suggested in the sample interpretation and ministry plan, please read the summary at the end of chapter 2, to refresh your memory of good protocol.

- God uses us to interpret people's dreams and visions. When He does, we see Him touch their lives with compassion and help.

# CHAPTER 6: ANSWERS AND INTERPRETATIONS

## Exercise 7.1: Nancy's shoes dream

"I was walking down the pavement with some friends (I think it was the outreach team). I was barefoot and I stepped in a muddy puddle. I couldn't see the bottom and I stepped on a parasite which went up into the ball of my foot. I couldn't walk properly and I was distressed. I couldn't keep up with my friends. I went home and went to bed. Soon my friends turned up and they had brought a doctor with them. He was a kind old man and he said, 'Your friends have told me about your troubles, it sounds like you may need quite a serious operation. Can I take a look?' He looked straight at my foot and said, 'Oh, this is easy,' and took the parasite straight out. He looked me in the eye and said, 'Don't go anywhere dangerous without your shoes on again.'"

### The interpretation

The interpreter might say, "This dream suggests you have been going into spiritually dirty territory, with a measure of lack of preparation. It speaks of picking up some hidden negative spirituality which, although it's affected you, is easily dealt with. You are in a loving community who bring God's ministry to you when you need it. There needs to be a conversation around what protection and preparation looks like for you."

Nancy needs healing and support, preparation, and protection.

### Possible applications and time frame

* An increase in an offensive strategy of prayer for Nancy, especially before ministry. A helpful prayer for Nancy to use might be St Patrick's Breastplate, an ancient Irish prayer of encirclement:

> *I rise today*
> *With the power of God to pilot me, God's strength to sustain me,*
> *God's wisdom to guide me, God's eye to look ahead for me,*
> *God's ear to hear me, God's word to speak for me,*
> *God's hand to protect me, God's shield to defend me.*

*God's host to deliver me:*
*From snares of devils, from evil temptations,*
*From nature's failings, from all who wish to harm me,*
*Far or near, alone and in a crowd.*
*Around me I gather today all these powers, against every cruel*
*and merciless force,*
*To attack my body and soul against the charms of false*
*prophets,*
*The black laws of paganism, the false laws of heretics,*
*The deceptions of idolatry. Against spells cast by... smiths and*
*druids, [and witches]*
*And all unlawful knowledge, that harms my body and soul.*[257]

- Nancy will benefit from cleansing prayer after ministry events.

- She will also benefit from regular one-to-one mentoring times to gain a sense of fellowship, support, and covering.

- Time frame: to begin straight away.

## Exercise 7.2: A pair of shoes dream

"My older brother and I were walking round a toy-shop [we were children]. He was saying, 'We have to buy you a "Buzz Lightyear". I tried to tell him that I did not need one, but he kept on persisting.... Finally we found one... he handed it to me.

"Instantly I found myself standing in a dirty little slum house. In front of me, my mother was standing, screaming at me, but I had no idea what for. I was scared and confused and felt that my life was in danger. Suddenly she pulled out a metal stick and began beating me with it... if I did not escape I was going to die. I ran out of the house, down the little dirt road.... I could hear her footsteps coming up behind me; I knew that if I did not keep running that she would catch me.

"[I ran]. My body ached with exhaustion and with each step I felt weaker... I [felt] a sharp pain in my foot... I started to stumble and I fell.

---

257     Quoted in Russ Parker, *Rediscovery of the Ministry of Blessing*, SPCK, 2014.

"I grabbed my foot… I saw that the soles of my feet were infected and maggots were crawling out… as I sat there, staring at the soles of my feet… the footsteps of my mother came closer. In fear I shouted, 'I told you I didn't need a Buzz Lightyear. I just needed a pair of shoes.'"[258]

### The interpretation

The interpreter might say, "This dream speaks of a level of frustration that you feel in your present context, because you notice a slight focus on presentation rather than authentic ministry. It also speaks of a lack of covering which is not helpful in the spiritual territory you will be moving into in your new ministry.

"The dream points out a key issue: your current apprenticeship location may not have equipped and prepared you to meet the challenges that are to come spiritually without some cost. You may like to focus on that and think about a degree of preparation in order to protect your personal peace and well-being for your current work and as you move ahead. Peace will be a key for you. You seem highly aware of the spirituality around you, and it's important to prepare for the spiritual environment you will face and to be aware that there is sometimes a need for cleansing and healing, both as we prepare to go out in the field and once we are there. This preparation and ongoing cleansing will enable you to outrun and outmanoeuvre anything that is a spiritual challenge."

This is a sensitive dream to be interpreted with love and care. The dreamer has not been prepared for some of what is to come.

### Possible application and time frame

- As the home context may have been a challenge rather than an equipping environment, an experienced ministerial mentor would be ideal.

- A time of inner healing may also be a helpful preparation before the dreamer moves ahead.

- There is a need for committed intercessors to pray for the dreamer.

---

258     Neal, *Journey into Love*, p. 16.

- Time frame: to be put in place within weeks (because the move in ministry is shown in the dream to be quick and unexpected), but there should be continuing support for this committed and gifted minister.

## Exercise 7.3: Genevieve's vision

"I saw you walking bare-foot on a pathway made of blue chips of broken glass. You were determined and resolute and you had a cloak of suffering wrapped around you. It covered your head, but you did not give up.

"Beside you was a meadow of grass and flowers. Jesus came and took the cloak of suffering from you and led you into the meadow. He took you to a crystal-clear stream and bathed your sore feet. He kissed them and you ran freely in the soft grass.

"In the middle of the field was a circle and in the middle of the circle was a pair of shoes. I was expecting to see a pair of strong boots to guard you against the shards of the journey. But in the middle of the circle sat a thick-soled pair of flowery flip-flops."

### The interpretation

The interpreter might say, "The vision suggests that your pathway hasn't been an easy one. But you have been resolute in the place of difficulty. You seem to have grown used to this way of living, but God is calling you to a place of grace, openness, and healing. He wants to set you free to dance – it's a summer season. The preparation and protection that He has for you supernaturally will keep you free to enjoy that sense of openness and life that He is bringing to you.

"The circle represents three things you may like to explore with someone: it's the place of covenant, with full provision from God. It represents the cleanness of the spiritual space around our hearts when we are walking in freedom. It also represents the circle of friends we put around ourselves, as we are discriminating about our life-giving inner circle."

Things have been hard for this dreamer, but God has something better for her than stoicism.

### Possible application and time frame

- The picture of Jesus taking off the cloak of suffering and kissing her feet suggests a need for putting aside old coping strategies and for healing. This is more easily done in specific counselling sessions, ideally with a prayer ministry component – replacing her "cloak" with healing and protection.

- Affirmation and love are implied needs for this courageous woman, so it is important to explore who makes up her circle of nourishing relationships.

- Time scale: ongoing.

## Exercise 7.4: Vision exercise – washing your feet

Interpret your own vision.

## Exercise 7.5: Channel Island dreams

The dreams were being presented as coming from God. In fact, they are largely life-processing dreams; although the second dream carries an extra component: it brings revelation from God. They are ministry dreams showing a need for healing and cleansing.

### Dream 1

"I was coming home from the beach. As I came into St Peters Port, your family were buying crepes from a market stall. I came up and smiled to you all to say hello, but Michael was busy: he was buying crepes for everybody, except me. I wasn't hungry but I was upset by Michael's attitude because he did not buy me a crepe."

### Dream 1: The interpretation for the minister

This dreamer is processing his feelings in these dreams. He is carrying some hurt and judgment because of a personal need to be included in your family and cared for. It is likely that he also wants to be invested in as a mark of favour.

### Dream 2

"We were in your home, eating dinner before midweek children's church. The whole team had arrived unexpectedly, so the portion you served me was smaller than I would have expected. I felt cross, because before we arrived you had already served out your own meals, which were bigger.

"Then I looked into your kitchen, where a lady looked up at me and smiled warmly. She beckoned to me and gave me food from a large dish which she had brought along."

### Dream 2: The interpretation for the minister

The dreamer is still processing his feelings, which have hardened into resentment and judgment, because he has noticed that you are naturally putting your family first when your own resources are low. But there is provision for the dreamer, who needs to be helped to go to God for His part of the provision which they are currently seeking from you. The Holy Spirit has seen the dreamer's genuine need and is on hand, ready to help and love them. If the dreamer stays focused on you and their disappointment, they will miss this loving and full provision.

The dreamer has not recognized that this dream contains God's assurance for them, that the Holy Spirit has seen their need and is an abundant source of supply. There are bountiful resources available to them.

### Possible application and time frame

These dreams carry a pastoral mandate for the minister to address these issues to help the dreamer come to God as the source of his supply. This should be done soon as the feelings are developing into bitterness and judgment. Because the feelings of the dreamer toward the minister are quite negative, the matter may be better dealt with by an effective and trusted third party using the dreams as a starting point.

Firstly, the dreamer needs to be shown that the dreams are processing his feelings. Then the third party might say, "These dreams tell me a little about your experience of church. I wonder if you haven't always found it easy, because there are some 'feeling' words in the dream. I'm concerned that something may have left you feeling upset. It might be good for us to talk about that. There's a beautiful picture at the end of the dreams, when God comes to reassure you that He's seen your needs.

"It shows some loving heavenly provision for you in the very place where you are already sitting."

## Exercise 7.7: Selja's dream interpretation

"In my dream I was in a hospital visiting a young man I didn't know. He was about twenty. Even though I didn't know him I felt compassion from God for him and I gave him a hug and kissed him. Then I was told by someone in the hospital that this young man was sick with a red rash on his body, but it was like a child's disease. It wasn't a grown-up person's disease. I woke up.

"When I woke up and I was wondering why I had wanted to visit this man even though I didn't know him."

### The interpretation

The interpreter might say, "God is showing you His own heart for your son who is in a time of healing because something from his childhood has affected him and he has been feeling sad and possibly angry. The care you felt for the man in the dream shows the compassion of God toward your son, His desire to be with him to comfort him. God used an unknown man as a symbol for your son, because he wanted to show you that it is His love and care for him and He has the situation in hand."

### Possible application and time frame

- Comfort and encourage the mother. The application and time frame for the moment of interpretation is to allow the mother time and a prayerful, gentle, loving place to receive God's comfort and reassurance.

- The dream highlights a need to pray for healing for the son from the issues of childhood. The mother told us that the father of the household left the family during her son's childhood, causing hurt and pain. If the interpreter has carried out the first application well, the mother will have a new place of faith to pray with a new heart of assurance and peace.

# Exercise 7.8: A mother's and a daughter's dreams which work together

### Daughter's dream

"The whole family were on holiday, including me, and Mum was being really stressy and rude to everyone, and so everyone was in a bad mood and tiptoeing around. She can get stressed but this was like tenfold; everyone just wanted to leave. Then I was at my parents' house while the family was on holiday and then they arrived home the day after saying they were all too ill to stay on holiday."

### The interpretation

The interpreter might say, "Your dream shows that you are picking up your mum's stress. The whole family is being affected to such a level that it's affecting their ability to enjoy themselves. It may be important for you to think about ways to prevent that stress affecting your well-being, and instead, pray for your family."

### The mother's dream

"Last night I dreamt there was lots of gunfire and screaming at our holiday park. I looked out of the window and saw that everyone was putting their lights on and going outside. I turned our lights out so it would look like no one was there. It was Islamic state. Also Abbie was in labour and I was talking to her on the phone and she was crying and wanted Becky with her. I also popped into some little church for a service and lots of my relatives were in there. I also dreamt about people who had loads of money and who were just talking about all the things they had."

### The interpretation

The interpreter might say, "Your dream speaks of your loving concern for your family and how that can sometimes have an effect on how you feel. Perhaps you've felt that, in the last season, your resources have been stretched. You may have felt unsettled in yourself. There are 'fear feelings' being expressed in the dream.

"The fact that you popped into a little church shows an innate understanding of where you can find the peace, welcome, and hospitality

397

for your soul to find peace and rest. There's a sense of belonging there for you when your reserves feel low."

### Possible application and time frame

- To help the dreamer to pray for her mother and about the effect she has on the family. But also to see that because the stress of the family also impacts on the dreamer and that she herself may need a place of peace.

- To lift stress from the mother by interpreting her dream and calmly recognizing her busy life, drawing her into God's presence. The mother may need some help to process her feelings and find a safe place for herself so that she can order and administrate the rest of the family.

- Time frame: at the time of interpretation.

## Exercise 7.9: A mother's traumatic dream

"I dreamt I was walking along a road and I saw my thirteen-year-old daughter lying dead in a ditch."

This dream symbolism involves death; moreover the death of a child. We don't interpret this symbol because the potential for getting it wrong and for hurting and frightening people is huge: love covers.

As I opened my mouth to say a general disclaiming "cover all" statement about this being an interesting dream and I wonder what it meant, God literally put the interpretation on my tongue and I saw the meaning of the dream. It was a surprise to me as much as to the dreamer.

### The interpretation

The interpreter might say, "This dream suggests that your own dreams for your daughter have died; it's not about your daughter at all but about your own hopes and dreams. It tells me that you feel sad that they have been thrown away."

### Possible application and timeframe

- Be very careful. The sense of this dream is that "my daughter is dead". Recognize how the dreamer is feeling. New hope and dreams need to be birthed. For example, "There is a Bible passage meditation which says, 'I know the plans I have for you... plans to prosper you and not to harm you, plans to give you hope and a future.'[259] That is true for both you and your daughter; there are new things to come for both of you."

- There is a deep need for ministry/healing and some exploration around the mother forgiving both her daughter and herself.

- Time frame: at the time of interpretation and in counselling.

## Exercise 7.10: Josh's dream

"I was in Granny's house and in the room were loads of werewolves; they were getting bigger and bigger so then I had to climb out the window, slide down a pole (guttering). Esther was there. We jumped over a wall to the neighbours and Esther brought out hot chocolate. We sat in their garden drinking it."

### Working interpretation

Josh has a safe place of wider family. There may be some generational issues of fear, manifesting in anxious thoughts and dreams which reflect an Ephesians 6:16 dynamic. The answer comes in the dream as the Holy Spirit is showing Josh a way out, with comfort and higher ways of thinking, initially through someone else who acts as a conduit between God and Josh. However, increasingly communication will take place between the Holy Spirit and Josh to bring comfort and peace at his own level.

### The interpretation if given to someone who isn't known by Josh

(This is the lightest touch of all types of interpretation. In Josh you have a minor who is not under your covering so an interpretation can only include edification, encouragement, and comfort.)

The interpreter might say, "It looks to me that you might feel like everybody does – a little bit worried sometimes. But this dream says

---

259    Jeremiah 29:11.

something amazing – it shows me you have people nearby to love and help you and that you are a resourceful and clever person who can make great decisions to keep safe and happy."

### Possible application and time frame

This interpretation can be given to Josh straight away to encourage him.

### Deeper interpretation

The interpreter might say, "This dream suggests you have been a bit unsettled sometimes, and it also shows how to stop those worries and any bad dreams. The way out (the window) is to find a new way of thinking, with joy and peace, and the dream says you need a bit of help to do that. It sounds funny but we have noticed that the Holy Spirit often appears in dreams as a blonde woman. Who do you think Esther is in the dream? The Holy Spirit. He has seen how you've been feeling and has come to be nearby to help you move to a new place of thinking and feeling (hop over the wall): a safe and comfortable place to be in God's garden.

"God has seen how you are feeling and has come to help you. The dream is an invitation to work with that and make some changes, and God will help you to do that."

### Possible application and time frame for the deeper interpretation

Because the dream highlights Josh's thinking patterns, Josh may benefit from chatting these through in a way that suits him in the coming weeks. There is a mandate to pray for Josh, that his dreams and his thoughts return to peace in an ongoing timeframe.

## Exercise 7.12: A prophetic summary for the crocodile dreams and visions set

There has been a flow of revelation coming from three churches which reflect and diagnose a certain type of spiritual attack (the "flaming arrows" of the enemy).[260]

The dreams are contained in the chapter text.

---

260   Ephesians 6:16

## Page 1: Summary

There is an assault on relationships between people which is adversely affecting the church itself. Anecdotally we are seeing discord around relationships in the churches.

Symptoms: spiritual lies, twisting of truth, misunderstanding and accusation, relational discord, the twisting and confusion of thoughts, verbal attacks that drag people down or influence others against them.

Two of the dreams helpfully outline the areas of pride, fear, legalism, and soulish attitudes which make people vulnerable to attack. And they show that as people reject fear and pride, and encounter the confidence that arises in a loving grace culture, being secure in God's provision, these attacks will cease.

> *I have forgiven in the sight of Christ for your sake, in order that Satan may not outwit us, for we are not unaware of his schemes.*[261]

> *In that day the Lord with his hard and great and strong sword will punish... Leviathan the fleeing serpent, Leviathan the twisted serpent, and he will slay the dragon that is in the sea [of our fallen human nature].*[262]

The book of Job refers to Leviathan as "king over all that are proud",[263] which is interesting, as dream 4 of our dream set referenced pride as making people vulnerable to its attack.

## Page 2: Dream and visions summaries

### Diagnostic dreams and visions

**Revelation 1:** a church member is experiencing discord and relationship difficulties in their workplace which are spiritual in origin.

**Revelation 2:** a high-level intercessor had a dream about a level of attack in the church which spreads and deeply affects many church members.

---

261     2 Corinthians 2:10–11.
262     Isaiah 27:1 (ESV UK).
263     Job 41:34.

**Revelation 3:** this dream suggests that the church is coming under an attack of these symptoms which could lead to some people leaving in order to find a place which feels safe but may in fact beach them.

### Two solution dreams containing safeguards, which are apparently "lizard" repellents

Dream 4: pride, fear, legalism, and soulish attitudes make people vulnerable to these attacks. Humility, fullness, and purity in the Holy Spirit protect people because they leave no room for the enemy.

Dream 5: confidence in God's goodness and a happy expectation of good provides a protection and repels the attack.

## Page 3

This page would detail each full individual dream and vision and its interpretation, which are present already in the text.

# APPENDIX 1: COMPLINE

Compline is a prayer of blessing which brings a place of God's rest, creativity, and His powerful presence into our sleep.

In our household, we made a deliberate decision to bring peace and rest into our night-times when our small children went through a short stage of having nightmares. Compline since has become a way in which we periodically end our days together. It's a beautiful part of our family tradition. The use of liturgy was new to me, as I come from an evangelical background, but I think there must be a Celtic heritage in me somewhere, because I simply love these gentle, reverent moments of prayer.

Compline is a simple way of setting a seal on the day and opening the door to a settled night. God's peace and presence still our hearts and liberate our spirits. We rest in the rhythm of His choosing, as God's light is reflected into the quiet of the night.

Compline starts with a focus on God, on His completeness in the face of our incompleteness, and we rest in His sufficiency.

Because of the tradition which gave us Compline, many like to quietly start and finish the prayers by making the sign of the cross (+).

The phrases in **bold** can be read together by those present, and those marked with a star (*) denote a change of reader: those who are taking part can each read a section.

## Compline One

+ **Be still and know that I am God.**

\* *Be still, relax,[264] sink down.*

\* *Let cares and defenses drop.*

\* *Be still. Let go. Be quiet.*

---

264    Hebrew: Be still.

*Peace be upon you.*
*Peace be within you.*

\* *My heart only be silent before God,*
*for my expectation comes from Him.*

\* *He alone is my rock and my salvation,*
*He is my fortress.*

**Peace be upon you.**
**Peace be within you.**

\* *My salvation depends on God,*
*He is my rock, my refuge.*

**+ The peace of all peace be mine this night,**
**In the name of the Father,**
**And of the Son,**
**And of the Holy Spirit**
**Amen.**

## Compline Two

**+ In the name of the Father,**
**In the name of the Son,**
**In the name of the Holy Spirit,**
**Amen.**

\* *The Lord is faithful to all His promises*
*And loving to all He has made.*

\* *The Lord is near to all who call upon Him*
*And watches over those who love Him.*

\* *Lord, I make you my dwelling place.*
*Command your angels concerning me,*
*To guard me this night.*

**I proclaim your love every morning,**
**Your faithfulness at night.**

\* *The Lord Almighty is with us,*
*The God of Jacob is our fortress.*

*He breaks the bow and shatters the spear.*

*\* Be still and know that I am God.*

**I proclaim your love every morning,
Your faithfulness at night.**

*\* The Lord Almighty is with us,
The God of Jacob is our fortress.*

**Peace be upon me,
Peace be within me.
+ In the name of the Father,
In the name of the Son,
In the name of the Holy Spirit,
Amen.**

# APPENDIX 2:
# WORKING UNDER ACCOUNTABILITY IN THE COMMUNITY OF FAITH

## Safe practice guidelines

*There is a proper time and procedure for every matter.*[265]

*For we know in part and we prophesy in part.*[266]

We suggest that you photocopy and give these guidelines to a mature person, who can hold you accountable to grow and to practise interpretation safely.

The guidelines can also give you a healthy way of operating in a peer group, as you grow and learn together and hold one another accountable.

If you have no one to help you, check your practice once a month against this list and ask, "What could I have done better?" Continue to seek out a wise and safe context in which you can grow and be held accountable.

### Good practice
Record each dream/vision interpretation for future reference in a voice memo or notebook. Keep it as a record to refer back to if necessary.

### Checklist
There are two broad types of dreams and visions which each need to be handled differently:

---

265     Ecclesiastes 8:6.
266     1 Corinthians 13:9.

- "Over-the-counter meds": those dreams and visions with a general, positive, non-directive level of interpretation. Your interpretation should be balanced by the usual "social norms" of communication: be polite, non-directive, humble, and non-intrusive. Don't touch the person you are giving the interpretation to, unless you know them well and it is part of your usual interaction.

| Type of dream or vision | Protocol to apply |
| --- | --- |
| "Over-the-counter" meds | |
| Encouraging revelation | Interpret and encourage |
| Calling revelation | Be general, not directive |
| Prayer/prophetic ministry revelation | Be general about the area for prayer, without being dramatic or raising fear. Simply suggest that their attention is being drawn to this area for prayer |

- "Behind-the-counter meds": dreams and visions that contain a degree of revelation which is pastoral or directive in nature. Again, the relationship you have to the dreamer or seer will set the degree of information that it is appropriate for you to give.

Record your interpretation for future reference.

Work in team.

| Type of dream or vision | Protocol to apply |
| --- | --- |
| "Behind-the-counter" meds | |
| Direction, correction, foretelling, and warning | Unless you are responsible for the dreamer or seer's discipleship or well-being in some way (parent, counsellor, pastor), be very general about the areas that the dream speaks of: "The dream speaks about issues of …" |

| Type of dream or vision | Protocol to apply |
|---|---|
| Dark revelations and nightmares | Don't interpret the content. Deal in a relaxed manner with the fear by bringing peace into the encounter. You may like to offer people the "Compline" prayer in Appendix 1. |

Give each person for whom you do an interpretation the following weighing summary which they need to understand in order to weigh the interpretation you have given them.

## Healthy checks and balances for those receiving dream and vision interpretation

Dreams and visions give us a tiny jigsaw puzzle piece from the picture of our lives. It's important to check it against our wider life context. Asking these questions before we take an interpretation on board for our lives is important.

Pass the interpretation through a scriptural filter:

- Does the interpretation line up with the teaching and loving values of the Bible?

Pass your interpretation through a trusted wisdom filter:

- What do trusted, mature, and godly people who know me say about it?

- Does it agree with other things which are true about my life?

Pass your interpretation through the source filter:

- Is this interpretation uplifting and loving?

- Does it sound like the God of love?

- Does this interpretation bring a sense of fear, control, and negativity?

- Does it sound like an opinion from the person who gave it?

| Godly wisdom brings: | False wisdom brings: |
| --- | --- |
| Peace and freedom of choice | Fear and control |
| Truth | Deception |
| Clarity | Confusion |
| Unity | Isolation |
| Love | Anger and hatred |

# APPENDIX 3:
# HELPFUL INTERPRETATION SUMMARY TO USE WHEN INTERPRETING DREAMS AND VISIONS

- Record the dream or vision.

- Who or what is the dream or vision about?

- What type of revelation is it and what is its source?

- What is the sense of the story?

- Which are the important parts of the revelation?

- They might be: key statements, items, people, places, colours, names, numbers, feelings, quality of light, or colour.

- Are they literal or symbolic, positive or negative?

## Types of revelation

Revelation dreams and visions from God:

- Edification, encouragement, and comfort revelation.

- Calling revelation. Prayer/prayer ministry revelation.

- Direction. Correction (cleansing). Foretelling revelation. Warning revelation.

Healthy life-processing dreams and visions.

Trauma dreams.

Hallucinations caused by an imbalance in levels of brain chemicals, drugs or alcohol abuse

## Protocol

- Are these "over-the-counter" revelations or "behind-the-counter" revelations? Adjust the amount of information you give and where you will be very general, accordingly. By adjusting that to suit the situation and type of revelation, you will express increasing maturity as an interpreter.

- Serve, don't sell. Simply see what God is doing or saying in the dream or vision and facilitate it.

- Never try to manipulate a conversation about faith.

- Sometimes listening is enough.

- Use neutral-space language when interpreting outside a faith context.

- Keep a bullet-point, dated record of the interpretation, in case you are asked to refer back to it at a later date.